BORDERLINES

OTHER BOOKS BY EDMUND KEELEY

FICTION

The Libation
The Gold-Hatted Lover
The Impostor
Voyage to a Dark Island
A Wilderness Called Peace
School for Pagan Lovers
Some Wine for Remembrance

NON-FICTION

Modern Greek Writers (ed. with Peter Bien)
Cavafy's Alexandria
Modern Greek Poetry: Voice and Myth
R. P. Blackmur: Essays, Memoirs, Texts (ed. with Edward Cone & Joseph Frank)
The Salonika Bay Murder: Cold War Politics and the Polk Affair
Albanian Journal: The Road to Elbasan
George Seferis and Edmund Keeley, Correspondence, 1951-1971
Inventing Paradise: The Greek Journey 1937–1947
On Translation: Reflections and Conversations

POETRY IN TRANSLATION

Six Poets of Modern Greece (with Philip Sherrard)
George Seferis: Collected Poems (with Philip Sherrard)
C. P. Cavafy: Passions and Ancient Days (with George Savidis)
C. P. Cavafy: Selected Poems (with Philip Sherrard)
Odysseus Elytis, The Axion Esti (with George Savidis)
C. P. Cavafy, Collected Poems (with Philip Sherrard and George Savidis)
Angelos Sikelianos, Selected Poems (with Philip Sherrard)
Ritsos In Parentheses
The Dark Crystal/Voices of Modern Greece/A Greek Quintet (with Philip Sherrard)
Odysseus Elytis: Selected Poems (with Philip Sherrard)
Yannis Ritsos: Exile and Return, Selected Poems, 1968–74
Yannis Ritsos: Repetitions, Testimonies, Parentheses
The Essential Cavafy
A Century of Greek Poetry, 1900–2000 (ed. with Peter Bien, Peter Constantine & Karen Van Dyck)

FICTION IN TRANSLATION

Vassilis Vassilikos: The Plant, the Well, the Angel (with Mary Keeley)

BORDERLINES

A Memoir

✕

EDMUND KEELEY

WHITE PINE PRESS • BUFFALO, NEW YORK

White Pine Press
P.O. Box 236, Buffalo, New York 14201

Copyright ©2005 by Edmund Keeley

Acknowledgments: I am grateful to the editors of the following journals for publishing excerpts from this memoir: *The Yale Review, The Ontario Review, Words Without Borders, Mondo Greco,* and *PEN America.* I am also grateful to my friends Karen Kennerly and Christopher Merrill for their generous reading of the completed manuscript and for their valuable suggestions, and to my wife Mary for her magnanimous accommodation of my long labor.

The epigraph is from THE COLLECTED POEMS OF WALLACE STEVENS by Wallace Stevens, copyright 1954 by Wallace Stevens and renewed 1982 by Holly Stevens. Used by permission of Alfred A. Knopf, a division of Random House, Inc.

The quotations by Miles Copeland in chapter Twelve are from *The Game of Nations,* Weidenfeld and Nicolson, London, 1969.

Publication of this book was made possible, in part, by grants from the A.G. Leventis Foundation, the Stavros S. Niarchos Foundation, the National Endowment for the Arts, which believes that a great nation deserves great art, and with public funds from the New York State Council on the Arts, a State Agency.

NATIONAL
ENDOWMENT
FOR THE ARTS

ISBN 1-893996-33-6

Book design: Elaine LaMattina

Printed and bound in the United States of America

1   3   5   7   9   10   8   6   4   2

Library of Congress Control Number: 2005920854

To the Memory of My Parents

Mathilde Vossler Keeley

James Hugh Keeley

Oh! Blessed rage for order, pale Ramon,
The maker's rage to order words of the sea,
Words of the fragrant portals, dimly-starred,
And of ourselves and of our origins,
In ghostlier demarcations, keener sounds.

—Wallace Stevens

ONE

About a year after my father was transferred from the American Consulate in Montreal, Canada, to the American Consulate in Salonika, Greece, my brothers and I began to speak to our parents in the third person. This wasn't something we discussed or planned. It just happened, as though it were the natural thing for us to do at that point in our respective lives (I was nine, my older brother twelve, my younger brother seven and a half). And it went on seeming natural, because neither my father nor my mother ever corrected us, not that year, 1937, not the next year or the year following, when war broke out in Europe and we returned to settle in Washington, D. C., where my father was assigned to the Special Problems Division in the State Department and was no longer the American Consul anywhere abroad.

"Can she give me some cash for the streetcar?" my older brother Budge might ask my mother to her face before he headed out on an excursion into downtown Salonika (his name was Hugh, but he was called "Budge" in the family, as I was called "Mike," for reasons that remain obscure).

"He's going too fast, I can't keep up," I might complain beside my father while trying to match his quick, short-legged circuit from the American Consulate door to the White Tower along the Salonika esplanade and back the long way around to our waiting De Soto.

When I think back on those pre-war years and the many years following, what seems as strange as this linguistic curiosity is my never having asked either of my parents, both of whom lived into their late eighties, what they may have said to each other to explain the perverse grammar that emerged from their offspring day in day out until each of their sons in turn went off to college. Long after the fact, when both parents were dead, I did ask my younger brother, Bob (his real name in the family and elsewhere), what he made of this odd grammatical distance between generations within our household, as though our intimate home life was governed by an unexplained narrative convention that prevented us from speaking directly and personally to our parents, our lives somehow threatened by an excess of subjectivity. Bob's response to my question: "I have no idea why we spoke to them in the third person, but that is what we did. All three of us. Idiotic. Though no more idiotic than their never correcting us."

At the time we were sitting in the living room of my brother's home in Washington, D.C., shortly after his retirement from the Foreign Service. Our wives had gone to bed, and when Bob stood up to replenish his glass with a final dash of bourbon, the mood easing further toward reminiscence, I was taken back to the bourbon nightcaps that had been the essential drink of choice in Princeton to keep our college bull sessions alive a bit longer those many years ago while he was in graduate school and I a neophyte instructor. Bob turned to tell me that he had asked our mother, at some point during her last years, about this linguistic curiosity in our family, and she had blamed it on the presumably dubious English of our maid and nurse at the time, Nartouie, known to our less tolerant Greek companions as the Armenian Midget.

"Of course it wasn't Nartouie's fault at all," Bob said. "Her English was devious, but not dubious. She certainly knew the difference between I, you, he and she. The problem is, we did too."

Nartouie wasn't actually a midget. She was well over four feet tall, an orphan refugee from the Armenian massacres in Turkey, stunted by hunger and poverty but eternally optimistic, eternally young, all heart, all cunning. At least that is what she became after my father took her in during his tour as Vice Consul in Beirut, Lebanon, and brought her to the winter never-never land of Montreal, Canada, to help my mother cope with three hyperactive sons, spoiled by adoring Syrian and Lebanese servants. Nartouie's diminutive size and her child-like view of the world kept her close to me and my brothers, more surrogate sister than nurse, and whatever the limitations of her English, Bob was right: she was never third-person distant with the younger generation or anybody else. It pained the three of us children in unspoken ways—the first death in the family—when, some days after Europe went to war and we moved back to the U. S. and into our new home in Washington, D.C., Nartouie escaped without notice and took the train to Providence, R.I., to become the bride, in a marriage arranged by an Armenian broker, to a man two heads taller than she was and wider by another half.

During those early years my mother might betray us to our father over some delinquency of ours—that was her one consistently unforgivable weakness in my childhood opinion—but not Nartouie. When we would violate the anopheles mosquito deadline that prevailed throughout the foreign community in northern Greece and stay outside past the sun's disappearance for another half-hour or so of soccer with our multinational companions, Nartouie was always there to lie for us.

"You were to get them back here before sunset," my father would say to Nartouie on his return from the office for dinner, his finger pointing menacingly. "If they get malaria, it's your funeral."

"When I went to call them in, one of them fell. We had to take care of him. Carry him back home."

"Which one fell? They all look perfectly healthy to me."

"Not one of ours. One of the gardener's boys. One of the Armenians."

"Nartouie, you're lying. Don't lie to me. I can tell when you're lying."

"I don't lie, Mr. Keeley. I am a Christian. I act like a Christian."

"I'm warning you. If one of the boys comes down with malaria, it's your funeral."

"I would gladly die for them, Mr. Keeley. My life means nothing to me. I have died once already. I—"

"O.K., O.K. But I'm warning you."

If there was a purely linguistic basis for the move from first to third person in our generation, such purity hardly plausible, the syntax my

brothers and I adopted had little to do with Nartouie's occasionally
quaint Near-Eastern English and much to do with the varied riches—
sometimes confusing and costly—of the polyglot world that our parents
introduced us into with the crossing from Canada to Greece. We spent
the first months of my father's new post on the outskirts of Salonika in
a rented villa with no particular charm that I remember except maybe for
its unattended, weed-studded clay tennis court that served to engender
in me a life-long obsession with the game, too rarely rewarded. During
the first spring in Salonika, my father moved us to a place called the
American Farm School some four miles outside the city limits, where he
rented a three-story house with a ground-floor living room that seemed
the size of a roller-skating rink, a second-floor garden patio open to the
unblemished blue heavens, and screens against malaria on every window.

My father's motive for this move was simple, my mother explained
years later: not so much the luxury of grand mosquito-free space (even
inside the house all of us slept under mosquito netting in those days) as
the proximity of a herd of Jersey cows, imported from the United States.
My father—Jimmy Keeley to the few who knew him intimately, James
Hugh Keeley, Jr. to the State Department, and Mr. Consul to the
Greeks—was not as familiar with cows as my mother was, he having
grown up in the care of three voluminous maiden aunts of Irish background in a Pennsylvania mining town, she having grown up on a farm
in upstate New York under the name of Tilly Vossler, though Mathilde
Keeley to the State Department and Mateeld or just "Maw" to my father
once they were married. Neither was as familiar with cows as I felt myself
to be from my persistent visits to my grandfather's dairy barn in upstate
New York whenever we visited that homestead during our days in
Montreal. If cows were my father's motive, I took that to be a product
of his passion for cream in his coffee and fresh butter for his bread, but
my mother, as usual more generous towards him than were his sons, told
me that he had wanted to be near cows so as to provide his children with
regular pasteurized milk. And to insure that, once we moved to the
American Farm School, he drew up a contract in which he agreed to pay
indefinitely for the upkeep of a particular cow with the best production
record in the herd whose milk henceforth was to be his and his family's

first of all, this arrangement what he called a "bovine scholarship" for the School's farm operation.

The American Farm School, enveloped in green close by Salonika Bay, was a high school for training Greek villagers in modern methods of farming, created while Northern Greece was under Turkish occupation at the turn of the last century. The creator was a white-bearded American missionary in his sixties named Dr. Henry House, who believed that the fastest route to the salvation of your soul was by way of the good works your hands could perform in tilling barren soil to feed your body—and to prove his point he bought a spread of once arid offshore land, with a single farmhouse for his wife and six Christian students from Bulgaria.

The school gradually grew to become an oasis of some hundred acres in free Greek Macedonia, and it was taken over in the Thirties by Dr. House's son Charlie, a graduate of Princeton '09 in engineering, who turned from sowing his wild oats to sowing the good word in an evangelist mode learned from his father. This he did first of all for the benefit of the school's Greek Orthodox students, who responded to his kindly manner if not to his largely incomprehensible message, and then for the benefit of anyone who arrived at the school gate with a survival problem and a capacity for hard work, whether a refugee from Asia Minor or from the Slavic territories to the north or from the Metaxas dictatorship then in command of the country. Charlie House, known as Turk House to his college classmates because he reached Old Nassau from the then-Ottoman Empire, was a man of gentle conviction and broad tolerance, with a talent for building out of stone and mortar on meager resources so as to put a roof over the exiled and dispossessed who came to his door for shelter and who remained faithful. He smoked cigarettes like every other local Christian, but always on the road outside the school boundaries in order not to displease his father's ghost.

For the under-aged new to Greece, as for the dispossessed, the Farm School was Eden. The pleasures in it started with the fields between the school buildings and the sea, known images of wheat, barley, and alfalfa, along with patches of tomatoes, cucumbers, sweet corn, and something called eggplant. The gold and green of those fields, the smell and taste of what the gardens produced, much of it familiar from my grandfather's farm in upstate New York, was startling nourishment for nostalgia. Then, on the hillside behind the School buildings, the unfamiliar colors of row on row of baby pines and blossoming almond trees and a neighbor's strip of dark green vineyard beside a spread of olive trees with silver in their leaves. And eventually you came to know the buildings themselves and their games: the dairy barn for more practice milking, the quadrangle of craft shops for after-school wood and metal work, the storage barns for caves and ladders, the farm machinery for hopping a ride into open country, and near the huge dormitory building, the playing fields for soccer and track and the garden reservoir that served for a swimming pool until its bottom and sides turned green, though that no obstacle for the foolhardy.

But most of all, what made it a vast playground were the young companions you discovered there, those old enough for action and adventure, children of the school staff living in houses of various sizes scattered on the grounds, the sons and daughters of Greeks who had come over from the Pontos and Smyrna with the exchange of populations in the 1920s, and Armenians who had fled the massacres, and former students from remote villages who had stayed on after graduation to teach the crafts they'd learned and to find a new life near the city. The language of the older generation was often mixed, Turkish and Armenian and even Slavic overtaking their Greek when privacy was called for, that Greek anyway partial or out-of-date. But the companions had their own language, Macedonian Greek spiced with vulgarities, wild metaphors, tall claims and grand threats, a language that remained distant enough from the elders to make for off-hour sport as loud and uninhibited as play in a first Eden ought to be for the uninitiated young. The sons of the American Consul learned that language better than their own.

"All right, masturbator. Christ and the Virgin! Are you a masturbator or what? I told you to kick the ball to me, you chunk of halva. Me, I say. Just give me the chance and I'll turn that goalie's eggs into cabbage."

"Hey, hey, it's almost nine o'clock. Rise up, rise up, you grandfather cock."

The difficulty was that the free-wheeling life at the American Farm

School did not begin until a few hours before sundown. Life in the real world began at eight in the morning when my father drove the ten kilometers into the consulate in the De Soto and on his way dropped the three of us off at the school he and my mother had chosen for our formal education, the German School. This, they told us, was the school highly recommended for non-Greek nationals by the city's foreign community, except for the French, who recommended a local school run by the French. Nobody recommended a Greek school, that apparently beyond the pale, even if the American Consul's children, by the end of their first spring and summer in the country, spoke a version of village Greek as though it were their mother tongue. In any case, it turned out that the French had a point, because the German School proved to be an abomination from several perspectives, most of all that of new students just in from foreign parts.

The first problem was that all classes in that school were taught in German, so the American Consul's children had to learn a third language, a ghastly-sounding language, to go along with their domestic English and their playground Greek. The second problem was that the teachers using this third language were political missionaries sent out from Germany to proselytize in more or less subtle ways for the Third Reich, as might have been suspected by foreigners of the older generation in that part of the world who kept up with the news during the years 1936 to l939, diplomats or otherwise.

My mother knew there was a language problem early on, because she had sometimes spoken German at home with her father and mother, my great-grandfather having settled in Allegheny County, New York, in 1857 as a thirty-two-year-old immigrant from Germany who eventually carved a farm out of dense woodland on a steep and rocky hill that nobody else in the county had yet cared to develop. My mother's German was not really *echt Deutsch,* but she could tell that ours was virtually incomprehensible when not simply mute, this sometimes a consciously self-determined rebellion against our fate as schoolboys. She tried to work with us on our German after school every other day, but when we finally revolted against that in violent unison because of the time it cost us away from the soccer field, we had a family conference that led to tears on both sides, though a degree of sympathy for the predicament of the younger generation was established when Budge made a speech protesting the inhuman weight of mastering three languages at once. I now realize that it was probably not so much his young rhetoric as the painful awkwardness of our parents hearing us address them consistently in the third person that led to a compromise. My father decided that it would be up to the German School to teach us proper German and up to my mother, meeting with us in group sessions two rather than three times a week, to work intensely on our grammar and vocabulary in at least the one language that it would be a disaster for us to lose: our native language, American English.

My personal problem with the German School wasn't merely a linguistic one. There was cause for severe stress in trying to get along with the teachers in that school. Some of them were kindly enough and only vaguely proselytizers, like the gourd-headed music teacher who made a point of not noticing that I and a few others never joined in the singing of "Deutschland, Deutschland uber alles" (I can't stay that I was deeply into international politics at the ages of eight to eleven, but I did know what my own national anthem sounded like even if some of the words eventually began to fade away). And when, out of the profound insularity that I brought to my history class, I screwed up the assignment to make paste models of the two designated Germanys—one that showed the country as it currently was and one as it was destined to become, we were told, when what was rightfully German territory established new borders—the history teacher, a low-pitched, white-haired, pig-tailed woman of a certain age who usually wore a dirndl, finally allowed me to substitute for the future Germany a crude paste model of the North American continent.

But a few of the teachers were bolder, more direct, for example the teacher who was assigned to tutor foreign students in verbal and written German, a rosy-faced Nazi with a brush of blonde hair and a sweet smile who could twist your ear to the point of drawing tears if your lettering was taken to be evidence either of dissent or mental deficiency. He always spoke softly as he twisted: "No, my child, you do not make an 'r' that way. Please. As I have already tried to explain, a German 'r' does not look like an 'n' or some other curiosity. Do you understand? Forgive me, but you must understand. You are not in America now but in a German School. The tail is small on the German 'r,' like a fishhook. Shall we try again? I think we had better try again." His teaching method worked indelibly: my handwriting still shows a German "r," a kind of scar on the page to remind me of this tortured phase of my early school days.

The gym instructor, who was said to be Count Somebody at home and who ended up a celebrated Luftwaffe pilot in the war—lean, skin pallid, a slash of black hair glued to his forehead in silent homage to the Führer—was no doubt paid well to be the most open Nazi in the school, since part of his assignment was to train and supervise the Hitler Jugend contingent that drilled in the afternoons and sometimes paraded with the members of the Greek youth movement called Neolaia. That organization, reserved for Greeks as the Hitler Jugend was reserved for Germans, had been recently organized by dictator Metaxas to promote martial coherence and group patriotism in the marvelously individualistic and generally undisciplined Greek secondary school students of those times. At the German School, gym class was an undisguised military drill, no room for games, all exercises by the numbers, discipline rigid, and much marching this way and that across the school yard as training for the after-school parades. Those who failed in concentration or rhythm earned a whack with a riding crop across the back of the knees, and those who spoke during a drill received a dressing-down in front of the class and special exercises after class for strengthening the arms, legs, and will.

My brothers and I were never party to the disciplinary exercises, though we learned about them from one of my brother's friends in the upper division who had made the mistake of swearing out loud in Greek during gym class, an act regarded by the teacher as blatantly subversive. The friend reported that during the harshest punitive exercise he was made to lean at arms length into the wall which surrounded the schoolyard and, under the guidance of the teacher's riding crop tapping the front of his knees, encouraged gradually to assume an ever greater angle and a straighter line until either his body or his will collapsed—and then to repeat the exercise. The American Consul's sons were spared such punishment, as they were spared all participation in the Hitler Jugend activities by decree of the school principal—short, round, bald except for a clownish fringe of curls above his collar—a smooth, amiable gentleman whom most parents considered a polished if occasionally pompous diplomat in those days but who came out of the war a man desperate enough to write some of those parents, my father included, for any help in clothing or food they might be able to spare for his distressed family. The principal's decree followed an interview with me and my older brother during which he explained in basic German that it would not be correct for foreigners who had no German blood to take part in practice exercises that were meant for those who would qualify for the Hitler Jugend, perhaps least of all the children of the American Consul, who would surely find such participation inappropriate. When I asked if having a German grandfather didn't allow us to qualify for the Hitler Jugend, the principal smiled. "But surely your grandfather is American, no?"

"Yes, German American."

"I'm afraid that isn't quite good enough," the principal said, still smiling. "After all, even Jews who are considered German citizens do not qualify for the Hitler Jugend. So you must not take it personally. Do you understand?"

I didn't really understand why I shouldn't take it personally, but I didn't want to admit it. And since my older brother didn't say anything, either because his German wasn't good enough or because his wisdom was greater than mine, I simply shrugged. Who, after all, wanted to go marching around after school hours and then parading in a stupid khaki uniform when you could spend that time on the soccer field at the American Farm School with your closest friends, even if they were Greeks from Asia Minor and Armenians who went to some other school or no school at all? And since there were now frequent special drill sessions even at noon, these reserved for the Hitler Jugend members preparing to perform during an upcoming visit by dignitaries of the Third Reich, we Americans and those of our kind were suddenly given an extra hour or so of free time to play marbles or ride the backs of streetcars or explore the upper city walls, in my case with the Turk and Jew and Dane and Yugoslav in my class who also did not qualify for the Hitler Jugend and the joint parades with the boys and girls of the Neolaia—all of us trying hard to show that we couldn't care less.

If my brothers and I felt half rejected and half privileged by the principal's exclusion, we decided that it was not a thing that we ought to make a subject of conversation at home, especially in view of the new freedom that it gave us to turn to our own devices during the lunch break and to get to the soccer field earlier than usual after school. The only problem was one of transportation: my father couldn't drive us home in the middle of his afternoon duties at the consulate, even if we had chosen to tell him about our new bonus in free time. And in any case, Budge was on a later and more demanding schedule in the upper division. He decided to find unspecified ways to occupy himself in town while waiting for my father to pick him up as usual, and that meant that my younger brother Bob and I had no choice but to make our way home by streetcar to their turn-around yard called The Depot on the edge of town and from there on foot across the expanse of open country to the Farm School oasis, a trip that proved to be full of unwanted adventure, imagined and otherwise.

Since our lunch allowance didn't include ground transportation, we either ate less on a given day or, when too hungry for that, rode free on the metal bar that stuck out from the back of Greek streetcars like some extinct reptile's tongue. This was an option that usually called for sharing the benefit part way with one or another of the ambitious or the needy or the unwashed who would jump aboard behind you and hang on tightly to bring you their garlic-rich breath and ripe armpit odor until the streetcar slowed to a stop again: foot messengers in a hurry or penniless soldiers on home leave or gypsy boys out to beg where others hadn't yet cleaned out the territory.

"Give me some room to breathe, masturbator, in the name of God."

"How can I give you room to breathe when there's barely room to stay alive on this thing?"

"If I fall off, you're going with me."

"Then you'd better not fall off, you sister, because I'll fall off on top of you. Your head will end up a squashed eggplant."

"Well at least stop breathing in my face. Your breath stinks."

"Ha. You think your breath smells of carnations? Who do you think you are anyway, Hedy Lamarr?"

The danger wasn't all talk. Later that year a fellow student in the class ahead of me, finding the streetcar tongue fully occupied with three riders, jumped aboard the rear-door running board instead, and when the streetcar suddenly jolted to a stop to avoid hitting a mule-drawn cart crossing in front of it, the student tumbled headfirst into the street. That cost him the fingers of one hand, sliced off by a rear wheel. What we said to counter the lingering fear that went with the image of our fellow student's bandaged stump of a hand was that the streetcar's tongue luckily stuck out clear of all wheels except maybe from a passing car and anyway provided the lead rider with a safe purchase on the streetcar's rear end, good as well for those behind him so long as you hung on tightly to the rider in front of you and came there with a prayer ready for the Virgin if you should fall off.

In any case, the more tenacious fear came with the three or four kilometer shortcut across barren fields from the army barracks beyond the Depot to the Farm School gate. If the empty fields belonged to anybody, it must have been to the ghosts of those buried in the ancient funeral mound half-way across that expanse, because the land was silent and deserted except for a few of the living who passed quickly through it, whether donkey riders on their way into town or itinerant shepherds heading for the hills or gypsies on the move to more profitable country. After a first quick exploration of the funeral mound, my brother and I kept plenty of distance between us and the one entrance we found: a tunnel that you wouldn't want to enter deeply even without the ghostly presences in there where the slash of daylight died, because the depths were now protected by the offerings of a makeshift public toilet, constantly replenished. We crossed those dry fields as quickly as we could but only when the horizon ahead was clear of gypsies our age or older who might try to charge us a toll for safe passage beyond them, or still more threatening, the sheep dogs that might come rushing at us so fast and savage as not to give their inattentive master enough time to call them off our tender waiting flesh. We'd been given the word by one of our Armenian buddies: if a sheep dog comes for you, stand there absolutely still. Don't move a muscle. And don't sweat, because the smell of fear turns a sheep dog rabid. Sure. Try it sometime.

We were lucky most days, but we were also careful. We found that if we had to, we could make our way through the gypsy children for a few drachmas thrown out on the run or a T-shirt off our backs flung into the leader's face or a cap off our heads sailed into the void, and during the warming season we learned to change our route so as to dodge the sheep dogs and their flocks heading for new pasture land. But the safest days were those when we timed our crossing so that we could cut back to the main road at some point beyond the army barracks and join up with the Farm School's horse-drawn milk wagon on its way back home from delivering afternoon cream and butter to the School's regular customers in town.

From a distance the wagon—boarded in and roofed to keep its cargo fresh—looked like a blue hut on the move just above the horizon, with a man in blue dungarees standing statue-still in its doorway in imitation of the Delphic Charioteer: Panayotis the milkman, beloved not only by those who had a passion for pasteurized milk but those who could become enthralled by stories about what it was like to lose a grand home in Smyrna during the Asia Minor Catastrophe of *1922*, all inlaid furniture and precious carpets, and cross from the Turkish coast to the nearby Aegean island of Chios on a raft made out of driftwood and a prayer. Bob and I were duly enthralled the first time, and the second, then did our best to pay attention thereafter, because keeping on the good side of Panayotis meant not only a long cool drink of the morning's leftover milk but safe passage home in a make-believe limousine.

"You boys can't imagine—how could you?—what it's like to run from a sword-wielding Turk ready to swing at your head or your ass before you manage to jump into the sea in the darkness of night to search like a blind man for any floating piece of driftwood and if you're lucky a second piece to tie to the first with your belt and hang on to as you paddle with your tired legs kilometer after kilometer until you see a few lights in a distant cove giving you the last gasp of hope that you're going to reach the Greek island of Chios, if the Virgin still be with you, and find a few Christians there who are willing to close up the holes in your body from your land wounds sealed for the moment by salt water so that what blood you have left doesn't spill out onto the shore of your beloved fatherland before you have a chance to thank your God for having saved you from dying an evil death as the plaything of your infidel enemy."

The story would change here and there in its details—in place of the raft, an abandoned rowboat miraculously drifting by just within your grasp, a Greek fisherman hauling you aboard his caique at the last minute—but Panayotis' fall from a career as an aspiring rug merchant to a milkman with a horse-drawn cart not his own was the suffering heart of every version, as was the Savior's grant of life-saving grace in a moment of desperate need, matched by the saintly Charlie House, who had taken Panayotis in as a young man with no interest in agriculture but a way with words. Nobody ever challenged the story of his survival. One way or another, like so many of the defeated Greek invaders and the dispossessed local Greek community, he had made it out of Turkey in 1922 and across to the mainland with no more than the clothes he was wearing, because, along with other Greek residents of Asia Minor trapped by the retreat of the Greek army, he had preferred the challenge of a solo sea voyage to the threat of a slit throat or a severed head at the hands of the Turkish victors. And anyway, that was hardly his only story. If you seemed to tire of that one, he would pull another out of his past history during those days of beauty and adventure in his village on the coast near Smyrna, the lost paradise that only a milkman with the heart of a poet could find a way to make you believe.

During the good days that brought us home in Panayotis' carriage, I would have enough time before the late afternoon pick-up soccer game to visit the cow barn and check out Polly, the family cow, and a few others with easy teats that Thanasis, the dairy manager allowed me to milk a bit for practice so that I didn't lose the art of it, strenuously initiated during my last American summer on my grandfather's farm. And some days there was time enough to climb into the rafters of the hay barn next door and to explore its recesses, what turned out to be a secret schoolroom for the study of certain mysteries in this new world of mixed peoples, some with peculiar habits and unfamiliar ways of communicating with others.

My teacher was a girl named Lisa, a year and a few months older than me, her father a teacher at the school who had come over from Asia Minor in the exchange of populations following the Catastrophe, she herself worldly and knowledgeable in ways that made her seem as learned as my adolescent older brother. We were brought together in the beginning by our mutual interest in cows and the new pasteurization machinery that the School had received as a gift from Charlie House's Princeton class. When we would become bored with the rituals of milking, Lisa and I would find a corner of the hayloft to make a nest, renewed as the hay diminished with the changing seasons, and sit or lie there side by side while she would tell me about rare things she knew well and I knew not at all. For example, I heard about the habits of gypsies, how you could learn from them to read the life-line in your palm so that you could predict a long and happy life for yourself, how you could recognize by the colors of their eyes those children in gypsy camps who had been stolen from their real parents during the night in another country, how you could know by the rise and fall of a gypsy girl's voice whether she was simply being friendly or planned to take off your pants so she could run away with them. And Lisa knew about shepherds and how they were able to make a sheep dog lie down on his back and whimper just by playing a certain tune on their flute and how they could make a village girl marry them by playing a different tune.

"I don't believe that," I would say. "Have you ever seen it happen?"

"You never see it. They don't play a tune like that if a stranger's there to hear it."

"Anyway, who would marry a shepherd and stay married? They're always going somewhere else."

"Why not stay married to a shepherd? Especially if you had one with a great flock. And especially if he would get tired of looking at his sheep once in a while and look at you the right way."

"What does that mean?"

But a question like that would make her turn her back and start to stand up, whether out of shyness or not knowing what to say in language I could understand. And I would move on quickly to another subject so as not to lose her company: gossip about the school bus driver who was always drunk when actually not behind the wheel and who, under threat of being fired, agreed to marry a woman in the neighboring village much older than he was but with the will to keep him sober and a dowry to put a roof over their heads, or maybe another story about the compassionate deaf-mute in charge of collecting the school's trash in a donkey cart who came down with pneumonia because he'd taken off his coat during the winter's single snow storm to cover the bust of old Dr. Henry House in front of the main classroom building. One afternoon I brought up the subject of Panayotis' escape from a sword-wielding Turk across the sea to Chios, and I asked Lisa whether she thought he really was a refugee from Asia Minor.

"Of course he's a refugee. Just as you and I are."

"I'm not a refugee. I'm an American."

"Well you're a refugee here because you were born in another country. Like my father. Which makes me a refugee daughter."

"But I can go back to America anytime I want. So it's not the same thing as your father."

"Well, the truth is, my father can go back to Turkey anytime he wants, but who would want to?"

"What I'm saying is I don't know whether to believe Panayotis because he always changes his story."

"That doesn't mean he didn't escape from the Turks. Maybe he's embarrassed to tell you what really happened. Maybe he killed somebody or something."

"He doesn't seem like a man who would kill anybody. He spends all his time telling stories."

"Well maybe he tells stories to hide how much he suffered. After all, he lost his childhood home forever. Just as my father did."

I had never thought of it that way, and it changed the way I looked at Panayotis. I still didn't believe all his stories, but from then on I always made a serious effort to pretend I did. I also began to feel that there were some things Lisa knew which I could never know the way she did because I came from the other side of the world and so did my parents and they had never lost anything I could name. And then a thing happened that made me feel Lisa was not only different from me because she was a girl and older than me and a refugee daughter who sometimes spoke in a language I couldn't understand but because she believed with all her heart in something mysterious called Fate. The thing that happened was Budge being bitten by a stray cat that everybody thought had rabies.

The cat, mostly white and Egyptian-looking according to those who ran into it, had come into the school grounds by the back road and had zig-zagged its way between several staff houses before it ended up crossing our front yard, where Budge was supplementing his allowance by working with the Armenian gardener to weed out the patch of sweet peas that were the main source of gift bouquets for my parents' cocktail circuit. The gardener hadn't liked the look of the cat. He said that it was moving erratically as it approached and that it stared at him in a weird way when it stopped, so he went after it with his hoe, grazing its back, which made the animal squeal hysterically and go for the gardener's leg. When my brother moved in to help him with his trowel, the cat got Budge's forearm in its teeth. Budge whacked it loose with a blow to the head and the cat ran off with the gardener chasing after it, hoe held high, sending the cat to the devil and the devil's mother as it disappeared around the corner of the house.

The gardener was lucky: he was wearing army boots that no cat teeth could penetrate. But that kind of luck didn't carry over to my brother. I can't remember exactly when it was in the afternoon that the cat had come into our garden, but it must have been well after work hours because my father was home, and by the time I got the news about what had happened and reached the kitchen doorway, my father was standing there near the sink studying the deep bright markings of the cat's rage on Budge's forearm, shaking his head, then talking in low tones to Nartouie, who was acting as the interpreter for my father's English and the gardener's Armenian. The gardener was red-faced, his voice hoarse.

"He says, Mr. Keeley, you have to burn it," Nartouie said. "There is no other way with sick animals."

"But tell him we don't know the animal is sick."

Nartouie translated.

"He says the boy will die if you don't burn it. He knows. He has seen people become mad from animals."

"Tell him I know all about rabies," my father said. "I've read up on rabies. The wounds are supposed to be cauterized, but by a doctor."

Nartouie translated. My father was looking at her as though he didn't trust what she was telling the gardener.

"Mr. Keeley, he says please. There is no time for a doctor. The boy will die a horrible death."

My father shook his head, studying the wound again. Then he let go of Budge's arm.

"All right," he said to Nartouie. "Bring me the poker from the fire-place."

Nartouie went over and held Budge's hand a second, the good hand. She tried to smile at him. Then she went out into the dining room.

"What is he going to do?" Budge asked my father.

My father had turned on the water in the sink and was testing the temperature.

"Cauterize the wound," my father said without looking up.

"What does that mean?" Budge asked.

"Sterilize it," my father said. "You just touch it for a second to kill the germs."

"He means he's going to burn my arm?"

"Not the whole arm," my father said. "Just the wound. It will only take a second. You mustn't be afraid."

Nartouie came in with the bronze-handled poker and gave it to my father. He put the black tip of it under the faucet and washed it with soap from the soap dish. I could see from my father's face that he was unhappy. He washed the full length of the poker slowly, carefully, then went over it with the dish towel as though it was silver and needed shining.

"It's going to hurt me," Budge said.

"It will only take a second," my father said. "You've got to be brave."

He put the dish towel away under the sink and went over to the stove to turn on the front burner. The gardener took Nartouie aside and whispered something to her.

"Hovaness says he will do it for you if you want him to," Nartouie said to my father.

"It's up to me," my father said. "He's my son."

Budge hadn't moved from his place by the sink and he hadn't looked over at me. I could see that he was frightened from the way he kept pursing his lips without saying anything. My father turned the poker tip back and forth in the gas flame, then brought the poker close to his hand to test the temperature, then put it back in the flame, then brought it over to where my brother was standing by the sink.

"It will be over in a second," he said to Budge, his voice low, tight, unnatural. He held Budge's arm and when he touched the wound, Budge screamed but didn't pull his arm away. My father touched the wound a second time and a third time, then flung the poker into the sink. It sizzled.

"That will have to do," he said to no one in particular. "I can't do it any more."

They took Budge into town to have his wound looked over by a doctor and to get him started on the course of rabies shots, one a day for forty days in his stomach with a long needle. The gardener and a crew from the school's maintenance department managed to track down the cat before dark and to cage it for observation. I went back to the soccer field and sat on the sidelines. I didn't have the heart to play. Lisa came looking for me there, and since my parents were in town at the doctor's, we had time on our hands beyond the mosquito curfew. We headed for the dairy barn. Lisa wanted me to tell her every detail about what had happened, and when I came to the business of the shots in the stomach she winced as though she was the one feeling the long needle. We were sitting side by side on a beam high up in the barn, our legs dangling over the edge well above what hay was in there.

"I have to tell you something important," she said. "But you've got to promise not to tell anybody else. Absolutely nobody else. I mean it."

"Sure," I said. "I promise."

"No, that isn't good enough. Here, you have to kiss my cross so the promise sticks or else the devil will take you and you'll die young."

She loosened a button on her blouse and brought out the cross she wore in there on a gold chain. She leaned forward so that I could kiss the cross.

"All right,"she said. "Now. What I have to tell you is, the cat that bit your brother also bit my finger."

"You're kidding me," I said.

Lisa clicked her tongue in the negative way. "Not at all. Here. I'll show you."

She held out her hand and put a fingernail against a mark on her fore-finger. She squeezed below the mark to make blood rise into it.

"The cat came into our garden before it crossed the road to yours, she said. I was on the porch, and when I saw it, I went down to pet it because I have a thing for cats, and it didn't seem to mind at first but then it turned its head suddenly and bit me."

"You're crazy," I said. "You've got to have that finger burned."

Lisa tucked her cross inside her blouse. "Never," she said. "They're not going to burn my hand with a poker or anything else. And they're not going to stick a needle in my stomach."

"But you'll go mad," I said. "You'll go mad and foam at the mouth and bite anybody who comes close to you, and then they say you'll die a horrible death."

"No I won't," Lisa said. "My life line is even longer than yours. A gypsy woman told me it would be my fate to live past the year 2000."

"What does a gypsy woman know? You've got to tell your father and have him take you into town. Or I'll tell him if you want."

"You promised not to tell anybody. You kissed my cross."

I didn't know what to say. I took her hand to look at her finger again. The mark was barely visible.

"You don't have to worry if I'm not worried," Lisa said. "Since it's my fate to live a long life, it means the cat probably isn't even sick."

"But what if it is?"

Lisa shrugged. "If the cat dies soon, that will be a bad sign. If it does-n't, maybe you'll start believing in gypsy women and how much more they know about fate than you and I do."

Two

I didn't tell anybody about Lisa's cat wound. And I didn't see Lisa herself for three days after our last meeting in the hay loft, because she disappeared into her house and kept to herself. Budge went to the doctor during lunch hour to get his shot in the stomach, and he would come back to school with a special look on his face, not exactly heroic, but with the look of someone who had just come out of battle with a difficult enemy, scarred but victorious. At the Farm School he was a celebrity among the children his age or younger and cause for persistent inquiry about his health among the adults, who would stop him on the road to the soccer field and, if women, kiss him on both cheeks or, if men, brush his hair back or pat his cheek with a friendly hand, gestures of good will that made him visibly uncomfortable.

I couldn't stand not knowing about Lisa, but I also couldn't bring myself to walk up to her house and ask her parents how she was when I had no plausible explanation for doing a thing like that and when she herself was so convinced that there was nothing wrong with her. Instead, on the third day after the cat came into our lives, I went looking for our gardener. I found him smoking a cigarette with some of the maintenance crew in their machinery shed, so I stood around outside the doorway until he was finished with the cigarette, then motioned him to come out so that I could talk to him.

"Where's the cat?" I asked him.

"Where do you think? The cat's in its cage."

"So it isn't dead yet?"

"Cats don't die so easily," the gardener said. "Cats have many lives."

"Well if it isn't dead yet, maybe it isn't sick."

"That is up to God. We will know soon enough."

"When is soon enough?"

The gardener shrugged. "Maybe by the end of the week. These things are not in our hands. As any good Christian knows."

I thought I was supposed to be a good Christian myself but I didn't want to show that I knew nothing about what was in whose hands by asking him where the cat was caged so that I could have a look at it. I found that out from Kirkor, one of his three sons and the one closest to my age who was by that time my best friend at the Farm School. Kirkor took me to visit the cat at the dark end of the pigpen. It was in a feed barrel set on its side between two rows of bricks and covered in front by chicken wire. The cat looked dead asleep, curled up at the back of the barrel with a paw across its eyes, but when Kirkor plucked the chicken wire in front with a stick, it raised its head and gazed at him. Then it went back to sleep. Chunks of something that might have been food scraps were scattered on the floor of the cage as though thrown there helter-skelter.

"That cat doesn't look sick to me," I said to Kirkor. "There's no foam around its mouth and it doesn't seem to care that we're here to look it over. All it wants is to sleep."

"My father says you never know," Kirkor said. "Sometimes the cat plays at being asleep or plays dead just to fool you."

"Why would it do a thing like that?"

Kirkor looked at me as though I was weak in the head. "So it can bite you better, of course. You think it's dead, and as soon as you get close enough to pick it up, it goes for you."

"Well it isn't playing dead now. You can see it's breathing like any live cat."

"Just be patient," Kirkor said. "My father says you've got to be patient with cats. Especially sick ones."

After that visit, I got up enough courage to go by Lisa's house and to ask for her at the kitchen door, where her grandmother hung out most of the day. The grandmother moved heavily to the hallway door and called out that the American was here to talk to Lisa, could she come downstairs for a minute. I could make out Lisa hopping down the stairs on the run. She came into the kitchen wearing a white blouse and a light blue skirt, colors of the Greek flag that made her look on holiday. She used my Greek nickname—Mihalaki—to say hello, but she spoke in the English her father had taught her, I suppose so her grandmother wouldn't understand what she was saying or maybe just to show off in front of her.

"You look very sad," she said, half smiling. "You see, I have not died."

"I didn't think you'd died. I've been to see the cat. The cat seems all right to me."

"Of course. Gypsy women do not lie."

"Well, Kirkor's father says we'll have to wait a while longer. Until the end of the week at least."

"Wait for what? Until this cat has little ones? Come, forget this cat. We will go now to feed the cows."

She crossed over and took my hand and led me toward the door. Her grandmother stared at the floor as we passed, pretending not to see our linked hands.

By the end of the week the cat was still alive and had struck up a kind of friendship with the manager of the pigpen who had been feeding it regularly. He reported that he was prepared to take it to his parents' village because they were in need of a mouser at home. Budge's doctor in town decided that he could stop the anti-rabies shots in his stomach, and that Sunday my father held a family conference to announce that we, the whole family, would be celebrating Budge's courage and good luck by taking a four-day trip to the mountains as soon as the house trailer he'd ordered from the United States was unloaded at Salonika harbor. He got out a brochure to show us what the house trailer looked like and then a map to outline the route we would take through the northern villages to climb up the mountain called Kastania, where he said we would be able to see clear into Yugoslavia. The trailer had only two wheels and was pointed in front so that it didn't look much more like a house than Panayotis' milk wagon, but it had a door that seemed big enough for Nartouie to stand in upright with space to spare, and there were windows all around it that looked like small house windows. The way my father answered our questions about things inside the trailer pictured in the brochure and how he was going to hook it up to the De Soto showed that he was very proud to be the owner of the only such portable house with kitchen in northern Greece, but when my mother asked a few practical questions about how the eating and sleeping arrangements would be organized to accommodate six people including Nartouie in such a confined space, he seemed deflated.

"Don't worry about things like that," he said to her. "We'll work it out. After all, families live in trailers full-time from one year to the next."

"Sure, if you're a refugee or can't afford a decent house. But this is supposed to be for our vacation. We're supposed to be doing this for fun."

"We're going to have fun. I guarantee it. Nartouie and the boys can sleep outside if necessary once we're set up."

"The point is, I hadn't expected Nartouie to be included in our vacation."

"That's to make it easier for you," my father said. "She can keep an eye on the boys."

"Well I'm not really objecting to the idea," my mother said quietly. "It's just a lot of people to feed and sleep in a small space."

My father looked irritated. "Well what do you expect when you go on vacation in a trailer? I mean I thought that was the whole point of ordering this thing from the States."

My mother stared at her lap. "There are just some things I have to think about that you don't have to think about when there are so many of us involved."

I was as excited as my father about this new possibility for adventure, but I hated it when my mother gave in to him so easily. She always seemed to do that in those days, have her say when she felt she had to but let his say prevail in the end. I have to admit that at the time I didn't really understand what went on between those two when we weren't around, and it is only in retrospect that I see she was probably disappointed that it wouldn't be just the two of them going off alone in that trailer for a while. The fact is that I never quite thought about them in that way until I was well into my adolescence and was assured by a confidante of mine—our occasional housekeeper in Washington, D.C. who replaced Nartouie—that my parents, who slept in separate rooms, did actually make love sometimes and especially on Sunday mornings when we boys were in Sunday school or otherwise occupied with our Sunday pleasures. The reason I was so slow to get this message may have been my never once having seen my father kiss my mother in our presence or even put his arm around her affectionately. And it wasn't until both my parents were dead and their correspondence over the years became part of my father's archive that I learned how deeply in love they appeared to have been in their early days together even if certain danger signs were also there from the start, and even if my mother kept a letter from another suitor named Van begging her to marry him only a few months before she married my father. The depth of my parents' feeling for each other showed clearly in the letters they exchanged while courting and as newly-weds, my father's curiously signed as "Daddy" from the start and my mother's signature changing from "Tillie" to "Maw" soon after they actually had children. Much of the correspondence between them in the years that followed was concerned with what they saw as the sometimes eccentric and distressing behavior, though never the faulty grammar, of their three growing offspring.

* * *

The arrival of the house trailer at the Farm School was a major event that September in *1937*. My father drove it up from Salonika harbor attached to the De Soto by a linkage fashioned in the school's blacksmith shop, and by the time it moved at slow speed from the main gate to the front of our house, it had gathered every child living on that side of the school grounds and some of their parents as well. The deaf mute named Yaya had pulled his trash cart over to the curb well before the trailer arrived opposite him, and he stood there at attention beside his donkey until the front door of the De Soto opened, at which point his hand came up in a sharp salute and stayed that way until my father disappeared up the steps leading into the patio, with his three sons following him in order of descending height. When my father appeared again in the kitchen doorway wearing his one-piece dungarees, he found the trailer swarming with little people trying to get a look inside the thing from one or another of its windows. Yaya had brought his cart over to block access to the back of the trailer so his donkey could have a look through the rear window after he himself had seen his fill.

An epic action followed: my father reversing the car and trailer down the curling driveway that led through trees and a stretch of flower garden to the garage at the lower end of our house. Though he had been an Army Air Corps fighter pilot and then instructor of cadet flyers during the First World War and was said to have performed for a spell as a circus stunt pilot in Texas before entering the Foreign Service, my father always had trouble on the ground when it came to backing a car. Even on the straightaway, he relied for guidance on instinct and his straight-ahead peripheral vision rather than on rearview mirrors or turning his head to see where he was going, as though the best procedure in backing a car was to make sure the front of it remained level with the horizon ahead. This predilection, and the peculiar dynamics of a trailer linked by bulb to the back of a car, could cause the kind of frustration that would turn him from a normally peaceful, soft-spoken, and conscientious public servant—cool enough, when called upon, to walk in a top hat beside visiting kings and prime ministers—into a raging first sergeant in command of a mentally retarded squad of slackers bent on defeating him and his ambition rather than the common enemy.

On most days involving the trailer's reverse progress, the delinquent squad consisted of his wife, children, and any household staff in the vicinity, but on this day it included other children, some of their parents, members of the Farm School staff, and the moaning deaf mute. Those old enough to yell advice did so freely, in turn or in tandem, whether in their native language or in broken English, suggesting which direction the steering wheel ought to go in order to keep the trailer from climbing the curb on this or that side of the driveway or climbing back off the curb before it crashed into a pine tree or cleared a broad swath through the sweet peas. Perspiration coursing down his temples, my father would poke his head out of the driver's window to see where the trailer had ended up, would then shake his head and sigh, and, in harsh language few could understand, would berate one or another of the gathered advisers who had guided him off a straight path, the leading voice of his advisers changing every time the failing became acute, my father's own voice still strong but hoarse by the time the trailer backed up against the garage door in a violent resolution. Yet, during the time car and trailer were freely in motion inside the boundaries of the road, his head at no point leaned out the window to gauge where his erratic steering might actually be taking him.

My friend Kirkor was there to see the end. "That new machine could become dangerous in a crowded village," he said to me. "It doesn't run straight."

"There's no need to worry," I said. "My father was an airplane pilot during the war. He can handle it."

"But this thing isn't an airplane. This thing is like a truck that could run people over and squash them flat the way you would rabbits crossing the road."

"It isn't a truck, it's a house. A traveling house."

"That's even worse. Anyway, what's the point of a house on wheels? Especially when they don't run straight."

"It's going to take us up the mountain where you can see Yugoslavia and we're going to live in it for a while away from everything."

"Who wants to live in a thing like that? It doesn't look like there's room in it to turn around."

"You're just jealous," I said. "If you could get inside it you'd see how much room there is."

Kirkor turned away. "You can have it all to yourself. I don't want anything to do with a thing as dangerous as that."

I woke up the next day feeling bad about having told Kirkor he was just jealous, even if I still half believed it, so the first chance I got, I asked my mother if I could have permission to bring him along with me for a look inside the thing now that my father had maneuvered it safely into the garage and had its wheels blocked. My mother was getting the downstairs living room set up for an afternoon gathering of her bridge group made up of foreign and domestic ladies from the town, and her mind seemed to be elsewhere, because what she said over her shoulder was that it would be all right with her if it was all right with my father, just the right message to kill the idea dead.

I decided not to disturb my father at his office that afternoon but to act on my own initiative when I got home from school, with the help of Nartouie, who turned out to be just as eager as I was to explore the trailer's dark insides. Her assignment was to find the key to the trailer wherever it was stored in my father's dresser, and my assignment was to use the key to open the trailer door, a thing she said she could not bring herself to do without permission. Once we had the trailer door open, our plan was for Kirkor to alternate with me as lookout to make sure the coast remained clear outside the garage so that each of us would have a chance to study the trailer's insides as long as we chose to. The one thing Nartouie and I did not want was a gang of kids or even adults traipsing into the garage behind us to explore our new mystery machine.

When I went over to Kirkor's house that afternoon to tell him what we had in mind, he greeted me with about the same restrained, self-protecting interest as the first time we'd met months before, and when I explained my plan for showing him the trailer's insides, he just shrugged.

"That's for you and your family," he said. "We can get along with the house we have. We don't need a house that has wheels or a fancy car to drag it to the mountains."

"I just thought you might like to see what it looks like inside. I haven't even seen in there myself."

"That's all right," Kirkor said. "It's for you and your brothers to play in. Seeing what's in there wouldn't do me any good."

It was the first time in my life I could remember being made to feel the prince to a friend's pauper, and I didn't like the feeling, not only because I'd been rejected at the palace gate I'd tried to open to him but because I'd suddenly been made to see that a gate was there between us. I went home to tell Nartouie that Kirkor wasn't interested in looking inside the trailer, that he told me it belonged to me and my family and wasn't anything he needed, so I'd lost my enthusiasm for exploring it myself. Nartouie said I was talking nonsense, I had no business paying attention to what Kirkor said, he had his life to live and I had mine, and he was lucky to have what he had, including me as his friend. She took me by the hand and led me down the driveway to the garage, then handed me the tagged key she'd picked up from my father's dresser. I stood there looking at it. Nartouie finally took the key out of my hand and opened the trailer door. I felt a little thrill go through me, part expectation, part pleasure in doing the illegal thing. It was dark in the trailer, but we could see that it had a wall-to-wall two-level bunk bed at one end and some chairs set at a table in the middle and a small kitchen at the near end that seemed to have everything you might need, at least for a vacation. The place felt the way I imagined the inside of a yacht might feel, and it smelled of new wood.

It was while Nartouie was looking through the cabinet under the kitchen counter that my father appeared in the trailer doorway. He stood there watching her bent backside with his hands on his hips, a preliminary posture that I had come to know during my spanking days, and though I considered myself beyond that prospect now, it still struck terror in me.

"How did you get in here?" my father said neither to me nor Nartouie directly but to the empty space above us, and very quietly, another danger sign.

Nartouie wheeled around and stood up. She wiped her hands on the sides of her dress as though they were wet from washing up. "I borrowed the key," she said finally

"You borrowed the key? How do you borrow the key without asking me or Mrs. Keeley?"

"I borrowed it to clean here a bit. I didn't think I needed permission to clean."

"It's spotless in there," my father said. "The thing is brand new."

"Yes, Mr. Keeley. Of course. But I did not know it was so clean. I expected dirt from its trip. All the way from America."

My father stood there shaking his head. "And Mike here was helping you clean, is that it?"

"That is right," Nartouie said. "But he was just going out and make sure nobody come in here who shouldn't come in here."

She moved over to brush her hand through my hair. I would have kissed her if I was the kissing kind in those days and if my father wasn't still standing there.

"Well I didn't know if there were thieves in here or what when I drove up," my father said. "From now on you don't open the trailer without letting people know ahead of time. Is that understood?"

"As you prefer, Mr. Keeley."

"It isn't what I prefer. It's the way things should be."

"As you prefer."

My father stood there shaking his head, studying her, his lips pursed. Then, suddenly, he smiled, first at her and then at me, shook his head a final time and turned away. When we heard the door to the De Soto slam shut outside the garage, Nartouie looked at me and made a face that said, What can one say? Then she bent down and finished looking through the cabinet under the counter. There was nothing in it as far as I could see.

* * *

As our vacation trip to Kastania mountain neared, the happy prospect became complicated in my imagination by the problem of brigands. It was from Lisa that I learned about brigands, as I had about gypsies. When I told her about my father's plan to take his family on a vacation in the traveling house as soon as he could arrange some days of leave, she said I'd better be careful not to end up spending the rest of the summer and maybe the fall and winter as well in a brigand cave like Miss Ellen Stone and her pregnant companion had done sometime around the year 1900. We were back in the cow barn when she brought the subject up, only this time sitting on bales of straw neatly piled up to make a high platform, the product of a grand new farm machine called a combine that Charlie House had brought to the school with further donations from his Princeton classmates, the first such machine to reach the country and maybe the first anywhere in the Near East. The bales were not that comfortable, not as easy on you as loose hay, but stacked up like that, nobody could deny the classy look they gave to that barn.

"The thing about brigands," Lisa said, "is people don't understand them. They fought against the Turks for our independence. And they robbed people in order to eat."

"Well there aren't any Turks here now, so why do they go on robbing people?"

"There were Turks here not so long ago. Maybe it takes time to get used to being free."

"I just wish they'd go back where they came from and stay away from Kastania mountain."

"But that's where they came from. Some from our Macedonia, some from Macedonia on the other side of the border. Miss Stone's brigands came from Macedonia in Bulgaria. Which is why old Father House became the go-between for the ransom money."

"I thought Father House came from America."

"Yes, but he also came from Macedonia in Bulgaria, where he was a missionary before he came here."

I had been trying to decide whether I really wanted to hear the story of Miss Stone and her pregnant companion in a brigand cave, but Lisa decided for me when she saw what must have been an intense geographical confusion written on my face. According to the story she told, Miss Stone and her companion were captured in Bulgaria just north of the border, where they were doing Christian missionary work in the villages, though she didn't know what work that might be since the villagers were already mostly Christian. Miss Stone was from America and had been a missionary for many years, and her companion was Bulgarian but educated in America and married to a preacher whose child was four months old inside her. The brigands were dressed half like Turks and half like Albanians, with their faces painted black, but they were really Bulgarians who believed in Karl Marx. The brigands were fighting for the freedom of Macedonia, and they needed money to buy weapons, so they took Miss Stone and her companion to the mountains and sent a messenger to the American missionaries demanding a ransom of many hundreds of dollars. The missionaries asked the American government for help, but the American government refused to deal with brigands, so a collection was taken up throughout America and England. It took many months to raise only half the ransom. Meanwhile, the two ladies traveled from one cave to another, with only a small fire for heat that choked them with smoke, and they were forced to listen to the brigand chief read to them every day from Karl Marx. When they refused to pay any more attention while the chief was reading, an agreement was reached: they would listen to Mr. Marx in the mornings, and the brigands would listen to the Christian bible in the afternoons. This way the two ladies kept from going crazy until the baby was born with the help of an old crone brought up from a nearby village dressed in rags and with years of dirt on her face who was forced by the brigands to act as a midwife.

"What's a midwife?" I had to ask.

"A woman who pulls the baby out, hlup, like this," Lisa said. "Don't you know anything?"

I decided I didn't know anything. Lisa went on to say that it was a girl the midwife pulled out, and when Miss Stone suddenly handed her to the brigand chief, he was miraculously transformed from a brigand into a father and refused to let anyone harm the child from that moment on, though some of his men were ready to kill her and her mother for screaming too loud. The brigand chief finally decided that half a ransom was better than none, so he sent a messenger to Father House to arrange the delivery of the ransom in gold coins because the American spoke Bulgarian and was thought to be a saint. To keep the Turks from confiscating the ransom, Father House fooled them by filling some bags full of lead and putting them on a train heading for the American Consulate in Constantinople.

"That doesn't sound to me like a thing a saint would do," I said quietly to my feet.

"Sure it is if you're a Christian saint. The Turks are Moslems."

"Well what if they opened the bags and found lead in them? They'd kill Father House and maybe the women too."

"The Turks were too slow for that. Father House was already in the mountains delivering the gold while the train was being loaded. And besides, he had God on his side. Which is why the two ladies and the baby were saved in the end, though they came out of the mountains with black faces from the smoky fires and despair still burning in their hearts."

I spent several bad nights dreaming of brigands and Turks in different costumes but all with the same blackened faces, and I finally got up the courage to ask my mother if she knew that there were brigands hiding out in caves on Kastania mountain. My mother said she didn't know of any such caves and doubted that brigands would bother us that far from the border, but anyway I wasn't to worry, because father had been notified by the Greek authorities that six soldiers would be assigned to guard us once we had established our campsite on the mountain. Caves or no caves, this news meant there really might be brigands somewhere in the neighborhood, but six soldiers to guard you: that impressed me. I slept reasonably well through the long wait of days and nights before we set out for the village of Verria at the foot of Kastania, with the house trailer bouncing behind us across the pot-holed plain as though on a rocky sea.

Verria is now a town that can boast as many concrete structures for housing small business enterprise and rising domestic tranquillity as you are likely to find so close to the northern border, but in those days it was a village mostly of mud brick dwellings and dirt roads that served the principal enterprises of farming and herding. The main road from Salonika—the beginning of the road to Athens—was possessed by horse-drawn carts and animals on the move, with no quarter given to other modes of transportation except in whatever good time a farmer or shepherd in the center of the road might choose to give you. But the arrival of a traveling house on the outskirts of the village was cause for the kind of initial surprise that cleared the way ahead, followed by a quick gathering of collective curiosity such as that usually reserved for visiting dignitaries on parade. You could hear people yelling to a neighbor that there was a small house going by, come out and see for yourself, and children with the largest ambition would run along beside the trailer and vault high to have a fleeting look inside its windows.

I found the attention thrilling at first, then embarrassing, especially when we were forced to slow down to a crawl and the children crowding in beside the trailer began to irritate my father to the point where he had to lower his window and try to shoo them off in a language foreign to them that merely roused high-pitched mock imitation in those urchins among them who were still uncultivated by public manners and due respect. But word that an American official was passing through must have gone ahead of us by telephone, because we reached the heart of the village to find a policeman standing in the middle of the dusty road waving his arms to clear the trailer of hangers-on and then to signal the way up the mountain with a long, precise gesture aimed at the single route ahead, and, as he stepped aside to let us pass, a final salute made for generals.

The lasting thrill came from the landscape that opened out below us as we curled our way up the mountain: a patchwork valley of green and yellow and brown stretching to the west and south as far as the shimmering purple range on the horizon, with thatched sheepfolds on the edge of rock cliffs in the foreground, here and there fencing in a wild playground of thyme and asphodel on both sides of the road, and far below a white-washed church to sanctify the opening of that fertile plain. We were close to the top of the pass that was to be our campsite when my father pulled over on a narrow ledge to let the boiling motor cool off. The six of us lined up with the trailer for a backrest to gaze out at the valley below, my father shaking his head not in consternation but wonder, and I remember looking out for the longest time at what had moved him, so that it took hold in my memory as one of the pre-war images of the country that survived, with total clarity, my going away and my coming back.

While we were still lined up there for the motor's cooling, my mother brought out a watermelon from the trailer ice box, and with the help of Nartouie cut it up in half-moon slices, one for each of us in turn but all of us under command not to take a bite until she, as family archivist, could take a snapshot to record this first gesture of harmony at the start of our vacation. We were barely into that slice of ice-cold pleasure when Nartouie, hovering on the edge of the family circle, called out "look" to signal a startling sight: three men in a row on mule-back, rifles slung over their shoulders, motionless as an equestrian sculpture, watching us from the high rock projection that cut off our view of the road about a kilometer up ahead.

"Brigands," I said, under my breath.

Unfortunately, Budge heard me. "Brigands. Who are you kidding? Brigands don't wear khaki uniforms. Those must be our soldiers."

He was right. Suddenly three more armed men appeared on mule-back, watched us a moment, then all six disappeared. And they stayed out of sight and were gone by the time we reached the rock ledge where they had landed out of thin air. Just beyond that, my father pulled over and stopped to explore what he called the lay of the land. We watched him cross a level spread of sparse brush to a point where he stood motionless against the sky, arms akimbo, then paced the cliff-face for a spell, stood again to gaze up the road ahead, and finally turned back toward the car at his usual fast pace.

"This is it," he said, climbing back in. "That's why they showed themselves over there by the cliff edge. You won't find a nicer spot before the road angles off toward the village up ahead and then starts downhill again."

Nobody argued. I guess everybody was now as ready as I was to escape from the car and face the good things waiting for us out there.

"What happened to the soldiers?" Budge said.

"They're probably up in the village having a coffee," my father said in a way that was meant to be funny.

As it turned out, they weren't anywhere near the village but had been watching us all along, and when they saw that we were setting up our camp, they must have decided to put up their small tents about a soccer field or two away on the far side of the road just out of sight. I found that out after we'd spent an hour or so getting the car and trailer backed into exactly the right position on the edge of the cliff to provide a view for those who might have a window to look out from, and after we'd gone along behind my father to gather up rocks of the right size to put in front and behind all six wheels. When the car was finally unpacked and the trailer ready for us to climb in, my father stood in the doorway and said it would be a good thing if we boys took a careful look around the campsite and the nearby territory to make sure there weren't any stray animals in the neighborhood and maybe gather up some wildflowers with the help of Nartouie, because he and mother were going to take a nap to recover from the long drive and would appreciate a little bit of quiet time to themselves.

Nartouie took Budge's hand and pushed Bob and me ahead of her in the direction of the road before any of us had a chance to protest. At the time I thought it downright cruel of my father to keep the trailer to mother and himself like that before any of the rest of us had a chance to check out our new home for the days ahead. I don't know how many years it took me, thinking back on that moment of disappointment, to realize how cruel it might have been to my mother, standing there with her eyes lowered to the dust, for my father to have done otherwise.

At one point in our survey of the campsite I veered off from the others and ended up on the far side of the road looking across a short open space at the soldiers camped out on the edge of the pine forest that covered the slope of the mountain over there, some of their mules hitched up to trees. The tents were well hidden in the brush, and I had to look hard to make out the figures squatting on the ground near them, their legs bound up in khaki leggings and their round caps lined with stripes like half a watermelon. I looked so hard and long that I didn't notice the one of them on guard duty who circled around from somewhere and came up behind me to make me jump out of my skin.

"So what have we got here?" he said, planting himself in front of me. "A bandit pretending to be a midget?"

I couldn't speak for the longest minute. "I'm not a midget," I said. "I'm the son of the American Consul."

"Well, now that's something," the soldier said. "Po, po. Excuse me."

He came to attention suddenly, raised his rifle to his shoulder, and saluted, all smiles. "So what are you doing here all by yourself, Son of the American Consul?"

"Just looking," I said.

"Well, why don't you come along with me so you can really have a look. And maybe I can get the corporal to let you ride one of the mules."

I shrugged. "That's all right," I said. "I can see fine from here."

44

"Come on," the soldier said. "We're not going to eat you. We like Americans. We don't eat Americans. We're here to see the Bulgarians don't eat you."

The soldier reached over and took my hand. I decided I'd better go along with him.

"Where are the Bulgarians?" I said.

"Who knows?" the soldier said. "All over. Up in the mountains. Their mountains, our mountains. Who knows?"

"And why do they want to eat us?"

"What kind of question is that? Because they're Bulgarians. What do you think?"

I didn't think anything. I was dumb about Bulgarians and just about everybody else who wasn't American like my family, except some Canadians, Armenians, Greeks, Germans, and the few other non-Germans who were part of the group rejected by the Hitler Jugend at our school—not that I could really see much difference between any of them. I didn't tell the soldier that but just went along with him until we came up against four other soldiers lounging between their tents, two playing backgammon, all four smoking. The two playing backgammon looked up for a minute, then went back to the board to talk to the dice in intimate language I sometimes didn't understand. The other two studied me. I freed my hand from the soldier on duty and stood there trying to look important.

My soldier guard put his hand on my shoulder. "Our little friend here, son of the American Consul, wants to know why Bulgarians want to eat Americans. What should I tell him?"

"Tell him for the same reason Bulgarians like the breast of the chicken," one of the others said. "And the cheek of the fish. They always want the best because they never manage to get it. Somebody always takes it away from them."

"Tell him anyway it isn't Bulgarians he should worry about," his companion said. "It's Turks. They eat whatever they can get, but they like young boys especially."

"Don't tell him that, in the name of God," the first one said. "That will just get us in trouble. Tell him everybody eats everybody else in this part of the world. We're all hungry for our neighbors all of the time."

He reached over to grab my leg, but I dodged his hand. I decided that was my chance to escape, so I took off for the road as fast as I could run. They were all laughing behind me, but I didn't stop to catch my breath until I was over the embankment and safely on the far side of the road.

The summer had turned toward fall those days, and it was cool in the evenings. Nobody had any trouble sleeping that first night as far as I could tell, including me and my brothers, assigned to sleep three abreast sideways on the back-end bunk-bed meant for two thin people sleeping lengthwise. My mother and father were above us, with a rear window and two side windows to take in the view. Nartouie had a mattress to herself on the kitchen floor. She was the only one you could hear snoring, but even that didn't cause a problem once my father got up and fixed the trailer door open to let in the fading sound of cicadas and the cool mountain air.

I spent most of the next day roaming the territory on our side of the road, a good distance from the soldiers' camp opposite and, on my father's instructions, well below the turn of the road leading to the village. There were some interesting rock formations on that side, outcrops you could climb a bit to get a higher look and openings in crags that you could pretend were caves even if they didn't lead anywhere, but I spent most of my time going for wildflowers of all kinds, none of which I could name. And when I brought Nartouie over to ask her help in naming them, I could tell she was either making up the names or speaking another language because they didn't sound to me like words in English or Greek. I asked her if those were Armenian names. She shrugged and said what difference does it make? It's what they look like and smell like that matters.

Some of them were too small to look like much to me, and most didn't smell at all, but I gathered up a bunch that probably included a thistle or two and took them to my mother, who thanked me for them and said it was an impressive bouquet, even if she couldn't give them any names either. I've been back to that mountain several times since, years after the war, when new trees had sprung up to replace some of the forest that burned to ashes under the German occupation, but the flowers were sparse where they had once flourished, and if some were the same, I couldn't recognize them any longer. The Greek flowers I know now—acanthus, hyacinth, carnation, gardenia—are hardly wild and anyway first came to me with their Greek names from poems, these mostly by poets living farther south who probably would not have known the wildflowers I found that second day on the mountain, except the one that most Greeks learn about in school because it is the flower called asphodel that Odysseus found in Hades, Homer's land of the dead.

Our second night on the mountain was terrifying. The wind came in as a mild breeze in the late afternoon and by supper time had cooled things down enough to send Nartouie inside to dig out something for us to wear over our summer T-shirts. I had hoped to sleep outside that night to get a good look at the stars, because I remember Lisa telling me that one thing you could count on when you reached the high ground of a mountain was seeing the dome of heaven in a way that made the stars you recognized seem so bright you'd think them new, and there would be plenty of others you wouldn't find anywhere else again. I had to wait almost a year before I came to see the stars that clearly, because our second night on Kastania had us inside the trailer and early to bed as the wind curling down a ravine from the mountaintop grew strong enough to make sitting out fun for some of us but apparently uncomfortable for the older generation, which went to bed early, too, with the trailer door shut.

It must have been about midnight when the howl from outside and the gentle rocking of the trailer got to Nartouie. I was sound asleep myself, and since she didn't say anything but just got up and went for the door, I don't think anybody realized that she was heading outside until the door opened and was suddenly picked up by the wind so that it went flying out of her hand and slammed back against the side of the trailer with a force that sounded like a gunshot and shook everybody awake. My father was up and out in a flash, and the three of us came out right behind him. Nartouie was cowering on her knees at the front of the trailer, one hand on the link bar to steady herself and the other at her neck to keep her nightgown tightly closed. My father was examining the side of the trailer, shaking his head.

"There's a hole here, he said. You put a hole in the side of the trailer."

"I didn't do it," Nartouie said. "The wind did it."

"Well you don't go opening a door in the middle of the night when there's a wind like this unless you can hang on to the door."

He was still examining the hole, running his finger around it, shaking his head.

"The wind will kill us," Nartouie said. "It will push us over the cliff."

"It will do no such thing," my father said. "The trailer is all blocked in place. Nothing can move it."

"I don't mind dying," Nartouie said. "What is death to me when I have died once already? But the boys. And Mrs. Keeley."

"Nobody's going to die," my father said. "It's just very inconsiderate of you to wake us up in the middle of the night like this and to put a hole in the trailer when we're up here where nobody can fix it. Now let's get back inside and try to get some sleep."

"I'm not going inside," Nartouie said. "If I'm going to die I want to die under the stars where I will be found like I am and not without my arms and legs at the bottom of a cliff."

My father stood there looking down at her, then turned away. "All right, suit yourself. I give up. How am I supposed to put sense in the head of a woman who simply refuses to grow up?"

The rest of the night was hell, anyway for me. I lay there listening to the wind, judging its strength by the measure of whether the trailer was rocking less or more, and when I would finally fall asleep, that never lasted long. The wind did not begin to die down to a breeze until the light came in from the kitchen window, and by that time I had woken more than once at the bottom of a cliff, breathing hard but with no arms or legs to help me sit up so that I could be sure I was alive and safe. Nartouie did not come back in until the wind was gone and the sun well on the rise, and when she did she sat on her mattress with her back turned to us, staring at the cupboard under the kitchen sink. My mother finally got up and went over to sit beside her, an arm around her shoulder, her voice too low for us to make out what she was saying. But it must have worked to bring Nartouie back to the land of the living, because she soon got up and began to make breakfast for those of us with enough appetite to eat.

The wind returned that afternoon and seemed to gain strength the closer it got to sundown. Before setting up the table for supper, Nartouie moved her thin and lumpy mattress outside on the lee side of the car and pinned it down in the corners with stones. My mother and father had a family conference between themselves, and my father then brought us boys into the action to remove the rocks blocking the trailer wheels so that he could move the trailer farther inland, a good half soccer field from the cliff face. When we had all the wheels safely blocked in again, Nartouie picked up her mattress from where it was now lying in the open and carried it over to her preferred spot on the lee side of the car and pinned it down with her own collection of stones. My father stood there staring at her, but he didn't say anything. When he turned away there was a look on his face that I had rarely seen, a kind of sadness that I might later have identified as an unspoken acknowledgment of inevitable defeat. After supper, during the hour before sunset, he worked on the hole in the trailer's side, taping it over with electric tape carefully, thoroughly, as though a wound in his thigh.

During the night, the wind was relentless again, sometimes gusting enough to rock the trailer so that you had to use your arms to stiffen yourself in place in that crowded and increasingly ripe-smelling bunk. I tried to ignore the feel of that wind, brave it out without a sound, torn between fear and what must have been loyalty to my father's image of possibilities, even if I'd seen that begin to fade with the dying sun. We were all up very early that morning, the whole family, outside to breathe in the sweet mountain air and see the dawn come in with what was now a cooling breeze. At breakfast father announced that we would be breaking camp that noon. We boys protested, but not with enough force to convince anybody, and Nartouie seemed ready to dance, clearing things up with some kind of Armenian song on her tongue to help give her motions an exuberant rhythm. If my mother was disappointed, she gave no sign of it but turned to packing things up with her usual quiet efficiency and grace.

Mid-morning my father put on his golf breeches and his fedora hat. He was never a golfer, as far as I can remember—in any case, those days there was no golf course within reach of Salonika—but his golf outfit was what he sometimes wore when he was on vacation or traveling for pleasure but had reason to wear something more formal than dungarees. The occasion that morning was a farewell visit to the squad of soldiers encamped across the way for our protection against those invisible brigands. As my father headed for the road, he picked up a stick brought in by the wind, longer than an ordinary cane, more like a crook a shepherd would use, anyway handled by him as an aid to walking with an authority that I thought extremely impressive. I ran to catch up with him.

"Can I go along?" I said to my father's back. "I can show him where the soldiers are. I saw where they are the other day."

"All right, come along. But brush your knees off and pull up your socks so you look halfway decent."

He waited while I pulled up my socks and brushed at the dirt on my grungy knees to no effect. Budge and Bob wanted to come along too, so we waited for them to tidy up their clothes a bit, then we all fell in line behind my father, each of us working hard to keep up with him without actually running. We crossed the road, lined up by some unspoken rule in descending order of age and height, and followed my father's fast pace across the stretch of no man's land toward the edge of the woods where the soldiers had their camp. A guard intercepted us part way across, not the one who had escorted me, so Budge had to explain in Greek who we were and what we wanted, and that sent the guard scurrying to find his corporal. By the time we got to the encampment, all six soldiers were there at attention to greet us. The corporal stepped forward and saluted. Using Budge as interpreter, my father thanked the corporal and his men on behalf of the American Consulate for the friendship they had shown our country and for the protection they had given him and his family, which would no longer be needed because we would be heading back to the village of Verria at noon. Then my father brought his hand up to his fedora and saluted sharply. It seemed to me a grand salute, no doubt given its style and shape from his service in the Army Air Corps, and as we turned away to head back toward the road, I suddenly felt very proud and showed it in the way I marched off solemnly in line between my brothers.

I didn't get a chance to feel that kind of pride again until the morning some months later that brought the King of Greece to the American Farm School during a visit to his northern domain and my father greeted him outside our house wearing his fanciest clothes, striped trousers and Eton jacket, the King in rather austere military khakis, cap and all. My father and Charlie House, who was dressed in the heavy black suit he wore at weddings and funerals, escorted the King on a tour of the school that took His Majesty within smell of, if not actually in touch with, every rough inch of the farm enterprise, from bull pen to pig sties to chicken houses, with a huge entourage behind the leaders that included most members of the school staff, their families, their pet animals, even, in the case of the deaf-mute, the donkey free for the day of his trash cart. The three Keeley boys, outfitted with jackets and wide-collared shirts, traveled for a while with their mother a discreet distance behind the American Consul and the Director of the School, both chattering away in English to the more or less attentive King, who used his riding crop occasionally to point a question regarding this or that curiosity he encountered on his way.

At some point brother Bob and I broke ranks to join our Armenian friends on the front steps of the dormitory building, Princeton Hall, where those few of our generation who had become bored with touring familiar territory had gathered to watch the dignitaries make their way back toward the Director's house for tea. Suddenly the parade stopped. I can't be sure who gave the signal for that, but I have my suspicions. In any case, I saw my father say something to His Majesty and the baton was suddenly pointing in the direction of Bob and me. My father then signaled us to come over. The second time he signaled, there was a degree of persuasive violence in the gesture, so I figured I'd better get moving, awkward as I felt in front of my Armenian friends about going over to the head of the line like that. I took Bob's arm in one hand and tried to straighten my hand-me-down jacket with the other as we crossed to shake hands with His Majesty, my eyes avoiding his at first and concentrating on his shining military belt. The King smiled formally and said, "I'm pleased to meet you, young fellow" in perfect British English, and I answered, "And I the same" in my village Greek. That made him let go of my hand and turn to shake Bob's, who said nothing. My father had a little smile on his face. Maybe he liked my having answered in Greek, even if he had no way of knowing what I'd said or the provincial tilt of my accent.

THREE

I remember 1938 as the best of possible years for the expatriate young. Much of the rest of the world had begun to be threatened by the prospect of catastrophic events, but in the small corner of Greece that I occupied with my family and friends, there was no sign of such threat that I, in my relative innocence, could see. By January of that year, the Keeley boys had settled into a passionless, if wary, routine at the German School that made their time there at least bearable, especially since the outcast companions excluded from the Hitler Jugend drill sessions remained an international medley of keen adventurers ready to devote their free time to roaming the city from its bay-side caiques to the high walls of the old prison guarding the slopes of Mt. Hortiati. And the Farm School remained an inexhaustible community of sandlot athletes, verbal fabricators, and pubescent instructors of both sexes—Lisa still the master spirit—some wiser than their years in the ways of animals and men but all given tirelessly to whatever open-air pleasures the season provided for their oasis.

Among the adults, my mother came into prominence that year as both advanced tutor and protector. She now had time on her hands to fill out our lessons in grammar with reading assignments in books that soon became our early literary Bibles—*Tom Sawyer, Huckleberry Finn, David Copperfield, Two Years Before the Mast*—and she managed to convince my father that each of us was old enough to merit a small weekly allowance for personal recreation in addition to our streetcar fare. It seems that after the rougher years of serving as the wife of an underpaid civil servant in hardship posts such as Damascus and Beirut and boring posts such as Montreal, with three boys to feed, clothe, and nurture and—given a hard-working, eccentric husband—to do so mostly on her own, she now had come into a certain liberating affluence. She not only had Nartouie to help her with the boys but also a sweet village girl named Rose for a full-time maid—dangerously pretty to the Farm School students but incorruptible—and a Consulate driver when she needed one (since she'd broken an ankle that was badly   repaired in Montreal, she never drove a car herself). Along with more leisure for tutoring, she now had the time and means to organize bridge parties at home, and cocktail parties, and grand costumed gatherings for both children and adults at Christmas and Easter in our huge ground-floor living room. And there was much of what you might want for your table right at hand in what the Farm School produced in the broad fields just beyond the spotless living room windows.

Yet certain constricting domestic habits stayed with my mother, whatever the territory, well into her middle age. In my father's archive, there are notebooks that record every penny spent on household items under some undesignated budget covering those years of Foreign Service residence in the Near East and Canada during the Nineteen Twenties and Thirties, no doubt a prudent move in times of minimum salary and economic depression, but the notebooks continue into the more prosperous late Thirties in Greece, when the American Consul was among the nobles at the local court, and each monthly list has the curious heading "Paid by James" or "Spent by James" or "Expended by James."

Since my mother had no income, who else would do the paying and the spending and the expending? She must have been acting as the family banker, at least when it came to what shopping my father had time to do in town. Were the notebook lists my mother's way of making sure that what my father spent on household items was not charged against some unspecified allowance he gave her as the family manager, or was it my father's way of making sure that his purchases under the family budget, including extremes of parsimony and manic buying, were duly recorded for her sake and his and finally for posterity? In any case, the items on the first pages of one surviving notebook, in my mother's round, precise script with the relevant drachma sums beside each item and each item crossed out with a single penciled line, serve for a sketch of our family's day-to-day mode of life in northern Greece: anti-freeze, fish-shrimps, flowers for Mrs. Diel, cod liver oil, cleaning and laundry (see bill), urine analysis, yeast, bird cage, tailor for Budge, movie, flour, lamp for boys, wine, bird seed, slip for MVK, wash woman, Budge for haircut and tram, medicines, tea, cheese and oil, bread, telephone, Rose for shoes, vegetables, butter, carfare for Mike, Bobbie's pencils, music book, stamps, gasoline for stove, tennis dance, Russian ball, Boy Scouts, dental bill, charity.

* * *

The best of that prosperous year came with the summer months, which were given over to exploring new places reached by novel means of transportation, though no one of which included the house trailer, which had been parked under a tarpaulin at the side of the garage through the winter and spring, waiting for its chance in imposed isolation, after which it mysteriously disappeared—anyway mysterious to those of us on the clueless side of puberty. Whether or not my parents still had privileged, private access to it on weekends by way of friends harboring it for them, as Nartouie once hinted to my older brother, remained beyond the range of my speculation or concern.

The first memorable trip that summer was to Mt. Pelion on the outer edge of the Thessaly plain, what my mother told us in preparation was the mountain where the fabulous centaurs, half man and half horse, lived in caves, also the mountain that two giant rebels in mythical days tried to pile on another mountain called Ossa and those two on Olympus in order to reach heaven, only to be killed for their attempt by the fatal wrath of almighty Zeus. Arriving at that mountain was clearly a thing to be anticipated with terror and wonder, but there was also much adventure in just getting there. These days Pelion is still one of the great asphalt journeys out of the inland gulf city of Volos through a valley of olive trees and up a green mountainside rich in cherry and apple orchards to villages of tower-like stone houses from another century with courtyards lined by gardenias and camellias and hydrangeas below precarious balconies. These overhang an occasional remnant mule path of cobblestones to show you how the traveler used to reach the emerald sea below and the broad stretch of deserted beach that is now blocked from your view to the edge of the curling waves by one after another of the tourist hotels that serve the hot sun-dusted towns of central and northern Greece for a seaside retreat to the once humble village of Ayios Yannis.

The start of our journey that summer was by a ship called the *SS Leon* out of Salonika harbor at six in the evening and docking in Volos at six the following morning. I don't remember the *SS Leon.* It must have been too large and ordinary to merit recollection. What I remember is the train that took our group—men only: my father, my brothers, Scoutmaster Theo Litsas and two other younger Farm School teachers— from Volos to the village of Milies halfway up to the pass that would carry us to the far side of the mountain and the open Aegean Sea. It was a toy train, available for passengers of all ages but diminutive enough to seem made especially for travelers under twelve and their midget companions. And it could go only one way at a time, on rails so close a child could walk them without stretching, the line tight by the side of the main dirt road that took farmers and their animals from one coastal village to another. It was a slow train, slow enough to ease through crossroads and to stop instantly whenever an errant donkey or flock of sheep decided to cut across its path in a sudden challenge to fate. There was thrill enough in that kind of encounter, but once the train began to climb up toward Milies, it would rise around one hairpin turn after another to emerge on the very edge of a ravine deep enough to pierce your breath momentarily and then call up the urge to fly free of all your earthly pastimes toward that heaven which those mythical giant rebels failed to reach.

At the village of Milies my father hired a car to take us to the far side of the mountain where the road ended at a village called Tsangarada high above the sea. The drive there was too dangerous to be fun until you got used to it, the road only wide enough for one car and no rails under you to guarantee that you'd stay in the center after you crossed the plateau at the top of the pass and started to wind your way in and out of one ravine after another with no railing between you and the rock gully so far below you couldn't bear to look after the first glance. But that made you focus on the distant sea, surely as blue the whole way as a sea could get outside a picture book, and on that day, the air so clear your gaze would reach what could only have been purple islands nuzzling one another on the far edge of the horizon.

Since the car couldn't go any farther, we abandoned it on the far side of Tsangarada and climbed aboard mules, each to his own, though brother Bob and I were assigned a guide to make sure we didn't fall off—what I remember as an unnecessary humiliation that I couldn't get fully out of my system until we were far along the cobblestone path that was to take us to the village of Mouresi and eventually down to the sea. But I also remember that I wasn't long into the clicking hoof-falls of that slow passage before it seemed the only honest way to travel on the face of the earth, and if I didn't know how to say so, what I felt was that man and the animal carrying him where he had to go were moving easily in rhythm with the natural landscape around them. And when my guide finally fell back a ways to smoke a cigarette, at least pretending to trust me to be on my own, I found myself bound to my mule as though we were one, dependent on each other's instinct with nothing man-made outside us to take that control away, and close, so close to the growing things around us that you sometimes had to reach out or lean away a bit to keep the passing branches gentle in their effort to caress your flesh.

Riding high that way through the village at the head of our mule train, I raised myself up straight as though nature's lord and master, not bothering to do more than nod at those who came out to watch and smile at the procession of strangers crossing the square in front of their tall church and their grand houses. According to Theo Litsas, these had been built by village dignitaries who had made their fortunes in Egyptian cotton and tobacco before the turn of the century and had then come home to make their village godly and beautiful at least until the dying enthusiasm for village life gradually brought on neglect and then partial restoration by outsiders hoping to capture a vanishing abundance. And as we headed down the steepest of paths between the last of the houses, our mules careful now but cunning in their ways, I still held my back rigid as I thought a cavalryman might but at a sharp angle towards the rear that was meant to challenge gravity and avoid a headlong plunge between the mules ears that seriously threatened my new equestrian mastery all the way down to the sea.

We parked the mules in the care of our guides at the edge of the beach. What had seemed white pebbles rimming an endless stretch of sand now, close up, were transformed into stones the size of your hand or foot and sanded smooth over the years by the winter waves rolling over them, so they were almost useless for building anything interesting but good for turning up ostrich egg shapes, squashed grapefruit, and if you were lucky, a slightly flattened honey-dew melon. We had little time for that kind of treasure hunt because my father said we were all filthy with dust and grime from the trip across from Milies and ought to take a dip to spruce up a bit before our official visit to the YMCA camp a short piece down the shore. There was no argument. That blue-green sea with its foam-tipped waves, more alive than any you would find in Salonika Bay, was new enough to draw you in with reckless courage, so that it made no difference to you at the time that you had to strip down naked to get there—bathing suits left at home for those so young they presumably had nothing much to hide—while the older generation changed into their swim trunks and shirts behind the shelter of rock outcroppings that here and there cut into the beach's long crescent. And once you were through the waves and into the soft roll of deeper water, nothing at all mattered except the feel of that sea, pure silver on your naked skin.

The embarrassment came when we were called out again to get ready for our early afternoon lunch at the YMCA camp. My father had promised to bring a snapshot back from our first swim in the Aegean for my mother's family archive album, so my father gave the camera to one of our mule guides after he'd got us all lined up, the young in front of the old, on a huge flat rock at the sea's edge where the only thing my mother's three sons had to protect their nakedness besides crossed legs and cupped hands was the spray that the merciful sea flung up to confuse what the camera lens recorded of our young flesh for the family's posterity. I think that is the moment I came to recognize one of the true privileges of being grown up: the right to determine on your own when you wanted to be naked and when not, especially while being photographed.

Lunch at the YMCA camp was boring but it didn't last too long. After my father made his official visit to the camp director and brought him a special message he'd received from Camp Cory in upstate New York, what he called the American patron and older brother of this beautiful new camp on the golden shores of the ancient Aegean Sea. The director was apparently so impressed by his visitors that instead of allowing us to eat with the campers near their bunk-tents—boys mostly my older brother's age but sounding rowdier—he put our group at a separate table near the outdoor kitchen. This meant that we ended up eating with the same grown-ups we'd been traveling with all along. It was very depressing, and Theo Litsas, the grown up all of us loved most, must have sensed our discomfort. Over the desert of chestnuts and apples, he announced that those of us who had the heart for it could join him in a climb to the top of Mt. Pelion, with a stop along the way at the cave of Chiron the Centaur. Five us had heart enough, and three of us said so raucously. My father agreed to go along at least part way, up to the first village that had a phone he could use to check in at the Consulate for any urgent messages and report to our mother that we had reached the camp safely. He said he'd wait there with some reading he'd brought along to join us on our way back.

Theo Litsas, a refugee teacher from Smyrna in Asia Minor, was a man who had the gift of knowing how to create the best of possible worlds for children and young adults, partly because he was wiser than most men his age, partly because he himself had never totally grown up. He was philosophical about life's possibilities, some said to an infuriating degree: all would be well tomorrow if you just relaxed and let things happen as they had to happen whatever your personal anxiety about the way things were or what you thought they might become. They say he managed to keep control of the unruly or delinquent under his charge at the Farm School and in his Scout troop by an old-fashioned mix of bribery and chastisement, but if that was so, the disciplinarian in him could be replaced by the clown anytime it became necessary to restore a proper balance between fear and compassion. He was a man with a wide forehead and bent ears, frizzy hair, and two gold teeth at the edge of his smile, his natural look leaning more toward comedy than authority. But he knew how to change his image, as the occasion required, to one of deep sobriety and contemplation, eyes closed as though in prayer, or to one of loose-limbed merriment, a vaudeville performer quick-stepping his way through life's ludicrous scenery.

His act that day during the hardest part of our climb was to keep us entertained by fables. We started out climbing on foot, with the mules along just to carry our casual baggage, but after leaving my father off in Mouresi to fend for himself with a local teacher who knew some French, each of us took a turn on a mule to catch our breath, then all of us stopped for a long rest in sight of the Chiron's cave at least a kilometer or two below the mountain peak. On the way up to that resting place, Theo Litsas filled us in on the history of the centaurs, creatures who were not exactly evil, he said, but who had a way of getting on the wrong side of the gods because they sometimes liked women and wine too much. That brought my older brother Budge out of the heavy-breathing silence that had been with him as head of the pack most of the way up.

"How can you like women too much?" he asked Theo.

"Don't you worry about that," Theo said. "You'll find out soon enough."

"I mean liking wine too much makes you drunk. But what does liking women too much do to you?"

"Turns you into a centaur," Theo said, showing his gold teeth. "Half man, half stallion."

"Only centaurs aren't real," Budge said. "They're myths."

"Well, that depends on whether you believe in gods and heroes," Theo said. "To gods and heroes they're as real as you and me. Heracles who was half god and half hero killed one of them for misbehaving with a woman. You believe in Heracles, don't you?"

"I don't know," Budge said.

"Well you'd better. And you'd better believe in centaurs. Because when we get up to that cave, I don't want any of you boys being impolite if we should run into Chiron. He's a centaur you've got to respect because he's a healer and he teaches children the truth."

Budge turned silent again and so did his brothers, especially since we had to work double-time to keep up with the rest. When we got to the mouth of the cave, the two teachers climbing with us barely looked inside before taking off toward the peak, now seemingly close at hand but actually on the far side of a col that appeared deep enough to make me wonder if we'd even get close to the top before the sun went down. At that moment Theo Litsas had Bob by the hand and was leading him into the mouth of the cave, which was barely large enough to take in the two of them together. I myself have never been one for entering unexplored caves eagerly however large their openings, and my having read an illustrated *Tom Sawyer* earlier in the year didn't work to ease my caution that day. But I wasn't about to let my younger brother discover something I would miss out on because of prudence, so I entered the cave a few steps behind the leaders, and Budge followed a few steps behind me. It was all jagged rock in there at first, no particular beauty to it, no dripping stalactites or curious formations, and the light too strong to allow a sense of mystery until we found ourselves so far from the opening behind us that is was hard to see much of anything ahead. At that point Theo Litsas knelt, motioned us to do the same, put a finger to his lips and held it there to signal absolute silence. We knelt where we were, gazing into the darkness. I found myself holding my breath. Suddenly Theo pointed.

"Do you see him?" he whispered to Bob.

Bob looked at Theo, then looked back into the darkness. He nodded. Theo turned his head to glance at me.

"Do you see him?" he whispered again.

"I don't see anything," I whispered back.

"You're not looking hard enough."

I tried. The darkness seemed to clear a bit as my eyes got used to it. I could make out a shape where the rock wall narrowed, maybe two shapes, but I couldn't figure out what they were. And nothing moved.

"He's asleep," Theo said. "We mustn't wake him."

He knelt there for a moment longer, then stood up slowly and began to back out, still holding Bob by the hand. I turned and took off for the light in the distance, trying not to run, failing in the end. When I reached the entrance Budge was standing outside waiting for us.

"I didn't see a thing," he said. "It was all just rocks in there."

Theo went over and put a hand on his shoulder.

"You only see what your heart wants you to see. Maybe you didn't really want to see Chiron sleeping in there. I can't blame you. Some other day maybe, who knows?"

Budge looked disappointed and turned to head uphill.

"I saw some shapes," I said. "I couldn't tell what they were."

"That's a beginning," Theo said. "When your imagination grows up a bit, you'll see things more clearly, I promise you that."

"There were two shapes," I said.

"Of course," Theo said. "Two shapes in one. Man and horse."

"I don't know," I said. "It was very dark in there."

"The secret is learning to see through the darkness," Theo said. "Someday you'll see all the gods and heroes you can't see now, I promise."

Theo caught up to Budge and put an arm around him, then motioned Bob and me to follow. When we arrived at the col below the peak there was still plenty of daylight, and we could see the mules and their guides part way up the slope on the far side and our two companions already at the top waving us on up. They were standing on a rock ridge, with nothing but clear sky behind them. I still remember the agony of that last part of the climb, the steepest yet, my breath short, lungs hurting, every uphill step calling on you to talk yourself into the next out of pride, but when we finally reached the ledge where the others were waiting and climbed up the one rock that would hold three small people at once, you could look out toward the far horizon where the sea vanished into a mauve haze and believe you were now really standing at the top of the world.

It was turning from twilight to deep dusk by the time we reached the shore below the Pelion village where my father had found himself a phone and a place to read but nothing new to report from the distant world of diplomacy, at least not to the younger generation. Our leaders decided that it was too late for a swim before dinner, so we had the country pleasure of eating and going to bed dirty, the bed a sleeping bag in a row of sleeping bags ranked by size, each of us to his own segment of beach that the occupant was left to clear of rocks and other impediments according to his taste, each provided with a canopy of mosquito netting to keep the local insects in their place. I remember the quiet rhythm of the night sea licking the rock shore as I fell asleep and the stunning brightness of the stars overhead the one time I woke in the middle of the night, but what I remember most was sitting up at the dawn's sudden coming to watch the slow rise of the blood-red sun out of the sea—primitive, hallowed sight—and its gradual change through the lighter shades of its ripening into the familiar sharp white that hurt your eyes to know.

The sun's rising signaled time for calisthenics on the beach, young and old lined up by height, with Scout Master Litsas trying without much conviction to keep our exercise in step, then a quick dip, then hot tea and thick black village bread with apricot marmalade for breakfast, and after camp clean-up and the morning's swim, an excursion down the coast in a caique skippered by a man calling himself Odysseus—more likely than not his actual name in keeping with a neoclassical tradition in Greece—who loved to announce his arrival near shore and his shoving off on a cruise by blowing three long mournful notes on a conch shell. He had been a fisherman since his teens, and in those days took passengers aboard only when it seemed the best catch available. But I learned years later that he eventually gave up fishing entirely in the travel-heavy postwar years because even dynamiting fish proved boring and unproductive beside transporting tourists wherever they chose to go in his territory, especially groups of foreigners that included his weakness: young women with hair the color of wheat to match his own.

This pre-war trip down the Pelion coast must have been as tedious for him as any involving fish, since the sea, flat as enamel, provided no challenge for him, and the passengers were all male. Yet for those of my generation it was rich with images of the unexplored, one encounter after another with aquamarine coves and offshore rocks in the shape of sea monsters and sea-caves full of dark secrets. We reached an inlet good for dropping anchor in time for a private swim before noon, the caique now a diving board high enough in the bow to teach you the price of physical arrogance, and on the way back to our home base under the relentless eye of the sun, a gift-offering to remember from Odysseus.

"Here. Take the tiller. Don't be afraid. Take it."

"I don't know how."

"You'll learn quickly enough. Just hold it steady against the current so you keep the bow heading for the tip of the point straight ahead."

"It keeps turning."

"You've got to brace yourself. Here, I'll help you a little."

"I can do it."

"Sure you can. Just lean back a bit more when you have to and move with it so you keep a steady rhythm as you go."

"See. I can do it."

"That's good. You're a born helmsman. Pray you don't take too much pleasure in it too long."

✵   ✵   ✵

There were other trips that summer before time ran out on learning the ways of the world outside school. There was a long hike with the Cub Scout troop up the slope of Mt. Hortiati to the whitewashed village of that name, built mostly out of mountain rocks and mud bricks by refugees from Asia Minor to escape the mosquito-infested swamps along Salonika Bay that had been their first home in exile after the 1922 Catastrophe that had brought milkman Panayotis and Theo Litsas to the Farm School along with others in the exchange of populations with Turkey that followed the disastrous Greek military campaign. The fields around Hortiati village were good for planting, and there was ample pasture land for sheep, sloping green meadows you could cross easily, the grass cut low by the grazing herds that seemed to be always just out of sight, though you could hear the tinkle of their crossing in the distance and smell where they'd been near your path, even when the afternoon breeze came up to cool your sweat and waft you with the odor of thyme.

From our spare campsite on the mountain—a few benches for resting after the climb to gather wild herbs, a few tables for learning to tie knots and carve small forked men, a few skeletal structures with airy roofs and canvas sides to keep the wolves at bay—you could look down on Hortiati village and think it so peaceful, so quiet, as to be asleep before sunset. But it was a village the gods chose not to protect from evil history. Six years later the quiet that was witnessed by the first group of Boy Scouts to camp on the mountain after the German army withdrew from northern Greece in October 1944 was of a different kind to what we had known. It had the aura of a makeshift crematorium and graveyard left behind by the Wehrmacht in September a few weeks before its departure, when it roasted some eighty local citizens of all ages in the sealed village bakery, slaughtered another sixty by hand, and burned the village to the ground in retaliation for the ambush of a German soldier by a guerrilla unit of the resistance hiding near the Roman aqueduct a good distance out of town. The village was rebuilt out of red brick and cinder block after the war, and the sheep returned to graze in the broad meadows when the hillside became safe again during the late stages of the civil war, though they were gradually crowded out by the arched and columned villas with their walled-in gardens for city dwellers in search of clean air and by the fenced-in crown of the mountain that was turned over to NATO for the topless towers of a radar station. But on a rare clear morning, the view could still give you Olympus rising high and sharp enough to display its late summer or early fall snow on the far side of Salonika Bay.

In 1938, September was the freest of months in some ways because that was when my father applied for a vacation leave long enough to take his family across the border into Yugoslavia for a journey into new territory that started out by train in a first class cabin that had dusty velvet seats on both its sides and its own door that allowed you to escape for privacy into a corridor that ran the whole length of the car. This was our first pleasure trip abroad as a family, though we shared it with three other families at various times, and if there were moments when it was luxurious by comparison to our Kastania and Pelion outings, there were also disadvantages for the young in a crowd that large and that well dressed. My brothers and I wore short pants, but most of the time with jackets and ties and knee-length stockings, and my father, always in a light gray business suit, showed he was on vacation only by wearing a large bow tie. For our excursions outside the train my mother put on a snazzy Twenties felt hat with a flower in it, pinned at an angle, so that I later came to think of her young image as that of a golden-voiced, if less careless, Daisy Buchanan. The others were all dressed and polished as though on their way to our Sunday hymn singing at the Farm School to count our many blessings and come to Jesus just now.

My father's best friend for important excursions in those days was a gentleman who had been the Yugoslav Consul General when we first arrived in Salonika and had recently been promoted to Minister to Turkey (in those days most Balkan countries and their neighbors were considered only of sufficient importance to have legations and ministers rather than embassies and ambassadors). Minister Adjemovitch was a tall, considerate, white-haired man with a sweetly-rounded accent in English and a fondness for patting your cheek. He always showed up for travel in a dark tie and vest and fedora hat.

I don't know whether the honorable Minister, who represented the government of young King Peter, was actually as close to the King as we all assumed from his demeanor. What I know is that he was so generous with the children of the American Consul, always ready with a handout from his pocket or a word in our defense to calm our father's nerves ("Really, Jeemey, the boys are only tired or maybe bored, so let them fight a leetle bit, who does it hurt?") that it seemed to us the King of Yugoslavia surely would have been pleased to have him a member of his court for as long as it lasted, which was for a much shorter time than anyone in our company of pre-war vacationers would have imagined in those heady cure-happy days. And that included the beautiful Adjemovitch daughter, Dani, a regal young lady Budge's age who wore her hair in pigtails sometimes rolled neatly against her ears but for this trip long and ribboned against her white silk blouse, her dark-browed eyes the kind that could make you feel more uneasily grown-up than you could understand the few times she let those eyes pass over you instead of over your older brother. Also included was her brother Vladi, the best of companions for Balkan travel because he knew how to read maps and pronounce impossible names, already a gentleman in his manners compared to me and my soccer friends, and whether or not more knowing about politics than the rest of us, already uncritically in love with the kingdom that he took such pleasure introducing us to and that he was within a few years of losing to exile forever, along with his adolescent king.

I remember crossing the border on our way to Lake Ochrid as the first and last time in my life that I saw a custom's official actually flush red while leafing through a stack of passports, more than half of them diplomatic, and then drop them to the floor in his hurry to stand tall and salute. The official was on the Yugoslav side of the border, and of course it was Minister Adjemovitch he was honoring in his passionate way, but that elegant diplomat refused to take the credit. He leaned over to tell my father softly, "As you see, my friend Jeemey, he salutes you to show we respect Americans in Yugoslavia. Respect them and maybe fear them just a leetle, what do you think?"

At Lake Ochrid we found a beach for sunbathing but no Aegean blue to whiten the spirit, and from there we turned north to Dubrovnic on the Dalmatian coast, a marble city so bright and empty as to seem full of radiant ghosts, then east through the mountains of Montenegro, sometimes with sloping snow that came down close enough for snowball war games during a stopover while our elders bargained for carpets and lace, then on through Kosovo to the Serbian town of Vranje, where we turned north again to our designated garden of earthly delights, a spa with the unpronounceable name of Vrnjacka Banja.

What I remember of that spa is the crafty neatness of it all, the lawns cut short and sharply trimmed, the flower beds made into circles and ovals and rounded triangles—anything other than uninspired linear forms—each bed thick with flowers arranged in clusters that shaped someone's extravagant pattern of colors and textures, the whole kept from spilling out of control by clipped bushes carved like fallen latticework. And everywhere benches newly painted for sitting to play backgammon and card games or simply to watch others walk the earthen paths from the hotel to the bath houses where the adults would go to boil themselves clean and healthy in water that smelled of sulfur or worse and tasted as bad as castor oil if you made the mistake of trying it out just to see what made it so special. I also remember the quiet of the place in its open spaces, no sound other than the momentary low-voiced talk of passing couples and a bird call every now and then from outlying trees.

The hotel was another matter, grand as any I'd come across in my young days, palatially off by itself on a hill with a carriage house below it, verandas everywhere for outdoor hanging around, but once you were inside the place, crowded with chatter in the public places and hardly ever free of the brassy music from a band that would waft its unfamiliar tunes into whatever quiet corner you'd chosen for a chance to catch up on how the Man in the Iron Mask was doing since you last left him cooped up in his dungeon. What I can recall of the dining room, besides images of some very ancient people in love with soup and nothing else, were the deserts. Two deserts especially, the one some kind of gentle custard in the shape of an overturned cupcake—a cross between creme brulee and ice cream that tasted the way cool aquamarine would if it had a taste—and the other a triangle the size of your palm, called a pancake by some at our table and a crepe by others, filled with crushed nuts and apricot jelly, whatever its real name a pancake you had to wait years to find again that thin around a filling that unexpected.

I can be exact about this. The Proustian recollection of that triangle's taste stayed with me through the war years but was not rediscovered in the flesh until the early summer of *1950*, when Marshall Tito decided to open the border between Greece and Yugoslavia to Americans, presumably a gesture of good will in response to America's support of his rebellion against Stalin. I took advantage of this gesture the day the southern border opened that summer by heading for the crossing between Evzoni on the Greek side and Gevgelja on the Yugoslav side, delivered there by my friends Bruce and Tad Lansdale in a jeep belonging to the American Farm School, where we had worked together the previous academic year. I saw this route north as my shortest to Austria and the Salzburg Festival, a reward I had promised myself after a strenuous year of teaching English and basketball to village boys, most of whom had only a primitive interest in education of any kind beyond the strategies of school soccer. I waved goodbye to the Lansdales as I crossed the border out of Greece—a jaunty wave, full of feigned confidence—and sudden-ly found myself carrying a heavy suitcase along a stretch of no-man's land between a steep hill and a gully on a dirt road leading God knows where, certainly nowhere that appeared to be inhabited by man or beast. I walked some distance on that road, and when the wilderness ahead continued to seem unrelenting, I decided to sit down on my suitcase and see what the fates might bring my way before darkness.

What they brought, bounding down the hillside out of a shack so natural to the high pastoral landscape that I hadn't even noticed it, was a soldier half a head taller than me and a good ten years older, wearing a red star and carrying a rifle that had an impressive weight in its look. He parked himself in front of me and spoke in a language that I only vaguely recognized from my recent tour of the remote Slavo-Macedonian villages in northern Greece but that had an authority in its tone that I found quite familiar and quite ominous. I just stared at the soldier, but with a rigid smile. Then he tried broken German on me, I suppose a remnant of his wartime service as a resistance guerrilla.

"You speak German?" he asked.

"Yes," I said. "A bit." (This was a lie; I'd recovered much of my child-hood German during the one assured gut course of my freshman year in college).

"So. What are you doing here?" he said.

"Nothing," I said. "Does it look like I'm doing something? I'm just sitting down."

"But you are here," he said.

"That is true," I said. "I am here."

"That is problem," he said. "Why are you here?"

"I am here because I am going to Austria."

"Austria? There is no Austria here. This is Yugoslavia."

"That is a thing I know," I said. "I have a transit visa. From your offi-cial in Salonika."

The soldier still had his rifle off his shoulder. "What is this visa you have?"

I opened my passport to the visa page and thrust it out. The soldier stiffened. Then he took it from me. It was clear he had a certain reading disability in his own language—or at least this particular version of his country's various languages. I wasn't exactly sympathetic, but I offered to help by pointing to the official stamp. The soldier closed the passport quickly and put it in his pocket.

"You will stay here," he said.

"I'm not going anywhere," I said. "I promise. Where could I go without my passport and visa?"

The soldier studied me. I thought I saw the beginnings of a smile.

"Maybe you go where you come from. Maybe not. We will see."

He turned sharply and headed back up the hill. It must have been close to an hour later when the soldier and an officer came down the hill side by side, and I took it as a hopeful sign that the officer was unarmed and that the soldier now had his rifle on his shoulder. I stood up as the officer approached. He reached out and handed me my passport, grinning.

"Good American," he said in German. "Welcome. All is good. You wait, no?"

"I wait."

"Good," he said. "Until we meet again."

I saluted him, a casual American salute, that of a Tennessee Williams character I had once played ending a long goodbye to his dying goldfish as he cleared out of his apartment and went out into the world of desire and despair. The officer saluted me back, then turned on his heel and headed uphill, the soldier following a step behind. Irrationally, I thought of my father. Absurdly, what I thought was that he might have been proud of my diplomatic cool during this encounter with our former enemy, though God knows I didn't feel cool at all.

It was almost another hour before the horse-drawn cart arrived with a driver and a new soldier in it. The soldier jumped down to hoist my suitcase aboard and signaled me to take the seat next to the driver, a glum, gray-haired gentleman who smelled of garlic and hard labor in the fields. During the endless ride into the town of Gevgelia, nobody said a

word because we shared no common language, the driver too miserably
self-absorbed in any case and the soldier too young to have fought the
Germans, not to mention the Croats or Michailovic. At least he kept an
amiable look on his face and at one point examined my cotton shirt
approvingly by running his fingers lightly over the sleeve. When we
reached the center of town, the evening promenade was in progress on
both sides of the street in opposite directions, the married or engaged
walking along slowly as couples, the rest divided into the two sexes who
remained nonchalantly unconscious of each other except by way of a
subtle play of eyes. The soldier took my suitcase despite my protests and
directed me to follow him down the center of the street, cleared of all
traffic until the end of the evening promenade. I drew the eyes of the
crowd as I went by, at least for the momentary surprise of my passing,
but the whole way I felt as others must have felt on the final march to
the guillotine.

The soldier stayed with me that night, parked in the corridor outside
my single room on the second floor of an eight-room empty hotel, and
he escorted me to the train station the following morning—in fact, into
the train itself that was headed for Belgrade, still carrying my suitcase. I
tried to give him a tip from the clump of dinars I'd picked up in
Salonika, but that brought a cold stare of disapproval that froze my
blood for a second. As I put the money away, he gave my arm a friendly slap, then disappeared down the corridor and off to his honorable
destiny.

By the time the train pulled out of the station, my compartment had
filled up with a group of uniformed officers and men belonging to some
red-starred unit—gendarmery, military, something more irregular?—
who were clearly in a free-wheeling celebratory mood, as though a ghostly troupe of combatants left over from V-E Day. It turned out that they
were on a weekend pass to Belgrade, cause enough for reckless hilarity.
At first they pretended to take no notice of their foreign fellow-traveler,
but when a bottle of slivovitz started making the rounds, it was thrust
my way with aggressive generosity. "America gut," one of them said. That
was greeted with general favor, and I was forced to take a second and a
third slug in praise of America. By the time we reached the outskirts of

Belgrade some hours later, half the unit was sound asleep and the other half raucously drunk, full of song and folk poetry. I was somewhere between, heavy in the head but lyrical in the heart, if still vigilantly silent.

On the platform in Belgrade the uniformed gentleman who appeared to be the senior officer though no more than five or six years older than me insisted that one of his men carry my suitcase and that I join the group for a parting drink and a plate of what sounded like *palechenka*. His German was insufficient to explain what that dish might be, but it wouldn't have made any difference: for the moment I was the captive of their hospitality, with no clear ground for escape. The place the officer had in mind was only a few blocks from the station, and we were settled in there with another bottle of slivovitz before I'd had more than a passing look at the city that was to be my home for the night. The truth is, I remember absolutely nothing about that night in Belgrade except for the restaurant, full of old-world European charm, a wood-heavy bistro kind of place with some quaint posters from the Twenties on the wall advertising cigarettes and cognac. And the plate of palechenka that arrived at our table, as though a gift of madeleine from the gods, had me beaming like the village idiot: crepe pancakes in lovely triangles full of the fruity taste that hadn't come my way for more than a decade.

I went back to that restaurant for another taste years later, after Tito's death and not long before Yugoslavia broke up into one country after another, and finally one ethnic region after another, each fighting to eat up some part of the other's territory or to keep from being eaten. The friends I had visited in Belgrade that second time, a Serbian poet and his wife, were both fond of Americans in those early post-Tito days, he working at the time to promote American culture under the U.S. Information Agency, she a professor and translator of Modern Greek literature. My particular mission was to join the poet Theodore Weiss in reading poetry in English at a factory devoted to producing blood plasma on the outskirts of the city during what most workers there chose to make their lunch hour while some others diligently sat in polite silence listening to verse in a language that was surely no more comprehensible to their ears than lines in Serbo-Croation or Slavo-Macedonian would have been to mine. What my Serbian friends hoped was that the mere presence of two writers who had traveled from distant America to read poetry with some attempt at passion to that unlikely audience—even poetry in a strange language from a supposedly materialist-capitalist country—might make the culture of that country seem to matter in some crucial non-political way.

But as we have come to know too well from the century just passed, history is not always kind to those with the best intentions. When my friends last visited me and my wife Mary in our Athens apartment as soon as the NATO bombing of Belgrade allowed them to travel south, their mood was edgy. What they had to say about the effect of the bombing on their lives wasn't pleasant—their house had been spared destruction, but it had often been shaken to its roots as in an earthquake, and they were still without heat and electricity—so I thought it best not to ask them if my favorite restaurant near the Belgrade railroad station was still standing. We talked about poetry and fiction and about my friend's new venture as a publisher who no longer had a current source of income other than his wife's unpaid salary, no public or private funds in hand to back his enterprise, no bank account even—"What banks remained that could provide for an account in Belgrade?" he asked rhetorically—but with supreme good will promised to publish a novel of mine in Serbo-Croatian as soon as he possibly could, by Christmas perhaps or anyway by Easter, whenever the chaos back home permitted the designated translator to complete her work and his new publishing house to reopen its doors. He had made this promise originally before the bombing began and he said he had every intention of fulfilling it now that the bombing was over. As we parted, his wife opened her pocketbook and reached inside to give me a present, what she called a souvenir of our days, a six by eight piece of paper of the kind her fellow Serbians had defiantly pinned to their chests as the NATO planes crossed overhead to bomb the bridges of her city: two black circles around a black center above the word TARGET in English.

FOUR

In the fall of 1938, the teachers in the German School of Salonika, Greece, must have been in a state of suspended elation. By then Hitler had easily annexed the country of his birth, Austria, and after the Munich agreement in late September that the British prime minister thought would bring peace in our time, the Führer had swallowed the best part of Czechoslovakia. His stop-gap non-aggression pact with Russia still remained some months ahead, along with his invasion of Poland, but it was clear at the start of the school year that Nazi Germany was well on its way to changing the map of Europe in keeping with what my pigtailed and dirndled history teacher had long since outlined for our paste model of a Germany-to-Come, rich in lebensraum. I had entered the sixth grade in the German School that fall, a bit ahead of schedule for my age by accident of birth, and I was quite impervious to the local and international political developments that would very soon alter the progress of my young life as it would everyone else's in our corner of the world and beyond. What preoccupied me then was my having begun to feel the first tremors of excessive ambition and to discover its costs.

For one, I found myself aspiring in an untutored way to become a star first of the screen and then of the stage. A major influence in this connection was my having fallen in love not only with the movies generally but with Shirley Temple specifically, along with many others my age, which some fan-mail source told me was almost exactly her age as well, I being appropriately her elder by two months. Another influence was the traditional Christmas pageant that my class was responsible for presenting before the parents of all grades in the lower school. The previous year I had taken part, along with my younger brother Bob, in a simpler theatrical event that involved six of us wearing white beards and dressed as Santa Clauses sitting cross-legged in front of a chorus of angelic girls dressed in white, each wearing a halo with a star rising from the center of their foreheads. As Shirley Temple's approaching puberty gradually limited her life on the screen and my too-distant passion for her began to fade into the world of hopeless daydreams, it was one of those Christmas angels come down to earth in my sixth grade class which made me think for a while that it was my fate to become an actor.

I had always considered myself subject to acute stage fright in facing any public performance, beginning with my having completely choked up reading "Now I am Six" at my birthday party relevant to that ghastly poem, but when I learned that Helga Trauger—could that really have been her name?—was to play the Virgin Mary in our Christmas pageant of 1938, I succeeded by way of spotless month-long behavior in the yard and shameless apple-polishing in the classroom to qualify for the role of First Wise Man in the pageant. That was the only one of the three designated Wise Men who had a speaking part. He was to arrive out of the wings under the sign "Der Osten" at the head of his two sage companions, cross the stage at a funereal pace, halt near the two-by-four marking the entrance to the stable and slowly ask the Virgin by the manger in his deepest German: "Where is he that is born King of the Jews? For we have seen his star in the East and are come to worship him." Bearded, sumptuously long-robed, the First Wise Man was then to move forward and kneel before the beautiful Helga Trauger, her luxurious brown hair parted in the middle and bound by a lace-trimmed blue bandanna that merely served to highlight the radiant ivory of her forehead and the limpid directness of her green eyes. Kneeling there, the First Wise Man was to present her with a cigar box wrapped in gold paper, then rise and step aside to allow his companions to offer her in turn their yellow and purple boxes representing frankincense and myrrh. That done, all three were to retreat to the west edge of the stable to make room for speechless shepherds and lesser adoring pilgrims moving in to fill the stable.

The rehearsals for the pageant were a torment of delight: the time assigned for the Wise Men to perform all too short, but many hours of just hanging around to watch Helga at fairly close quarters after she had positioned herself by the manger with her stooped husband and infant doll, her head held proudly high to receive the parade of her worshipers, her gorgeous blue gown spread over the several bales of straw that I had personally arranged to provide for her perch through my connections at the American Farm School. The one chance I got to monopolize her attention was when I found occasion to explain to her in some detail how straw was baled by way of the marvelous new machine called a Combine that had come to Greece from America, a monologue that she accepted with more or less patient if less than angelic grace. The rest from me was silent adoration.

That lasted through the best part of opening night. What happened then has been suppressed for some years and therefore remains a touch clouded. What I recall is feeling rather weak-kneed as I came out on stage to take in, without actually seeing, the large audience of parents, relatives, and fellow students as they acknowledged with muffled sounds the arrival of the Three Wise Men, and the knees weakened more as I crossed with my companions to present the golden gift box from the East to my green-eyed madonna. I spoke my lines in a German so practiced as to have the ring of parody—though now, alas, surely inaudible beyond the front rows—and I don't know whether on kneeling before the proud Virgin my foot caught the edge of my robe or I simply buckled under the pressure of the moment, but as I stumbled down before her, I almost ended up in her lap, and the gift box went flying out of my hands to graze the bald forehead of her infant doll and to fall with a thud on the stage beyond her straw bales. It may have been pure guilt projection, but what I was certain I heard as I went down, along with the gasp from the audience, was the lovely Holy Mother muttering "Dummkopf," and whether actual or not, the look on her face, as I gathered myself to retreat to the side of the stable, said that searing word and more.

It took me a while to decide how best to cope with the humiliation that followed on this dramatic failure. My parents, mother and father both, were very understanding in their way at the social gathering after the performance, my mother telling me, as she squared my robe on my drooping shoulders, that I looked truly elegant in that wise man costume, and my father telling me that he was truly impressed by how well I now spoke German. But their no doubt generous gesture in ignoring my having almost collapsed into the Virgin Mary's lap and my having hurled a missile at the Christ Child's head only seemed to make my shame that much more inconsolable. I thought of going to Lisa to let my heart speak out, seek her wisdom about how I could bring myself to face my classmates again with head held high, let alone the limpid-eyed Helga, but something told me that bringing any remnant of that dying passion into the open might damage my relationship with the only person more or less my age that I still fully trusted—anyway, the only woman.

I ended up going to Theo Litsas instead. He was a man of the theater in his fashion, and I figured he would be sympathetic about how to deal with a loss of nerve before an audience that I took to have been dominated by severe teachers, the parents of others, and jealous students. When I told my tale to Theo I could see that he had trouble keeping a straight face, but being a man of rich experience with the young, he managed in the end to assume a proper sobriety. Putting his arm around my shoulder, he said that one such episode meant absolutely nothing in an actor's life, in fact was a normal state of mind for those new to the profession and even for many experienced actors who were known to vomit regularly off-stage in order to settle themselves before heading into the bright lights. He also said it was necessary to be philosophical about such occurrences, philosophical especially in the ancient Greek way, taking to your heart the teaching of Heraclitus.

"You know Heraclitus?" Theo asked. "Do they teach him in your German School?"

"Hera who?"

"The melancholy philosopher they called him. But don't let that bother you. I think he was melancholy just because he knew too much."

"They don't teach us ancient Greeks in that school," I said.

Theo looked at me somberly. "Well, remember what this ancient Greek says: You can't step into the same river twice. And the way up is the way down, as the way down is the way up. So if you fall one day, the next day you are sure to rise."

"I will never fall like that again," I said, "because I will never be an actor again."

"Nonsense. You are clearly a born actor. And I can tell that you have been captured by the magic of the theater just as I was at your age."

"Not me," I said. "My feet don't work right up there in front of people."

"Nonsense," Theo said. "The time will come when you won't even know you have feet. You will float across the stage as happy as a dancer."

He was right in a way, but it would be years before a moment of that kind entered my life, and talking to Theo that morning, mostly avoiding his eyes, I was at an age when my sense of future possibilities did not carry much beyond the week ahead. I decided then and there to shift the focus of my ambition to excellence in athletics, specifically in track and field, beginning with the sixty-meter dash. This thought was inspired by my having won a medal the previous spring at the Farm School junior track meet that included a potato race and a sack race for those ten and under. I had failed in the potato race out of excessive zeal (the winner, younger brother Bob, slower than me because his legs were shorter, turned out to be more careful and balanced in picking up potatoes with a soup spoon), but the sack race proved a cinch once I figured out that quick short hops rather than huge leaps gave you a better chance of controlling both the uncooperative sack and your shackled feet so you didn't fall on your face again before you got very far. My parents, as the official Americans on the scene, were recruited to give out the medals in our junior category, cause for pride in my brother and me but cause for some suspicion outside the family, at least among those who hadn't actually watched us win our races.

Running a sixty-meter dash in the next age division a year later called for a mature and serious training program. I would get up an hour earlier than usual in the pre-school hours and make a dash in spurts for the soccer field, then run the sixty-meter course as many times as I could before my gasping breath gave out. It was lonely, demanding work, hard on body and spirit, and I found after a while that it was boring as well. I decided it might be easier if I had some companionship, someone to talk to, someone to urge me on by competition, so I made a point of going to visit my friend, Billy Compton, the son of a teacher at the other school run by Americans in Salonika, Anatolia College.

Billy Compton lived near a school track that was usually kept in better condition than ours at the Farm School, but I didn't get to try his out even once either with him for company or by myself, because on the way to the track we got into a scrap the cause of which I do not exactly remember except that I must have said something challenging which infuriated my friend enough to cause him to give me chase at a speed so threatening it recurs in my dreams. The chase was over ground meant not for human travel but for the growth of newly planted shrubs and flowers, with the result that I tripped over a sudden hollow of dug earth and landed full force on my left arm so that it bent the wrong way. I can't say that I heard it snap or that I even felt intense pain, but I felt enough to make for the kind of show while I was down on the ground that I hoped would keep me from being punished in some violent fashion for my big mouth. Billy Compton hovered over my curled body, and as I lay there moaning, his rage was gradually replaced by uncertainty and then concern. When he finally helped me up, I knew there was serious trouble ahead, because the arm wasn't at all right. I held it against my belly, my back bent as though to protect it, and walked back sullenly to Billy's house to call my father for help.

I had always been reluctant to bring medical matters having to do with personal injuries or sickness to my parent's attention unless heavy bleeding or blatant nose dripping and coughing were involved. Even knee scrapes meant immediate sighing and head-shaking from one parent or the other and treatment with stinging peroxide for cleaning the wound by my father, followed by scalding iodine, while anything beyond a sniffle meant bed for some days and bad food, all sour juices and boiled cauliflower. But an arm swelling at the elbow could hardly be hidden for long, and my solemn attitude toward it was the only way at that moment I could exonerate myself before the friend I had somehow grievously insulted.

After Mrs. Compton, the sweetest of young white-haired women, outlined the situation to my father by phone, he was there in the De Soto before I'd had a chance to figure out exactly how I would explain the cause for this intrusion into his office time. My father came over and looked at my unsheathed arm as though I was holding it there severed from my shoulder, shook his head, sighed, didn't touch the arm, didn't ask me how this thing had happened, shook his head again, asked me where it hurt, and when I said it hurt all over, he sighed again and made a face as though it was his arm that was undeniably broken.

The doctor he took me to had an office in the old part of the town, half way up the hillside that ended at the Seven Towers prison in the old city walls. My father told me I had no reason to be afraid, this was a very experienced doctor, recommended to him by his Greek assistant at the consulate because the doctor had an excellent record in the military, having dealt with many wounded arms and legs during the First World War and the Asia Minor Catastrophe that followed. He was also good with horses, having served for years with the cavalry. It turned out that his office was on the ground floor of a building that looked as though it had once been a barracks of some kind, maybe even a stable, because the long corridor leading to his office had filled-in window spaces along it and half doors that had been sealed shut and were now part of a display area that offered a series of photographs of mostly naked men showing off protruding bone fractures here and there or body parts rendered unnatural in shape by disease or accident, all presumably cured in that ghoulish place.

There were more photographs on the walls of the doctor's office, but I chose not to look at those. The doctor was in there alone, a big man, rugged, with a puffy, damaged face that might have been handsome once, dressed not in a doctor's uniform but in khaki trousers and a sleeveless white shirt that allowed thick black hair to show at its neck opening and along the length of the doctor's brawny arms. He reached for my father's hand as we came in, smiling, showing three gold teeth. He had obviously been expecting us.

"Ah, Mr. Consul General. Now what do we have here? I understand there's a problem with the boy's arm."

I didn't bother to translate for my father, because the doctor motioned him to take a seat, the only one in there, then turned to me, still smiling and patted me on the head. He leaned forward to touch the good hand that was gripping my injured arm, the smell of his sweat wafting me from his armpit, and told me to let go a minute and just relax. Then he slowly rolled up my sleeve, took hold of the injured arm and suddenly yanked it straight. I screamed, on the edge of passing out. My father jumped out of his seat and came over.

"What the hell," he said to the doctor. "What are you doing?"

The doctor stared at him. I came back down off the ceiling.

"He wants to know what you're doing," I said to the doctor, almost inaudibly.

"Tell him I'm checking to see if the arm is broken and where. Excuse me, but what does he think I'm doing?"

I told my father what the doctor had said. My father's face was red, the forehead perspiring.

"You tell him if he does that again, I'll break his goddam arm for him. I mean it."

I told the doctor that my father said he shouldn't hurt me like that again.

"Tell your father that of course it is going to hurt. Tell him that the arm is broken and has to be set."

I told my father that the doctor said the arm was broken.

"I know it's broken, for Chrisake. There is no excuse for doing that to a broken arm."

My father had turned paler. The doctor was looking at him and he was looking at the doctor. I didn't say anything.

"I mean, Mr. Consul General, you are the Consul General but I am the doctor."

"What's he saying?" my father asked.

"He says he's the doctor."

"I don't give a goddam who he is," my father said. "He pulls your arm like that again and I'll break his for him. Right here and now."

I didn't want my father to get into a fight with a man that much bigger and uglier than he was, so I told the doctor that my father just hoped he wouldn't have to pull my arm like that again.

"What could I do?" the doctor said. "A broken arm is a broken arm. And the two pieces have to be put back together again. Does he want me to leave them separated so they rub against each other? Then you'd really feel something you wouldn't like."

To me my arm didn't look as though it was in two pieces, but it was beginning to feel that way.

"What's he saying?" my father asked.

"He says he has to put the pieces of my arm back together again. So it won't really hurt me anymore."

"Well you tell him he'd better be very careful about what he's doing or there'll be all hell to pay."

I didn't know how to say that in Greek, so I just told the doctor that my father hoped he would be careful with the two pieces of my arm.

"Of course I'll be careful," the doctor muttered pretty much to himself. "I'm always careful. I'm careful with horses even when they can't be saved, so why wouldn't I be careful with the son of the Consul General?"

He nodded at my father as though he'd got the message, and the truth was, he became much gentler when it came to manipulating the arm so that it's pieces fit together again just above the elbow, and I did my best not to show how much it hurt. Then we went down the hall to another room where a man in a white coat with very bad breath wrapped the arm in gauze and a mixture of plaster he made up in a basin. When the plaster dried, the arm was solid as though made of stone and in a bent position. It was pretty heavy, but once it was in a sling, I didn't have any serious problem with it, and I found that it was the cause of much attention when I showed up at school the next day. During recess I let a lot of people sign their names in ink on the plaster cast, even Helga Trauger. Especially Helga Trauger.

But of course that broken arm put an end to my athletic ambitions for the rest of the school year. I had no choice but to focus on my work in the classroom, with the hope of earning myself one of the three prizes given out at graduation to those who had done superior work in one or the other of three major subjects: arithmetic, history, reading and writing. Arithmetic was clearly out, not so much on grounds of difficulty as irrelevance to the way my heart of hearts beat, and history was out because of my persistent confusion about the complex story of what had been going on, from the German point of view, in various countries of Europe during our century and the last. It was a story that in any case ignored the two countries—America and Canada—whose apparently simpler, if now fading past, present, and future still occupied a fairly coherent portion of my brain. That left reading and writing. Though a slow reader in any language, German most of all, I figured that the prize requirement in this subject was relatively uncomplicated: a four page essay in neat script on any subject having to do with European geography. The only problem was finding a subject sufficiently compelling to get me to the bottom of the first blank page, after which I assumed the writing would continue to the next page more or less by itself with only modest urging on my part.

I can't remember what subjects or how many I tried out, but I remember that no one of them filled a blank page since I knew very little about the huge territory called Europe, and this failure to get a decent start was enough to drive me to my mother for help. I went to my mother rather than my father not only out of a natural impulse in that direction but because I carried a bit of dialogue in my head that I had heard one morning at the breakfast table. It began with my father leaning over his freshly-made yoghurt to hand my mother a letter he had written: "You're the writer in the family, so tell me if you think this will get me a promotion or get me fired." I don't know what was in that letter, but I remember my mother shaking her head now and then as she read it and suggesting that this or that sentence didn't sound quite right, and I also remember my father silently taking the letter back from her to write something in the margins as he went through it, then returning it to her for a second read.

It must have been at least a decade after her death before I discovered, on entering the labyrinth of my father's files, a reference to three articles that my mother had written between 1925 and 1928 for a New York magazine called *Travel*, their titles intriguingly exotic: "Willing Guest of a Bedouin Sheik," "Syrian Hillsmen Who Defied France," and "Mighty Ruins of Ancient Heliopolis." It moved me to learn then that she really had been a writer, even if her budding career had apparently been cut short in 1928 by the arrival of a second child and then a third child only a little more than a year later, and maybe incidentally by my father's transfer from the hot sands of Syria and Lebanon to the chillier landscape of Montreal, Canada, I suppose from my mother's perspective not much more exotic and inspiring for a travel writer than her hometown in upstate New York, which she had left, soon after graduating from Alfred University, for the other side of the world and the unrestricted adventure of YWCA work in Istanbul, Turkey. The photograph albums from that period in her life, immediately after the end of the First World War, show nothing of the Waste Land panorama of futility and anarchy leading to the despair that her generation has been pictured as suffering in its search for the lost center of belief. Her search, with other young ladies her age—sometimes in their YWCA uniforms, sometimes in elegantly playful hats and flowing dresses, sometimes in bathing costumes—was for yet another unknown city or site: Batoum, Tiflis, Seraglid Palace, Smyrna, Salonika, Vienna, Venice, Florence, Rome, Lucerne, Paris, and after she met her American husband-to-be in Istanbul, trips to Sofia, Budapest, Prague, Berlin, Aachen, Coblenz, Rheims, Oberammergau, the Holy Land, the Pyramids, Athens.

I was still at an age that spring of 1939 when it wouldn't have occurred to me not to tell my mother the full truth, so in my increasing anxiety about the contest ahead of me I simply went up to her one afternoon on getting home from school by streetcar and milk wagon well ahead of my father's return from the office and told her that I wanted to win one of the German School prizes at the end of the year and needed her help. She told me that trying to win a prize was a fine idea but that it would mean a lot more to me if I won it all by myself. I explained that I was supposed to write an essay about the geography of Europe only I didn't know anything about Europe since I hadn't grown up there and hadn't even worked on the paste models of the place that our geography teacher had assigned the class.

"Well what about Greece?" my mother said. "I think you know Greece well enough by now, don't you?"

"I didn't know Greece was in Europe," I said. "They never told me that in school."

"Well it is and it isn't," my mother said. "But I think for what you want to do, we can say that it is."

"So what should I write about Greece?"

"Well that has to be up to you," my mother said. "You should write about some place that has made you feel good, made you feel excited."

"Swimming at the beach?" I said. "Riding the Combine?"

"I don't think that would pass as geography," my mother said with a little smile. "Some place you've been that's maybe a bit unusual. That you won't easily forget."

We went over the places I'd been that I was sure I wouldn't forget easily—Kastania Mountain, Pelion, Vrnjacka Banya—but they all seemed places too large to fit into four pages. And then my mother said something that sent a little thrill through me.

"Can you think of a place where you discovered something that you are pretty sure nobody else in your class has discovered?"

I knew that place immediately: the tower on the border of Mt. Athos that once belonged to an Emperor but now belonged to writers from Australia named Joyce and Sydney Loch and that was haunted by a monk who had killed himself by falling or jumping off its high balcony to the rocky shore below in the Middle Ages. The tower was square, and from a distance its two windows below the roof looked like blank white eyes, with that balcony between them for a toothless mouth, but it was even more terrifying close up, especially after the lady from Australia got through telling you about its history and showed you the open hand print that had suddenly appeared on the wall in front of her husband one afternoon part way up the second flight of stairs leading to a third flight that brought you to the creaky boards of that balcony where the monk's gray-white skull was preserved in a glass case because to the local people it was a holy relic but to a boy of eleven from another country it was a thing that turned your heart to stone even in the bright light of noonday. Which was the only time of day this boy could find the courage to climb those stairs. And once out on the balcony, he might glance at the skull sideways a minute but still not turn his look upwards to the slate roof where Mrs. Loch said her maid had ended up dancing naked one night in front of the whole village after the tower's ghost had apparently turned the maid's brain inside out so that a priest had to be called in to exorcise the demon that had gone on living inside her for some days thereafter.

Getting all that into German was not easy even with the help of my mother and the English-German dictionary she handed me when it came to certain unknown words that seemed essential, but the subject proved to be enough to fill four pages and more after I gave some space to a description of the seaside village where the Lochs lived and a bit of background on Mt. Athos and its many monasteries that were not open to anything female including cats and hens, and some biography about the Emperor who built that great creepy monster of a tower for the last of his wives while he went off to a cave on the Holy Mountain so that he could end his days as a holy hermit. I don't know where I went wrong—maybe not stopping with strict Germanic discipline at exactly four pages, maybe not rewriting one of the pages where the script went a little out of control under the pressure of what I was feeling at the time—but the fact is, I didn't win the prize. What I won was a special mention by the Principal at the graduation ceremony "for showing unusual improvement" but no book in German such as that presented the winner in Reading and Writing, a girl with dirty-blonde pigtails and thick eyebrows who wrote an essay on the Austrian Alps. I told myself I didn't want a book in German anyway. But that wasn't the last time in my life I lied to myself after ending up an also-ran.

My real consolation prize was the news my father brought into the kitchen a few days after that graduation in early June, *1939*, while I was still lifting a bucket of water up and down, up and down, in the regular afternoon sessions, under my mother's supervision, that were gradually allowing me to bend my mending left elbow open and closed at almost three-quarters of its normal capacity. The news was that my father had been granted the two months of required home leave he said was in any case long overdue. We would sail out of Piraeus on the first American

Export Lines ship that reached Greece in late June or early July and return on the first ship heading back to Greece in September. And with this announcement my mother turned from me to give my father a hug—no kiss, just a brief hug, I suppose because I was watching them too intently. Then my father addressed me. During this leave we would take a trip across the whole of the United States, from Washington, D.C. to Los Angeles, California and back again by a different route, visiting all the National Parks that were worth visiting along the way, so that my brothers and I could get to know the best of our great and vast home country. This we would do—and here my father glanced over at his wife for a second—in our own house trailer, a larger model of the one that had disappeared not long since from our garage outside.

I couldn't wait to bring this news to Lisa, I suppose partly to show off, partly to let her know how much smarter I would be from all I would learn on the road by the time I got back to Salonika at the end of the summer, if surely never smart enough to know as much as she did. I decided not to mention the house trailer. I found Lisa working on the flower bed in her back yard and told her I would meet her in the barn whenever she could get free from her chores, and we agreed to make that an hour before the sun's descent would signal approaching mosquito time. I was too excited to go to the soccer field, so I just wandered around the school for a while, then checked out the farm machinery to see if anything new had arrived from the U.S.A.—it hadn't—then helped with the feeding of the animals until I saw Lisa coming down the road toward the dairy barn, her dark short-cut hair neatly trimmed, head high, breasts high, her gait the straight-ahead no-nonsense kind that didn't show any of the tentative self-consciousness that I had begun to see in some of my mostly pigtailed mostly still flat-chested schoolmates—that is, until she spotted me and slowed down abruptly, her head turned a fraction, her smile curious, what I might have seen at a later time as a touch flirtatious.

"So. What is so important that you aren't any longer afraid to come looking for me even with my grandmother watching from the porch?"

On the way to our private corner of the hayloft I told her what was so important. Lisa didn't say anything until we were sitting side-by-side on our separate bales of straw high up in the barn.

"You're going away then," she said. "Just like that."

"My father has to," I said. "He's been expecting it. He said it should have happened a long time ago."

"And you and your brothers have to go with him?"

"Well, it's a family thing," I said. "They call it Home Leave."

"I mean, I'm sure you could stay here if you really wanted to. I'm sure Mr. and Mrs. House would take care of you for two months."

"My father says he wants to show us America. He says it's time we got to know our country. The whole country."

"How can you get to know it?" Lisa said. "It's too big a country to know in two months."

She was no longer looking at me but staring at her feet. She seemed upset.

"Well, I already know some of it," I said. "My grandfather's farm and a few other places. Anyway, we'll see as much of it as we can in two months and then we'll come back."

Lisa shook her head. "You won't come back. That's the trouble."

"Of course we will. Why do you say a thing like that?"

"I just know you won't," Lisa said. "I feel it."

I nudged her with my elbow. "That's just gypsy stuff. We have to come back. Everything we have is here."

"I know what I know," Lisa said. "Besides, my father says there's going to be a war."

I didn't know what to say to that. War wasn't a thing my father and mother talked about, at least not in front of my brothers and me.

"My father hasn't said anything about a war. And that's the kind of thing he would know about. He works for the American government."

Lisa glanced at me. "You think I don't know that? Anyway, what difference does it make? You seem so happy to be going to America, so go ahead. Go to America with your American parents who work for the American government."

"I'm not so happy," I lied.

"Yes you are," Lisa said. "I can tell."

We sat there without saying anything. I picked up a few blades of straw and used them to tickle her bare calf because I didn't know what else to do. Lisa reached down and stopped my hand, then let go and sat up straight.

"Well, you might as well come here so that I can kiss you goodbye," she said. "Who knows when I'll see you again now that you'll be getting your things ready to leave."

She was looking at me now in a way that wasn't her usual way. It made me turn to gaze at my knees.

"Can I at least kiss you goodbye?" she said

"Well, I'm not leaving right away. But sure."

I sat up and leaned toward her and gave her my cheek.

"Not like that. Don't you know how to do it better than that?"

She took my head in her hands and kissed me on the mouth, her lips a little open—not long, but long enough to make me feel something I'd never felt before. Then she leaned back against the bale behind her.

"Now go along to your American parents. But don't you forget that to me you're just a poor Greek like me, and that's the way I'll always think of you. Whether it makes you happy to think that or not."

※　※　※

We left the Farm School for Athens about ten days later to spend some time looking at the ruins there while we waited for the SS *Exachorda* of the American Export Lines to arrive in Piraeus. During those last days, I saw Lisa here and there on the school grounds but not alone again because I told myself I had to spend all the free time I could getting my things together and deciding what I could fit into the small suitcase my mother gave me for the trip to the States and what I simply had to leave behind. On the day before our last at the school, I made the rounds to say goodbye to my closest friends, the Armenian gardener's children first and Kirkor most of all, though he was just as shy as I was about making a big thing about my going off for two months even if it was to America. And I stopped by Theo Litsas' house to say goodbye to him and his wife and to receive a hard hug from both, and then Lisa's house to say good-bye to her parents and her grandmother and to shake Lisa's hand when they called her down from whatever she was doing upstairs. She didn't say anything special to me that I could remember, I suppose having said what counted that day in the barn. But her eyes said something to me that hovered between sadness and pride, and though I couldn't describe it to myself then, it was a look I carried with me to Athens and way beyond.

Because my parents seemed very impressed by some of the ruins we visited in the capital city, I tried to be impressed myself, but wandering through stones and columns on the Acropolis in the morning heat was not an experience that joined other more stirring encounters with the Greek landscape that settled into memory, even with my mother explaining as best she could the history of this and that temple and the gods and goddesses who once lived in them but were apparently driven out first by the Christians and then by the Turks, who blew the roofs off those temples so nothing was left of them to see and not that much of their walls either. What I remember best of the Athens of those years was the Zappion Garden, where there was a photographer with a box standing on three legs who disappeared under a black cloth to take your picture after spitting on his hands and where there was another man with a box on wheels who ladled out homemade vanilla ice cream that had something in it sticky enough allow him to pile up layer on layer of the stuff on a cone the size of his thumb.

That garden, really an open square lined by benches at one end of the Royal Garden, was the most peaceful place in the center of the city. There was no sound of traffic close by, no chatter of linked girls out for shopping, only the sound of cooing pigeons waiting for a handout. You could see whole families sitting quietly on a bench, the youngest children crawling all over their parents with melting or crumbling goodies, the older ones paying much quick attention with the eyes to those of the opposite sex passing by but no sign of interest in facial expression or posture. Most in the oldest generation were sitting in the outdoor café at green metal tables drinking water, some beside little cups of coffee, some beside preserves on a glass plate, some with just a glass of water for its own sake. And the strollers strolled by slowly, heading into the tall trees and thick foliage on the edge of the square or coming out of one garden path or another into the open to cover their eyes against the sudden light and to dodge the soaring pigeons. Even the Evzones at the other end of the garden looked cool in their summer uniforms as they marched with slow, casual formality to take their place for the changing of the guard in front of the Parliament Building, no sound from them other than the clicking rhythm of their hobnailed *tsarouchia* on the marble sidewalk. If there were other soldiers on guard against an unseen enemy somewhere, we didn't see them, and if there were any distant drumbeats of the coming war, we of the younger generation didn't hear them.

I now have a suspicion that my mother did, even if she never said so in our hearing. There was a moment before we left the lower end of the Zappion Garden, my father already on his way back toward the far corner of the Royal Garden to check in at the American Embassy close by, when my mother, apparently sensing that her three boys had tired of ruins and the dry passages between them, handed us over to Nartouie with enough cash for her to buy us a cool drink or anything else reasonable we might want at the outdoor cafe while she took a stroll on her own to visit Hadrian's Arch just in sight ahead. That decision seemed to please Nartouie as much as it did us, bored as she no doubt was by then with the dusty remnants of ancient Greece. And she didn't seem especially worried when my mother failed to reappear by the time we were finished with our lemonades and roasted peanuts and had begun to get restless just sitting around that green table with nothing to say to each other. Nartouie eventually gathered us up and led us down the path my mother had taken. We found her sitting in a slash of shadow from the Arch, which, at a good two stories high and crowned by its own temple-like columns, was very impressive in its way even if there was nothing but open space behind it. She was sitting on the marble curb that protected the Arch from the street beyond, leaning on her arms, her legs stretched out and crossed in front of her, her gaze not on the Arch at all but on her own feet, and so intense that she didn't notice us coming up on her until Nartouie had us stop in a casual line a few yards in front of her.

I could tell from the expression on my mother's face and two damp lines that she'd been crying, though she immediately tried to hide what was there behind a strained smile. Without a word she stood up, dabbed at her face, brushed herself off, and came over to take Budge's hand to guide him around the Arch toward the road leading up to the Parliament Building and the white-stockinged Evzones, with the rest of us following close behind. I could never be sure why she'd cried that day. Recalling the moment in later years, I told myself she must have had a premonition that our idyllic life in Greece was now over, that the possibility of war was real, that she would be facing harder days ahead in the grayer civil-service life that awaited her back home. But even that kind of premonition, if reason enough for melancholy, didn't seem cause enough for her going off by herself like that to end up crying. It was shortly after her death, when I inherited the photo albums she'd kept of her travels over the years and our occasional family outings, that I came across what struck me as a revealing snapshot in the first pages of the first album, dated August, 1919, this one covering her trip from New York State via Canada, Gibraltar, and Greece to her assignment with two other young ladies as YWCA social workers in what she labeled Constantinople, Turkey. On the page devoted to Greece, there are several snapshots of the Acropolis, one of the temple of Olympian Zeus, and one of Hadrian's Arch, with a horse-drawn carriage emerging through the Arch ahead of a man in jacket, tie, and straw hat.

So she had been to that grand site twenty years before, almost to a day. What had it meant to her then? And what touch of nostalgia had brought on those tears in 1939? Or was it a quick review of what had become of the adventurous young lady of 1919 during the two decades since she'd left her small-town home for unknown regions, given her time not only to YWCA service but to much travel in exotic places, had more than one man in her life and more than one marriage proposal, settled for a foreign service clerk working for his bachelor's degree in night school, tried her hand at free-wheeling journalism for a while, bore and bred and half educated three children while living in Syria, Lebanon, Canada, and Greece, and had now ended up where? Somewhere in her husband's shadow, as in the slanting shade of that high Arch, with how much life of her own outside that of her children, her household chores, her semi-official, unpaid responsibilities as a Foreign Service wife? I never found a sufficient answer, and she herself never gave me one beyond the abiding image of her tear-stained face that day.

*   *   *

The SS *Exachorda* of the American Export Lines proved to be a grand ship in my eleven-year-old opinion—as grand as any I had seen at close quarters, even if it was built mostly for transporting goods rather than passengers. It was the largest ship in the harbor of Piraeus, tall enough to give you a full view of all the lesser ships around and a stretch of the neighboring coastline. There was nothing going on in the harbor to see, mostly small craft for island hopping or transport caiques and just one small warship that was getting a new coat of paint on one side of its hull, but after we were aboard and had our things stowed away in the cabin set aside for the children and Nartouie, there was much room for exploration inside our new home for some days to come. The engine room was closed to passengers until the captain sent word that it was all right for the children of the American Consul to have a quick tour under the eye of the chief petty officer down there, and then there was the bridge with enough shining objects to interest even those of us who had no affection whatsoever for engineering, and there was deck space for walking at a good speed back and forth or for shuffle board and ping-pong. But the deck turned out to be mostly for sitting out in a deck chair to take in the sun and, when the sea got rough, for watching others get sick over the railing until you did yourself.

The real discovery on that ship was another American family that was heading home from Lebanon, the only other passengers I remember. My parents knew that family because they had served together in Beirut, but they were new to me because I had left the region at the age of three. In any case the only member of the family I was really interested in getting to know personally during this trip was the daughter, who was a year or maybe two older than me, a difference that I took to be insignificant but that proved to be something like a generation in her mind. Her name was Fay, and she was taller than me by half a head, hair dark as it comes and falling into an easy roll close to her shoulders, her forehead high but teased by a curl where the hair parted, her eyes gray-green under the thin black curve of her brows, her lips—never mind, she seemed to me gorgeous beyond words. And she proved to be unapproachable except in a formal family way until at least half-way through our journey.

The problem to begin with was again my older brother Budge, who seemed, at that age, to appeal irresistibly to any girl a bit older than me whom I happened to find irresistible, Greek girls excluded, maybe because he was somewhat shy about his American way of speaking Greek or maybe because a girl like Lisa found him too American in other ways. But not Fay, not this tall, elegant, distant girl, the first American girl I had been close to in my life (not counting a cousin in upstate New York), though "close" is hardly an accurate way to describe the few times in those first days aboard ship when I would approach her to try and get in a friendly word only to find her so absorbed by whatever had her preoccupied at the moment—a magazine, a cup of tea, most of all, some kind of vivid conversation with my older brother—that I had to settle for a quick look from her and a little smile that seemed to me to hover dangerously on the border between tolerance and indifference. The other problem was rough weather in the open Atlantic after Gibraltar, when Fay took to her cabin for what seemed like days, I suppose to avoid the embarrassment of vomiting in public, a thing that didn't seem to bother anybody else, including some members of the crew. When she finally appeared on deck, it was to bundle herself up in a light blanket and either lie there pale in a deck chair with her eyes closed or bury her lovely head in a book.

It was a book that finally brought me within talking distance, a book of poetry. We were by that time so far into our journey home that I decided I had to be more forceful and direct if I had any hope of getting this American girl's attention long enough to make some kind of significant impression on her. When I next found her parents taking a stroll so that there was an empty deck chair beside their daughter, I simply cut over from the section of railing where I'd been keeping my vigil and sat down at the foot of that chair.

"What are you reading now?" I asked bluntly.

Fay looked up. "Now? Now I'm reading poetry. What's wrong with that?"

"There's nothing wrong with that," I said. "Personally, I love poetry. That is, when I'm in the right mood for it."

The little smile appeared. "What kind of poetry do you like when you're in the right mood?" Fay asked.

She had me there. The only poetry I could remember were some lines from "Winnie the Pooh" and Kipling's "If," my father's favorite poem, the one he used to recite on the open highway with the trailer bouncing behind us, along with some lines from "Hiawatha."

"Kipling," I said. "Not always. Sometimes."

"What do you like by Kipling?" Fay asked.

She seemed actually curious.

"Well the poem I like best is 'If.' At least it's easy to remember."

"'If'?" Fay said.

"You know, 'If you can keep your head when all about you are losing theirs and blaming it on you?'"

"I know the poem," Fay said. "I can't say that it's my favorite. In fact, I don't like it at all."

"Well, it isn't my very favorite either," I said. "I just happen to know it well. But my father likes it."

"That's because it's a poem for men," Fay said.

I didn't know what to say to that. I'd never thought of it that way.

"What poetry are you reading?" I finally said.

"Elizabeth Barrett Browning. Some of her 'Sonnets from the Portuguese.' Here."

She handed me the book. I looked at it, even leafed through it, with what I hoped would demonstrate intense interest. I had never heard of Elizabeth Barrett Browning or any of the other poets in that book.

"You can keep it if you want. I've read through the thing once already. It gets boring the second time."

"I wouldn't want to take it from you," I said.

Fay shrugged. "Take it. I have plenty of other things to read."

She reached to the deck and picked up another book she had lying there. I had no choice but to keep the poetry book, and anyway it gave me an excuse to sort of spread myself half way on the deck chair beside her and read a few of the poems in it until her parents showed up from their promenade to stand over me with the kind of solicitation that made me deeply uncomfortable. I thanked her for the book and thanked them for nothing in particular and took off for our cabin, where Nartouie was lying in bed in profound anguish, facing what she assumed was another confrontation with early death. I took to my bunk and had a go at the poetry book, and though I didn't understand much of it, every now and then I came across some lines that were musical enough to touch me and even to stick in my mind after I took a turn at memorizing them. My idea was to use some of those lines, most of them by a man with the weird name of Algernon Charles Swinburne, to impress the lovely Fay when I next had a chance, but nothing came of it because I could never again find her alone enough to give me the courage I needed to recite poetry like that in the open air. She did say hello to me in a different way when we ran into each other during the final days of the trip, and on the last day, when everyone moved out on deck to have a look at the Statue of Liberty and the New York skyline, she made room for me to come up against the railing on the side of her opposite to where Budge had nestled in. It was a special moment for me, more special even than seeing that huge statue or all those tall buildings crowded in against each other, but it was over before I really had a chance to drink in the full feeling of being that close to her and sensing for the first time the sweet smell of her newly washed hair.

And that was the end of it. Fay and her family headed for Princeton, N.J., and I headed for Washington, D.C., with that poetry anthology in its stained jacket wrapped for protection in a T-shirt at the bottom of my suitcase, the only book from my early reading years that stayed with me long enough to make it into the personal library I began to build as an English major in college. Though Fay settled down in the green-trimmed, magnolia-rich town of Princeton for the rest of her life, as I did for the better part of mine, she lived among the castles on the West End side with her Wall Street husband, and I lived on the East End side in the section where farm land had gradually been taken over by middle-class housing. When our paths more or less crossed over the years, we remained at a distance, not out of choice so much as a difference in the company we kept—except for one time I remember when we happened to end up at the same West End garden party and I made a point of crossing the vast lawn between us to touch her arm and ask if she still remembered me.

"Of course I remember you. You're the naughty child who fell so in love with poetry that you never returned the book I gave you."

"You're right. I was stupid. I thought you actually gave me that book."

Fay lifted her broad shoulders in a little shrug and showed me her old half-smile.

"Don't look so guilty. You didn't steal it. Anyway, it was only an old poetry anthology."

She turned back to the ancient lady she'd been talking to and I moved off as casually as I could toward my side of the lawn.

FIVE

Close at hand, the cluster of giant buildings in 1939 New York was striking enough by itself to create a new land of mysterious living in the mind of a boy just in from farm land bordered by a rock-crowned mountain and the swampy shore of a sometimes murky bay. But what opened out to even greater possibilities for the imagination were the extravagant, other-worldly pavilions of the World's Fair in the Flushing plain. The architecture in wonderland shapes, the miniature cars swirling fast over and under the curling maze of projected highways, the open-ended images of travel through space—it seemed a corner of America more than a century ahead of any other land in the universe, including those you'd seen in the movies, and never mind if you could tell that much of it was pure make-believe. My brothers and I, ready to give ourselves over to a uninhibited discovery of the America we knew almost not at all but now wanted to make our own, were allowed only a day of that futuristic vision when it should have been good for a week or two, the first of our disappointments that mid-summer. The second came when we moved on to Washington, D.C., and learned that a thing people there called the international crisis would cost us our planned trailer trip to explore the length of our home country because my father was suddenly assigned to a new Special Problems Division of the State Department and had to report to work after his first weekend in our nation's capital.

Somehow we ended up living in a trailer anyway, a motionless trailer on blocks parked near the Tidal Basin with other such trailers serving transient civil servants in desperate need of temporary housing. It was not a satisfactory substitute for a home from the point of view of the younger generation, even after Nartouie suddenly disappeared one August morning on her way to Providence, Rhode Island, to meet her pre-arranged fiance, thus freeing space in the trailer that had been taken up by her folding cot where the kitchen table stood in daytime. At first my parents tried to make our new mode of living seem a camp experience, each of us with daily chores to keep things tidy inside and outside the trailer, each sent out on missions as though into the forest primeval to fetch this or that from the nearest grocery store or to fill this or that container from the water source on the edge of the campsite. But we had much time on our hands that August, time for learning to throw a baseball and a football in the strip of grass border beyond the outer line of trailers (kicking the foreign soccer ball we'd brought with us roused hostile glares even from adult onlookers), and time for just sitting on our haunches waiting for something exciting to happen, as though stranded settlers on the covered-wagon road to an invisible West watching out for a possible Indian attack.

The serious action began with a Saturday trip to visit the White House and the Capitol Building, my mother serving as our guide through the corridors of the new history opening out in front of us and the democratic ways of President and Congressmen and Supreme Court justices that were meant to challenge what we had vaguely learned abroad about kings and parliaments and dictators ranting in various languages. The buildings along Constitution Avenue were truly impressive, and some of them even looked Greek, though their columns and walls had apparently been scrubbed cleanly white. And at the foot of the Capitol Building we found flowers in the Botanical Garden that none of us could name. Then the Mall, as grand an expanse of city green as any that had come our way, the Athens Royal Garden included, with the Washington Monument at the far end for a view of the city and an acrophobic thrill when you reached the top that made it more than worth the long climb up there to test the weakening soccer muscles in your legs.

It was on the way to the Lincoln Memorial beyond the end of the Mall that I learned that day's most complicated lesson for a newcomer to that region of America. By the time we came down from the Washington Monument, my mother was in a bit of a hurry to finish our tour and get us back home for supper, but we decided to have a toilet stop anyway, and since I happened to be last in line, I told the others to go on ahead toward the Lincoln Memorial and I'd catch up with them after I'd done my business. By the time I came out, they were a good distance in front of me, and instead of running to catch up, I slowed my walk to take in the feel of that great open space in front of me leading to the river, then stopped for a minute to look back over the green expanse of the Mall behind me to focus again on the curious, castle-like structure called the Smithsonian Institution with the Lindbergh plane in it that my mother had told us we would have to save for another day. The sun was getting low by then, and I could see that the Mall was now almost clear of wandering sightseers, but it didn't occur to me that I was out there beyond the Washington Monument more or less alone until I turned around to find myself facing four black kids who had come out of God knows where to stand there facing me the way I meant to be heading, kids not my age but not much older either, standing there in a casual line, smiling, just smiling, and one of them, the tallest, slowly shaking his head as he smiled.

"Where you think you goin', boy?"

"Nowhere special," I said. "The Lincoln Memorial."

"Is that right? Hear what he say? He goin' to the Lincoln Memorial."

"That's what he say," the kid next to him said. "The Lincoln Memorial."

I decided to smile and keep on going at a slightly new angle. The line shifted in front of me and closed in.

"Now what's you hurry, boy? That Lincoln Memorial aint goin' nowhere."

"I'm meeting my mother up ahead," I said. "And my brothers."

"You hear what he say? Say he meetin' his muvver. This muvver be meetin' his muvver.

"I don't think he got a muvver," the kid next to him said. "You think he got a muvver?"

"No sir. Not this muvver."

I tried going around the line again. It moved in closer.

"I don't think this muvver be goin' anywhere," the taller one said. "What you think?"

"No sir," the kid next to him said. "He aint goin' nowhere. He be where he shouldn't be. I mean to say he shouldn't be right here, that's for sure."

"That's right," the tall one said. "This muvver be far from where he needs to be. 'Cause this where we be."

I'm not sure who hit me first, but the blow went straight to my jaw, and another went to the side of my head and knocked me down. When I started to get up, I felt another blow graze the side of my head. I knelt there waiting, and when I looked up again, they were gone, racing one after the other toward the edge of the Tidal Basin and, by the time I got myself up and brushed off, out of sight behind the trees and shrubbery over there. My jaw was sore and so was the side of my head, but there was no blood anywhere as far as I could tell, so I decided that gave me an excuse not to tell the others what had happened.

I didn't understand what had happened, so what was there to tell? These were not gypsies blocking my way home on the back road to the Farm School, intent on one thing only: the loose drachmas in my pocket or the shirt off my back. And once I knew that, I could learn how to keep out of their way. These black kids hadn't made any move to rob me or hold me up for a toll. All they seemed to want was to make me feel stupid, dumber than they were, smaller, and since I felt that I didn't yet speak their language, I had to keep my mouth shut not to appear even stupider than I was. I didn't believe they really thought they owned the territory I was crossing any more than the gypsies owned the flat land surrounding that ancient tomb in Greek Macedonia, and since I didn't own it either and hadn't pretended to, there had to be something else behind their quick attack and equally quick disappearance into no-man's-land. The only black people I'd ever seen at that time were the hired hands who worked on my grandfather's farm in upstate New York, good farm hands who did what they were supposed to do well according to my grandfather, didn't talk much or bother anybody, and moved on eventually when they'd picked up enough in wages to settle wherever they'd come from originally or wherever they thought their best luck might lie ahead. This gang of kids seemed to belong to another world, with unfamiliar borders.

It took me some months to begin to grasp the local history that lay behind this first encounter with the racial divide in the nation's capital, and not until I reached college to learn the larger context of that history. During my five school years in Georgetown, I came to see that M Street, the setting for several local race riots, was what separated the black world in our neighborhood from the white world that supplied the students in the public schools I attended, and I also came to know how Southern in their prejudices the old Washington residents on my side of the border were during those years. I don't know how long it took after that time for the boundary between black and white in the city to shift so thoroughly as the result of the gradual exodus of white residents to Virginia and Maryland that my high school ended up serving black students mostly, no longer as Western High but as the Duke Ellington High School for the Arts. In any case, by then my college courses in American history and the civil rights movement had given me much of what I needed to understand the difference between nomad gypsies on the make in Macedonia and black kids in the District of Columbia looking for a way to exercise their frustrated pride.

My first taste of Washington public schools came in September, when we moved out of the Tidal Basin camp grounds to a row house on Lamont Street and into the school district that put residents on that street into Central High and Powell Junior High, the former Budge's domain—as it had been my father's at one time—the latter mine, and with Bob now assigned to the local elementary school, each of us had to confront his American education entirely on his own, and this divided schooling did much to keep each of us in the younger generation moving our separate ways most of the time during the years following. The possibility of starting out in a new school in a new country that fall had not remotely entered my imagination, even after what Lisa had predicted in her parting gypsy mood. It was during a quick trip to Wellsville,

N.Y., at the end of August to visit our Vossler grandparents there that my father called a meeting of our family around my grandmother's kitchen table to bring us the startling news that it seemed likely war was about to be declared in Europe and to explain what this growing danger would mean for our immediate future. The first thing it would mean was that we would not be returning to the American Farm School in Greece as planned but would be living for a while in Washington, D.C., a change of direction that I found as hard to accommodate initially—despite Lisa's premonition—as I would have word that my parents were getting divorced and leaving us in the care of our grandparents for the time being. It didn't help much to learn from my father that he planned to begin house hunting in Washington with all deliberate speed and expected us to be settled into a comfortable home soon after we returned to the city. I slept badly that night and the next and the next after that, and it didn't do my state of mind any service to overhear my father's daily reports to my mother on what sinister things were happening in Europe and how confused the people he worked with down in what he and his State Department friends called Foggy Bottom seemed to be about our anticipated role in "developing events." I saw images of those events as great forest fires that would gradually spread south from Germany to climb Kastania mountain and cross the Macedonian plain to devour the city I still considered home territory.

During the first days of September I had got up the courage to write Lisa a postcard in a version of Greek script and in the simplest of sentences, whatever the spelling, that I hoped would be good enough to convey my painful state of mind: "I gave your address to a girl here who wants to write a Greek girl. She will write you in a little while. There is going to be a war now, so we won't be going back to Greece until it's over. This makes me very sad. My father may have to go back. We here listen to what is happening on the radio. With love, Mikis." Originally I'd planned to send a postcard with a picture of the Washington Monument on it that I'd borrowed from my mother, but I ended up needing all the room I could get for my script without taking up valuable space for an address. When I'd finished my handiwork, I gave the card to my mother and asked her to put the right kind of stamp on it for Greece in addition to the one cent printed there already. She glanced at the card, saw it was in Greek, turned it over, saw who I'd addressed it to in English but didn't say a word about that one way or the other, just went across the room to tuck it away in her purse. Though I didn't know it at the time, that postcard got through to Lisa safely with an additional two cent stamp, because she showed it to me some eight years later on a beach a few kilometers beyond the curfew barrier that had been set up during the Greek Civil War to seal off Salonika from the sometimes still dangerous countryside on its outskirts. And some three years after that, the postcard came back to me in an envelope that had no return address.

✳ ✳ ✳

Powell Junior High in Northwest Washington had advantages and disadvantages over the German School in Salonika. The most important advantage was the fact that the teachers were not Nazis and generally managed to control their students by persuasion, appeals to pride, special assignments after class, and election to some office rather than by the threat of physical discipline. Another advantage was that the school encouraged competitive games rather than military drills, the latter remaining the prerogative of the Washington high school cadet corps. And there was the advantage of all classes being held in your native language, imperfect as your grasp of that might be depending on your background and history and quirky mode of addressing your parents. The major disadvantage—no, it was more than that: a serious obstacle—was the ever present requirement of conformity that students imposed on themselves. One thing this meant for you, as a newcomer from abroad struggling both to become and to seem an American, was that you had to learn to deal with the conception of others as to where you belonged and didn't belong, what you were or were not, and where you might tread or not tread, lessons that sometimes appeared easy because you were bluntly made aware of what others thought about you, sometimes not so easy even in appearance because you were forced to calculate accurately the shifting grounds of acceptance, let alone popularity.

My first lesson of this kind came when I was called to the blackboard in English class to write an assigned sentence there and identify its sub-ject and predicate. As I remember, the sentence was "In the Christian religion, baptism is a ritual involving water." I had no problem identify-ing the subject and predicate; the problem was the number of "r"s in the sentence and the "p" in baptism, which came out as a "b" then and almost ever after. The English teacher—Miss Englehart, I believe she was called—was my favorite, not only because she was young and blonde and very pretty but because she usually spoke gently in class and took extra time to help you out if she thought you had a problem she could deal with that wasn't a matter of congenital deficiency. On this occasion, she corrected my spelling without a word and told the class that I had marked the sentence correctly, then asked me in her gentle voice where I had learned to make my "r"s that way.

"In the German School," I said. "In Salonika, Greece."

"Well, that's interesting," she said. "Maybe sometime we can work on those 'r's a bit to make them easier to read."

"Very interesting," a voice said from the front seats.

"Very German," another voice said.

"Heil Hitler," another voice said.

Miss Englehart turned to the class, her voice no longer gentle.

"All right, enough of that. Unless you want to spend your afternoon writing Heil Hitler up and down this blackboard."

Nobody said anything, but the damage had been done. I had now been baptized "The Nazi," and I heard the name in shrill mockery every now and then when I passed certain of my classmates in the corridors of that school, girls as often as boys, which hurt the most. It took half the year to clear the air of that slur, and I managed that only when arduous practice after school on the basketball court had taught me this new sport well enough to earn me a place on one or another pick-up team, which in turn led to my joining a group of my contemporaries who had begun to experiment with the minor sins of those on the edge of puberty.

The leader of this group, Bernie Schultz, was partly responsible for restoring my good name. He was two years older than me and a class ahead, and though I was tall for my age, he was taller and muscle lean where I was merely thin. Bernie was already a cigarette smoker, thought to be wise about girls, and tough enough to stand up to anybody his size and larger. He was Jewish, but nobody dared call him Jewboy to his face, and when he heard one of the friendlier guys on the basketball court refer to me as The Nazi in a way that struck me as more congenial than malicious, Bernie took me aside and lectured me.

"Don't you let anybody call you that, you hear me? Even if they're kidding."

He had me by the shoulders and he was serious.

I tried to shrug. "I don't give a damn. Anyway, he didn't really mean anything by it."

"Whatever he meant, don't you let him call you that. Ever."

"What am I supposed to do about it?"

"Knock him on his ass. What the fuck do you think?"

"I don't know how to do that."

"Christ. I guess I'll have to teach you that as well."

He meant having already taught me how to shoot baskets way out beyond the foul line and how to twirl in a layup from the far side of the basket. He'd also taught me a certain amount of locker talk that I was still trying to sort out. But what he had in mind this day was taking me to the closest Boy's Club in our neighborhood and teaching me how to box. That took another month of occasional afternoons when he sparred with me until he decided I couldn't take the punishment any longer and some afternoons in between when I practiced on my own with a punching bag. Other times I simply shadow-boxed on my way to school or late in the day in the back yard on Lamont Street.

By the time Bernie decided that I'd learned enough, I felt quite confident about protecting myself, but I never had to use what I'd learned in an aggressive way, not at Powell Junior High, because it got around that Bernie was my protector these days, and that was enough to kill my Nazi nickname. It must have been well into the second half of the school year before Bernie and I got to trust each other enough to talk about personal matters in more than a general way. I remember in particular a follow-up to a conversation that he had initiated during the final stages of his training program to make me an acceptable pick-up basketball player. It started with an off-hand remark one afternoon when I had played reasonably well but began to fade on the court late in a tight game.

"What's the matter with you, for Christ sake?" Bernie said to me when we came to a break. "Getting too much nookie these days?"

"What's that?" I said

"What's what?"

"Nookie."

"What do you mean, what's nookie? Nookie is nookie, for Christ sake."

"Well, I know what it is in general. I mean specifically."

Bernie stared at me. "You're something, you know that? You're really something. Just off the farm, is that the problem with you?"

I think he realized he'd touched a sore spot, because I turned my back on him and picked up a basketball to shoot a few on my own, and the next chance we got to be by ourselves, he moseyed up to me and told me to sit down beside him on a bench because he wanted to tell me a few things.

"I know you've come from another country over there, so I thought I'd better tell you a few things about the situation here with regard to poontang."

"With regard to what?"

"Poontang, pussy, nookie, whatever you want to call it. Anyway, the point is, making out."

"Well, I'm not completely stupid," I said. "I know how animals do it."

"That's a beginning," Bernie said. "A good beginning. I accept that. The point is, where you go from there with humans."

I didn't say anything.

"I mean, the point is, when you go out with a chick over here, you got to know what you're doing or you may get your teeth knocked out. You know what I mean? I mean you got to take it slow."

"I understand," I lied.

"I mean you got to start at the top and slowly work your way down. You know what I mean?"

"Right," I said.

"You start with some smooching, you know, enough to get things warmed up, and then only when you think things are ready, you head for the boobs."

"What's smooching?"

Bernie looked away. "What's smooching. I mean, what can I say? Smooching. Kissing. Feeling around a little but not really."

"Right," I said. "We call it something else over there."

"Well, whatever you call it, you got to do it right or they clam up on you over here. You know, you can't just sit there beside them and head for the boobs. You got to be a little romantic. Even if it hurts. Which is something you can use later."

"What's that?"

"That it hurts. You can tell them that eventually. I mean if it goes on too long without getting anywhere. You can tell them you got hot nuts or whatever you want to call it."

"Well how long should this smooching go on?"

Bernie considered the question.

"That depends on who you're smooching with. For some it takes a long time before you can move on down, for others not so long. And for some you just have to take what you can get without really going anywhere, you know what I mean? However much it may hurt."

I nodded. Then I got up and stretched. Some of it made sense to me but not all of it, only I knew that any more questions would likely get me in above my head to the point where Bernie would lose patience again.

"Thanks, buddy," I said. "I mean it. I'll keep all that in mind."

And I did, to the end of the school year, without coming anywhere close to putting what Bernie had taught me into practice. The most I could do was give a quick glance toward this or that lovely passing bobbysoxer in the school corridors, or a longer gaze in the classroom, and wonder with yearning what it would be like to smooch a little with that sweet thing the American way. Then, as the school year ran out, I became preoccupied with another kind of yearning: getting myself elected to public office, which seemed to be the one sure route to being accepted by your classmates in that school, male and female alike, and maybe even gaining their respect as a fellow American. This opportunity came my way as the result of a project in the Current Events class that was meant to give us a first-hand knowledge of the democratic process in our country. The teacher, a white-haired lady with a slight lisp named Miss Henderson, had prepared us for this by assigning us the American Constitution to study, and some almost unreadable sections of the Congressional Record, and a collection of speeches by famous men in moments of crisis, beginning with Lincoln's Gettysburg Address. We were then given a test on the make-up of the Federal Government, and the teacher told us that the six in our class who did best on that would run for office in an election for President, Vice President, and Speaker of the House, the reward for those who won the election being a trip to the real Senate and House of Representatives while in session and the posting of their names and public offices beside the blackboard until the last day of class.

Six names appeared on the blackboard one morning—four girls and two boys—and it was hard for me to believe given my bad spelling and the way I wrote "r"s, but my name was there among them, though I was sure it would have been at the bottom of the list if Miss Henderson hadn't put them up there alphabetically. When she read them off to us, some in the class exercised their democratic right to cheer after the first name, and then the second—both girls—and then before Miss Henderson came to the third, my name, she put down the chalk and the eraser and came to the front of the class to stand there silently for a second and then to tell us how ashamed she was that people our age, all too soon to be voting citizens of our great republic, were still so childish as to mock a process that had provided the world with its first and only true example of a working constitutional democracy.

That lowered some heads, and general silence reigned. Miss Henderson then returned to the blackboard and divided the six names there into two parties, the Whigs and the Tories—I don't know on what, if any, democratic principle of selection in the case of the girls, but a boy ended up at the head of each slate. The teacher made me the Whig candidate for President and Jason Ripaldo the Tory candidate. My opponent, who had the reputation of being a grind at times and a cut-up at other times, right away objected to being a Tory, for reasons I didn't fully understand, something about his not wanting to be considered a limey.

Miss Henderson asked if I had any objection to being the Tory candidate, and when I said I didn't really give a damn one way or the other, she put the chalk and the eraser down again and turned to say "That is simply no way for a presidential candidate to talk," then wiped my name off the Whig slate as though the sight of it disgusted her, and shifted me to the Tory slate.

I'm sure that gesture earned me some votes in the long run, but there were serious problems ahead. We were given a week to prepare for the election, each party allowed to campaign as it chose but each slate to stand as a group and receive a single vote on election day, when each party would be allowed to present its case in a five-minute speech by one of its members, chosen by party caucus. At the Tory Party caucus to plan strategy that afternoon, I had no idea where to begin except to plead that I not be the one to give the speech on election day in view of my unresolved terror of facing an audience from a public stage. The two girls on my ticket, both among the brightest in the class though neither of whom I had given more than a passing glance now and then, dismissed my plea out of hand: Jason Ripaldo was certain to be the speaker on the Whig side because he surely wouldn't let anybody else take center stage, and neither of my companions was prepared to be the one to challenge him. Their mood was that it had to be man against man, even if they didn't quite put it that way. How could I disagree? As far as other strategy was concerned, they didn't have any more of a clue than I did, except to offer to try and persuade some of their girl friends to vote for our ticket. From their point of view, strategy was up to the party leader.

I turned to Bernie for help. The problem there was Bernie being in a class a year ahead of me, and the only other buddy he had in my class, another member of the pick-up basketball group nicknamed Sliver because of his emaciation, seemed simple-minded most of the time off the court and had very bad breath, either because of his junk food eating habits or his indifference to brushing his teeth. Still, Bernie decided that I had no choice but to make Sliver my campaign manager, and this proved a terrible mistake. Sliver went around that week trying to get people to vote for our ticket, but he couldn't provide a single good reason why anyone should do so except that Bernie had told him it was the

smart thing to do, and I'm certain his lack of conviction and his breath
alienated most of those he approached. The only hope was that some of
the girls—most of whom gave him a wide berth—would follow his
advice out of pure compassion for a campaign manager that miserable
and undernourished.

But the crucial problem proved to be the speeches on election day. I
had thought of consulting my parents about what I ought to put into
my speech, but I was already developing the habit of keeping my life outside the house on Lamont Street as private as possible so they wouldn't
start worrying about any difficulty I might have making my way in my
own country and also because some of what I was learning didn't seem
to me the kind of thing you talked about with parents in your own
home. So Bernie ended up providing me with the main argument for my
speech, which was that I had traveled widely in foreign parts and therefore had the kind of experience that a candidate for President of the
United States on the Tory ticket ought to have. And when I checked this
out with the candidates for Vice President and Speaker of the House on
my ticket, there seemed to be general agreement that this was as good an
approach as any other we might come up with since Ripaldo had never
set foot outside of Washington, D.C. as far as we knew and therefore had
no international experience whatsoever.

By the time I got up in front of the class, I had convinced myself that
it was important not to let my side down—in fact, I had also convinced
myself that I was actually the candidate who ought to win. This made it
easier for me to face that restless audience without feeling like an idiot
babbling about green fields in distant places nobody had ever heard of.
And when Miss Henderson recovered the coin she had accidentally
tossed over the heads of the two presidential candidates and reported
that I had won the toss so that I was now the designated first speaker,
this struck me as a very good omen, and that further calmed my nerves.
My speech was quite short, but I managed to get in some mention of my
experience with people of various kinds—Greeks, Armenians, Jews,
Yugoslavs, Turks, never mind one other nationality I thought best to
leave out—and my acquaintance with animals of various kinds, especially
cows and mules, and my travels to places high in the mountains and

down by the sea, including crossing the Atlantic ocean and back in an American Export Lines ship. I also got in a mention of how much I had come to know the Hellenic World, which was a great place for a president to get an education because it was the Cradle of Democracy, a way of putting things that I had heard my father use on several important occasions while we were abroad.

The speech was a disaster. I don't know what my classmates found worse: what I had to say or the stiff way I said it. Anyway, the response was leaden, except for some embarrassingly enthusiastic clapping by Miss Henderson that finally silenced the room. And the minute she finished, Ripaldo stood up all smiles, all casual hands in the pockets, all well practiced generosity. He said he didn't want people to hold it against his opponent that the gentleman had come to America recently from a German School, that was his parents' fault, not the candidate's, but there was something else that really bothered him. He just didn't think it would be right, especially when the U.S. Constitution made it illegal, for the class to elect as President of the United States somebody born in a foreign country somewhere on the Asian continent who had lived abroad most of his life and had associated all the time with foreign peoples of different kinds, when one of the candidates, yours truly, was a pure American, born in Alexandria, Virginia, who had lived all of his life in the nation's capital and would be very proud to go on living there in the White House on good old Pennsylvania Avenue, just a ways down the road from where you and I, regular residents of the District of Columbia, were situated at that moment. He said he and his Whigs were all real Americans, ready to serve their country from the day they were born until they volunteered as American citizens for service in the Army or the Navy, or in the case of the girls, in the nurse corps or some other such way of showing their love of their native land. And another thing, he promised that if elected he would make sure every person who lived in the nation's capital and therefore couldn't vote at the present time would get to vote like all other white people in the country. What more, he asked, could you want in a President of the United States who would also represent the District of Columbia for the first time in history?

Ripaldo and the Whigs won the election by a three to one margin, what Miss Henderson, in congratulating them, called a significant land-slide. And before I could recover from the shock of losing that badly, Ripaldo was at my side to shake my hand and give my arm a thump as though to say that this stunning defeat couldn't have happened to a nicer guy, foreigner though he might be. The girls on my ticket tried to pretend that it didn't really make any difference, it was all make believe anyway, but that isn't what their faces showed. It took me several days before I could think rationally enough about what had happened to see that Ripaldo must have known all along what line I was going to take in my speech, because, smart as he was, he couldn't have made up all that business about my foreign connections on the spot, simply on the basis of what I'd said in front of the class that day. Maybe his parents had helped him out when it came to what the U. S. Constitution recorded about the foreign born and his pitch about residents of the nation's capital not having the vote he promised to give them, but all that jazz about being a pure American ready to serve his country from the day he had come into the world in Alexandria, Virginia? And another thing, how did he know I'd been born in a foreign country, let alone in territory he'd identified as Asia, I suppose to bring China and Japan into the picture? I'd never mentioned to anybody where I was born as far as I could remember—except, maybe to Bernie in explaining at some point that I was an American by birth even though born in Damascus, Syria, because my father was a U.S. government employee, and then talking a bit one day about where I had grown up and how I had become friends with Jews and Turks and other foreigners like me that the German School had separated out from participation in the Hitler Jugend drills.

I wasn't ready to believe that Bernie had betrayed me—why would he do a thing like that? Or Sliver—he wasn't cunning enough. But what if it was somebody else they'd talked to casually about where I'd been born and where I'd grown up? What if Ripaldo's campaign manager—the golden-haired Janice, among the most popular girls in the class, who was the candidate for Vice-President on his ticket—what if Janice had wangled that bit of information out of Bernie or somebody Bernie had talked to about me? And if that had happened, what was the payoff? It became so obvious that I decided I just had to give up thinking about it.

And the more I tried, the harder it became not to think about it, not to believe that somebody had been talking behind my back and somebody had ended up betraying me for a date with Janice or a smooch or God knows what. And the more I thought about that, the more it isolated me.

My father gave me a holiday from my suspicions during the last week of school by announcing at dinner one evening that we would be moving the following week to a larger and better furnished duplex house in the Georgetown school district that was supposed to be even better than the one we were in. And once we were settled into this Fulton Street house near Wisconsin Avenue, he planned to arrange for my brother Bob and me to go for part of the summer to Camp Cory, the Rochester YMCA camp on Lake Keuka in upstate New York, not far from my grandfather's farm, and following that outing away from the family, he planned to solicit a month's leave from the State Department in order to take the whole family on a trailer trip out west as he had promised us the previous year.

That news was enough to kill further thoughts about political disasters and possible betrayals and their influence on my attempt to adopt the ways of my American homeland—that is, until I happened to spot Bernie a few nights later across the street outside the Calvert Grill on Connecticut Avenue, which was my local avenue for taking the kind of fast walk that usually cleared my head of unholy thinking. He was standing there chatting away with some guy I'd never seen before, and Janice was there too, next to Bernie, not exactly leaning on him but close enough to show that she was with him rather than the other guy. I hadn't really finished my walk but I turned around and headed straight home. At the next pick-up basketball game, half of me was so relaxed and half of me so angry that I played like a young pro until the first break, and at that point, when Bernie came over to put his arm around my shoulder, I told him I'd be seeing him around.

"What you mean, you'll be seeing me around?"

"I'm moving," I said. "Over to Georgetown."

"You can't do that," Bernie said. "We start the pick-up tournament next week. And when that's over, I have in mind working up a hard-ball team in the sand-lot league."

"I don't know how to play hardball," I said.

"Relax," Bernie said. "I'll teach you."

"What's the point? I'm moving. So I'll see you around."

"So that's it? You'll just see me around?"

"Right," I said. "And by the way, I saw you with Janice the other night. Maybe you can teach her hardball instead of me."

Bernie took his arm off my shoulder.

"Now what's that supposed to mean?"

I shrugged. "It means what you want it to mean. Anyway, I think you know what it means. So like I said, I'll see you around."

I turned and took off. When I looked back, Bernie was still standing there gazing after me, and then he too turned away. Over the years I've sometimes wondered whether I was right or wrong about Bernie, whether I was fair to him in the end. But he didn't come after me to say anything later that day or the next, and as it happened, that was the last I ever saw of him.

Six

The duplex house on Fulton Street was a fine house from my point of view, with a living room, dining room, and kitchen on one floor, three bedrooms and a closed-in porch on the second floor, and a full basement with a bed down there for overnight friends and at one end of it a place for storing bicycles and athletic equipment. The closed-in porch outside my mother's room was where Bob and I slept. It wasn't exactly private, but it had quite a lot of space for two people still growing, and since it was at the back of the house up there by itself, you had a nice view of the cement alley behind the house, where we convinced our father to put up a basketball ring above our garage door. That is where I spent a good part of my mornings and afternoons early that summer, which was before I got to know the neighborhood and its underage residents well enough to take part in some of the less obvious pleasures those Northwest streets in the nation's capital had to offer the restless young.

The first high point of that summer in 1940 after the move to Fulton Street was the month at Camp Cory on Lake Keuka, adopted American brother of the YMCA camp that we had visited on the shore below Mount Pelion. Though Cory was also a YMCA camp, it was said to be open to all religions, and whatever Christian mission it may have had was kept in the background except for the public services on Sunday and the nightly vespers. The latter were followed by discussion sessions that counselors were supposed to hold in each cabin under their supervision, with an opportunity on that occasion to speak about spiritual values and modes of behavior appropriate and inappropriate for campers living away from home in close quarters with others their age, though it was taboo for anybody to complain about the bed-wetters, who, the counselors said, shouldn't be held responsible for something they couldn't help doing. This was a principle that certain among the senior campers argued ought to hold for the other individual activity in bed that had a name well-known to me in Greek but several new names in English and that was apparently sometimes rampant among those thirteen and over. In any case, the spiritual tolerance in camp did not extend to the rituals of all religions, as became evident one day when a fellow camper nick-named Goopie was heard to insist that the regular Thursday menu of pork and potatoes was actually chicken and potatoes, "because if it ain't chicken, just pass it along, I don't even want to smell it."

Outside of praying and eating, most of an ordinary day at camp was devoted to group activity that was meant to improve what they called your personal skills while you also improved your capacity for communal participation, whether learning to swim or sail or canoe or practice first aid or life-saving on the junior level or learning to work with others on various kinds of handicraft projects that involved using your hands in ways thoroughly unfamiliar to them while others watched your awkwardness, whether carving or braiding or hammering something together that never quite fit. And there were sports like soccer and soft-ball to develop a sense of team spirit (which in the first instance meant no show-off individual dribble runs down the length of the field and in the second instance meant a lot of loud banter you had to learn that was supposed to encourage your side and discourage the other side), along with tennis, paddle tennis, archery, and ping-pong to develop keen personal competitiveness within the rules of communal sportsmanship. Then there were canoe trips sometimes three-days long to visit another nearby Finger Lake such as Canandaigua or Seneca where you could work on your outdoor camping skills under greater physical and mental stress. And the evenings were taken up with communal games and shows and sing-alongs so that you never had a chance to feel alone and melancholy and abandoned by your parents, who with some justice had sent you to that camp to give themselves a few weeks of relative privacy to develop their own personal skills in a non-communal context.

If you ever wandered off alone at Camp Cory, someone was always there to track you down in a friendly way and bring you back to the group before you had a chance to feel left out of things or unappreciated by your fellow campers or inclined to become a loner, and that included going to the toilet, which was a shared public event at any time of day or night on whatever toilet bowl happened to be free among the ten or so lined up beside each other in what was called the Brown House. One of the true pleasures of hiking over to a neighboring Finger Lake for some time on another shore and some contact with open nature was the chance it gave you to find a subtle moment to escape the line of dug latrines and drift off from the campground to relieve yourself in total privacy under the eyes of God alone, so long as you did it quickly enough not to earn an unspoken demerit for an unexplained absence during the enduring crusade to make you feel a regular participating member of this or that collective group.

For someone trained to sing songs of nationalist or religious inspiration in several foreign languages, the communal sing-alongs in the evenings at Camp Cory were a revelation and a joy. Some of the songs were merely sweetly sentimental or rhythmically exuberant—"You are My Sunshine," "Dinah," "My Bonnie Lies Over the Ocean," "Shine on Harvest Moon"—but some were gloriously chaotic and silly:

> In a store in Palamore there lived a mean old man.
> His name was Mr. Dunderbeck and he could surely can.
> The place was filled with rats and mice, and skinny-tailed
> cats a few,
> So Dunderbeck invented a machine to grind them all to stew.
> Oh Dunderbeck, oh Dunderbeck, how could you be so mean
> To ever have invented the sausage meat machine.
> They'll all be ground to sausage meat
> In Dunderbeck's machine.

One day a boy came awalking, awalking in the store.
He bought a pound of sausages and laid them on the floor.
The boy began to whistle and he whistled up a tune
And all the little sausages went dancing round the room.
Oh Dunderbeck, oh Dunderbeck, how could you be so mean...

One day the darn thing busted, the engine wouldn't go
And Dunderbeck climbed into it, the reason for to know.
His wife was having nightmares and walking in her sleep.
She gave the crank an awful yank, and Dunderbeck was meat!

When a new group came into the camp, the night's festivities would end with the famous mantra that Camp Cory had adopted from an ancient Buddhist text sent them by a grateful former camper who had become a deposed Siamese Prince: "Owha Tagoo Siam," the new group encouraged to repeat the mantra faster and faster until it became the single phrase "OwhatagooseIam."

The evening get-together that most everybody in camp looked forward to with both heightened excitement and seriousness—and that included me—came at the end of each two-week session when new members of the honorary society called the Sons of Cory were initiated by previous members of the society during a solemn, torch-lit ceremony around the main campfire. There was talk of that society from the first days that a newcomer arrived at the camp, but you were never given a clear idea of how you became a Son of Cory, except that you were told it was the highest honor available to a camper, and membership was determined by a secret ballot among former members then in attendance. I assumed it was like the Boy Scouts, where you collected merit badges for completing this or that task or perfecting this or that skill, so during my early days at the camp I made a point of passing the swimming test—which I could do with hands tied behind my back—and getting my proficiency in canoeing, that one not so easy, and then focusing on handicrafts, which I mastered only with great difficulty given the sometimes erratic way my fingers behaved except when holding a soccer or basketball.

By the end of the first two-week session, it was obvious to me that I hadn't done enough to earn honors of any kind, so I skipped out on the Sons of Cory ceremony, but during the second two-week session I made what I thought was a significant advance by getting my qualification as both a junior life-saver and K-boat skipper, thanks to the sheer luck of running into Bruce Lansdale as my instructor. Bruce's father, who had been the YMCA director in Salonika during the 1930s, was the reason the two Keeley boys were at Camp Cory, and Bruce, three years older than me, had been among my few American friends in Salonika during the short time our paths crossed there at the Farm School and the German School. Bruce was now a counselor at Cory, and one of the sailing and life-saving instructors. I could work with him in Greek, swear at him in Greek, get bawled out by him in Greek, learn or unlearn what I had to without anyone knowing how badly I was doing, and finally I could make it a matter of pride in a Greek sense that he get me, an old buddy from foreign parts, through the very rough passage, even at the junior level, that led to a sailing or life-saving qualification. Besides, Bruce was by nature a masterful teacher and generous to a fault.

The trouble was, none of that mattered in the end, as I discovered when the ceremony for designating Sons of Cory came around at the end of our second camp session. It was a very moving ceremony from my novitiate point of view, especially when approached with edge-of-the seat anticipation. Almost the whole camp was gathered on several rows of benches set up to circle the main campfire, low now and providing the only patch of light as we sat there quietly waiting for the Sons of Cory to arrive out of the darkness in torch-bearing procession to form a line between the front circle of benches and the smoldering fire. The designated leader, perhaps the oldest camper of the group, anyway the tallest, carried a sword rather than a torch, and he stepped forward to say the sacred words that all of us eventually memorized:

> When in the days of old the knights of the Round Table gathered around the board, none would dare sit in the great chair, "Siege Perilous," in which any impure one would be struck dead. No, none, until Sir Galahad came forth crying

"I will sit in the chair. If I lose myself, I save myself." And as all expected to see him struck down, a shaft of light brighter than any day came upon him, visible only to Sir Galahad. He could see what others could not see and his strength was as the strength of ten because his heart was pure.

The leader then raised his sword. "With the touch of this sword, I will now induct those who have proven worthy of joining the Sons of Cory in the image of Lawrence Cory, who dedicated his life to serving his fellow man before he was killed in the First World War and who died with a heart that was pure." The leader then made a full circle of the campfire, paused in front of a camper in the first row and touched his shoulder with the sword. The camper looked startled, but he stood up slowly and was escorted to take his place at the end of the line of torch-bearers. The leader continued to circle as though searching the audience, heads turning to follow his path, then reached into the second row of benches to touch another camper's shoulder with his sword. The suspense continued almost unbearably, nobody saying a word, then suddenly ended after the fourth induction, when the leader returned to head the line of torch bearers, and the procession of old and new Sons of Cory marched off into the night.

By the end of my session at camp, I had figured out that getting the equivalent of merit badges was not good enough for membership in the Sons of Cory, and anyway, it turned out that you had to be a senior camper to qualify, which for me was a year away. I realized that somehow you had to convince those torch-bearing knights that your heart was pure, but just how you did that remained a major mystery to me. I promised myself to begin by working on my purity during the year ahead so that I would have a better chance of showing the right spirit to qualify during the summer following, assuming I could persuade my parents that Camp Cory was where I ought to spend the summer of 1941.

Of course it was impossible for me to know as a junior level camper that purifying the heart or the mind or simply promising yourself to try harder to avoid sin from one week to the next would become a much more complicated enterprise once you turned thirteen. And the fact that

I succeeded in becoming a Son of Cory the following summer proved less gratifying than I hoped whenever I looked into my secret heart. My parents having agreed to allow both me and Bob to spend as much time on Lake Keuka as we might wish that second summer was clear evidence, given the cost, of their need for some relief from the strain of raising three boys in adolescent transit (though Budge was then engaged in some serious vacation study that would help him get admitted to Princeton the following spring and with that move more or less outside the family circle). From the start of my second stay at Cory, I concentrated not on earning this or that physical qualification but on improving my spiritual health with a view to earning the sword's touch on my shoulder in the image of Sir Galahad. I took an active part in prayer sessions both formal and informal, I read the Bible almost as often as the Dickens and Twain I'd brought along, and I went through the Boy Scout manual diligently until I gave it a rest after reaching the passage advising conservation in place of self-abuse. My main effort in daylight was devoted to presenting a friendly, committed, even compassionate face to my fellow campers, especially those older than me. That my inner life was at times in turmoil, with regular surges of lust, guilt, failed conviction and renewed longing, I somehow managed to conceal from everybody but myself, and when I sought relief from those abiding sensual images in bed at night, the pleasure in it was too quick and too passing, just another challenge to my conscience the following day.

It was in the fourth and last go-around of the Sons of Cory ceremony that the lead torchbearer stopped between two campers on the bench in front of mine and reached through to give my shoulder the consecrating touch. I got up and followed him with weakened knees, feeling a glow in my face that had nothing to do with the campfire we rounded or with his torch. But as I stood in line beside the others chosen that evening, my humble smile hardened again with further recognition: pleasing as it was for me to stand there in front of my less fortunate campers with Galahad's halo over my head, I knew that I had gotten away with something that felt like fraud, and that was not pleasing at all, that night or the next—one of the rougher interludes in my crossing from puberty to adolescence.

*　*　*

The trailer trip my father arranged to educate his sons about the geography of America took place during a more innocent season, when I was still able to remain cool and relatively pure in spirit even in those moments that called for painful heft and saintly tolerance in responding to my father's eccentric mode of backing a trailer into its nightly resting place. The landscape of the trip has suffered from memory's layering, pushed farther underground by recollections of a summer working at very odd jobs across the country from one national park to another with my college roommates in a borrowed Lincoln Continental—blivet stacking at Mesa Verde, blister-rust control at Yosemite, hop-picking under the shadow of Mt. Rainier—and later visits to the mid and far West on the reading and lecture circuit. What I remember first of all from that 1940 family trip by trailer are the undying days of driving to cover every mile of the carefully planned route that my father had outlined for us map after map. There was the occasional stopover outside some acquaintance's home along the way—some relative who had helped to bring up my father in his motherless early years or someone now retired who had served with him in this or that post—but night after night was spent in one after another trailer camp considered safe for a five-member family on its own, living off its own resources in crowded circumstances without apparent need or opportunity for communication with other living things except the occasional deer that would cross our path in terror or a friendly bear that would nose in close searching for our garbage.

What I remember of the landscape during the trailer trip are the few places where we camped long enough for the mind to etch in exactly where we were or that were curious enough to be recorded in the small photo album of our journey that my mother put together at the time, kept stacked away for years with the other albums passed on to me after her death: Lincoln's log cabin in Illinois, the Petrified Forest in Arizona, the Grand Canyon cheated of some of its grandeur in misty two-inch by three-inch prints, a mule trip through cowboy country to a great natural bridge shaped like a rainbow, two fully-feathered Indian chiefs waiting patiently to sell onlookers a Navaho rug, our latest De Soto, liberated from its trailer, going through a tunnel cut out of a giant redwood tree in California.

I don't know how many of these curiosities would have remained in memory without the album—some surely—but what stayed with me unaided was my wonder at the great dimensions of the farmland we traveled through, so different from Greek Macedonia, one broad stretch of fields in this seemingly endless state bordering an equally long stretch in the next until we reached the Rockies, and after that, more open country mile after mile, the land often uncultivated and dryer but full of its own imaginative contours and coloring, until the next mountain range before the vast expanse of the western sea, all of it so impressive in size and variety yet so unfamiliar and daunting that finally coming to see this great new country of mine was cause for both pride and awe.

But what I remember best of all from that summer were those moments when our family took a break from the relentless pursuit of our itinerary, pulled the trailer well off the road and climbed out of the car for a picnic lunch at a high point where you could search out the plain below and pretend for a moment that you were exploring its secret passages leading wherever your imagination might care to take you. Or the edge of a forest where you could lie out for a while as though to nap while you catalogued the different bird sounds overhead and sometimes the distant sound of unknown animals. Or when the lunch stop was by a stream and all of us would strip to wash in its chilling current, my mother and father a bit upstream but not so far that we couldn't hear their playful agony at the water's touch as they doused each other in their nakedness. And most of all, those moments when my father would rest his arm on the open driver's window ledge to sing to himself this or that song I had never heard before, though always preceded by "It's a long long way to Tipperary, it's a long way to go," my mother not joining in but watching him with a little private smile when he wasn't looking her way. I don't think those two were ever so happy again.

✳   ✳   ✳

In 1940, a schoolboy recently arrived from abroad and fairly new to the nation's capital, even when working hard to become as American as his fellow Americans, was quite unaware that entering the school district in Northwest Washington defined in the south by M Street and in the north by the meeting of Wisconsin and Massachusetts Avenues meant crossing into divided country still haunted by the issues of a civil war that was supposed to have ended almost a hundred years previously. The remnant battle lines were relatively quiet at the time, with only the occasional race riot on M Street, and the members of the younger generation, both white and black, rarely ganged up on each, content usually to spend their excess energy in separate juvenile efforts to outwit the Seventh Police Precinct—that is, until the excitement and disruption and rationing that came with America's entry into the war a year later brought on more precarious juvenile activity, both inside and outside the law.

It was the division among resident whites that a newcomer to the territory, even one used to a mix of nationalities, had to learn to accommodate. The dividing line among residents in this school district proved to be R Street, roughly between Gordon Junior High and Western High. The southern region, dominated by Georgetown and including some streets in the area known as Foggy Bottom, was the poorer of the two in those days, bordered by slum land and industrial failure, inhabited mostly by old Washington families providing various services for the city and living at best in run-down Federal-style houses or cheaply built two-story row houses, some with "1/2" after their number. Blacks lived on the southern fringe of that southern region and went to their own schools across town. The northern region, where I lived, was made up largely of recent apartment buildings, newer vintage duplexes, and Tudor-style single-house developments, and among others it served rising entrepreneurs, the transient military establishment, and government employees, some life-long, some in town only for what was soon called the duration, including State Department officials and Foreign Service officers of my father's rank or above.

The whites in the southern region spoke the language of Virginia and states farther south, though with a particular Washington flavor that pronounced "out" as though spelled "oat," and this region's orientation was that of the increasingly dispossessed, the older generation for the most part revealing the religious fervor of evangelical Christians, along with the attendant prejudices, and—though even that generation couldn't vote—the politics of the conservative South. Those growing up in the region, males in particular, were only minimally interested in educating themselves outside the local Boys Club, though most suffered their way through high school because of the inter-city athletic program for white students and the access that heroism on the playing field provided to the best-looking girls in the school.

The older generation living in the northern region, because it was both more varied in background and less stable, was seen to be relatively cosmopolitan and progressive, most expecting their sons—sometimes even their daughters—to prepare for one of the local colleges and just possibly for West Point or Annapolis or the Ivy League. Yet their influence on those growing up in the neighborhood was not much more pronounced than that of their counterparts below the divide. For the adolescent young in the region, going to school had its obvious social rewards whether or not you took the school work to heart, and for some it actually provided a road to intellectual self-discovery, but outside school was either play time in some competitive arena or party time at some collection point beyond the possibility of serious interference by the older generation—in my case, the low arch outside the Alban Towers Drug Store on Wisconsin Avenue, within sight of the grand arches of the Washington Cathedral.

The predominant mode for proving yourself worthy of membership in the Alban Towers crew was proficiency in sandlot athletics and proper respect for the local heroes of that pick-up league, followed eventually by an unembarrassed interest in girls and their possibilities. One sandlot, good for touch football, was the undecorated garden behind the Alban Towers Apartments. The other was a vacant lot across Massachusetts Avenue, behind the house of the one Greek connection I found in the neighborhood, Plato Cacheris, who came into fame in later years as the distinguished lawyer who cleverly and authoritatively represented Fawn Hall, Aldridge Ames, Monica Lewinsky, and Robert Hanssen, among other demanding assignments. After I settled into the neighborhood, Plato, a year or so younger than me and closest friend to my brother Bob, was the only person I let know about my Greek background, and it was through him and his family that I kept a lingering contact with the foreign country and foreign language that still remained a vibrant if private source of wistfulness. After my experience on Lamont Street, I made sure that I toured the sidewalks of Fulton Street and Wisconsin Avenue without a past that would seem curious to my American contemporaries—no talk of the Farm School, the German School, my knowledge of other peoples and places, nothing more exotic than my having moved in recently from another part of Northwest Washington. But often when I was on my way home from the sandlot behind Plato's house, I would stop in for a few minutes to say hello to his mother—a dark beauty with all the warm gestures of her Mediterranean upbringing—and practice my Greek with his grandmother, whose face would feed me sunlight at the first sounds of my village dialect. The conversation with those two always brought on a restorative waft of nostalgia that would wipe away any remnant guilt I might be carrying about hiding my foreign past, though the talk could sometimes be unsettling in other ways.

"You know, Mr. Mike, the children of our people over here are losing their religion," Mrs. Cacheris would say. "And their language."

"Well, it's natural. They're now in their own country, I mean the country where they were born, and—"

"It's not natural. It's unnatural. How can they live without their religion? And how are they going to talk to their grandmothers and grandfathers if they lose their language?"

"Well, their language is now English and they don't often have anybody to talk Greek to outside the home. I mean I myself—"

"They don't want to go to Greek school to learn the language even once a week after their other school. They say it's boring. The priests who teach them are boring. How can they say a thing like that?"

"Well, I guess most priests aren't trained as language teachers. They're trained to sing the liturgy. And to give you spiritual advice."

"What spiritual advice?" the grandmother would say. "Who listens to the priests? Who goes to our church except at Easter? And these children are already finding ways to avoid their own kind. Some of them even refuse to marry their own kind. Can you believe a thing like that?"

I could believe it, but how could I say anything about it when I was having enough trouble making my way with my own kind, especially since I still couldn't be sure exactly who my own kind was? At least after a winter on the basketball court and a summer of softball at camp, I could pretend that I knew the right lingo to talk to the local Alban Towers crowd and most of the right moves for the kind of grubby hardball played on the neighborhood sandlot behind Plato's place, though I let it be known right off that I preferred to spend most of my time that early fall in my back alley preparing for another basketball season. To make the point convincing, of an afternoon that September and October I would invite this or that Alban Towers drifter to join me back there for one-on-one in order to show off all that Bernie and my obsessive practice had taught me so far.

But touch football proved to be the local sport that brought the newest and youngest of the Alban Towers crew into contact with the older and more respected members. The star of the pick-up game on the broad lawn behind the Towers, the model of aspiration in all ways, was a sixteen-year-old blond kid named Billy Garfield, who, in most young eyes, had the looks of a movie idol and the ease on the field of an All-American. He could pass almost the full length of that lawn, he could fake around anybody dumb enough to come right at him, and he could make all players on his side feel it their destiny to play better than they were able simply because they were on his side, or worse if on the other side. Billy Garfield was, in short, the hero of possibilities that appeared to be beyond the rest of us in the Alban Towers crew, however indifferent he was to anything outside the playing field and however mediocre his performance in school.

It turned out to be Billy Garfield's much younger sister, Beverly, less sure of herself and therefore more approachable, who became the close companion of my early days in the neighborhood, as was true of most others of both sexes who were roughly my age. Her talent was dancing, nurtured at some point by her older brother who had taught her, well ahead of the rest of us, the Washington, D.C. version of the Lindy called Catting. Beverly's arena was the basement of her home on Woodley

Road, where we would gather in the afternoons after the football season to listen to the latest record by Glen Miller or Tommy Dorsey or Benny Goodman or Harry James. And once we had overcome our shyness, we would pair up and practice the quick swivel steps and back and forth rhythm of arms and sudden overhead twirling that older zoot-suited and bobby-soxed schoolmates had made the symbol of hedonistic abandon on the local high school dance floors and soon in the private club gatherings of our nation's capital. "Tuxedo Junction," "How High the Moon," and "In the Mood" were the tunes with the right rhythm for Catting when you first started out, not too fast, not too slow, though we soon moved on to quicker rhythms, and then, catching our breath, on to the much slower, sometimes almost motionless, chest to breast and cheek-to-cheek versions of a fox-trot, under lyrics that could break your young heart with the first pangs of unrequited longing: "I'll Never Smile Again," "All the Things You Are," "It Had to be You," "The One I Love."

The pairing was always in flux, at least that first season, partners changing more or less according to who was there and most ready, and since it wasn't until the late winter and spring that we dancers found the courage to take up practice kissing with one or another partner under the guidance of what the older girls called "Improving Your Technique," those early days on Woodley Road were at the most passionately vicarious, with the lyrics of the Great Bands our solitary access into the world of deep romance.

That, anyway, was half the story. The other half was the underground life of the region that sometimes had its roots in Georgetown, sometimes as high up as Calvert Street, but rarely spread as far north as Woodley Road, just beyond the Cathedral grounds and the ritzy St. Alban's School. At least in my education, the dividing line between innocence and the fruit of the forbidden tree was around R Street, below Dumbarton Oaks and Montrose Park. That was the Georgetown neighborhood where one of my fellow students at Gordon Junior High named Jeanie Grant lived with her divorced mother in a two-room top-floor apartment in somebody else's house on Q Street. Like my friend Lisa, she was well ahead of me in knowledge of the ways of the world, but the culture Jeanie came from made for different manners and different gestures, some of which I could only distantly comprehend, and she was apparently more or less alone among her contemporaries in providing access to certain of the dark pleasures available to those entering adolescence in that border region of the nation's capital.

I had come to know Jeanie late in the school year at Gordon, when she was shifted to the desk next to mine at the back corner of the room in English class to separate her from someone up front with whom she'd evidently struck up an undertone dialogue that didn't bother the rest of us because we couldn't hear it but clearly rattled our English teacher. She was an ancient spinster named Miss Cunningham, a saintly woman for continuing to teach as long as she had in view of the generally indifferent and sometimes only partially literate students she had to face day in day out, though she had long since taken on the attentive demeanor of a cobra ready to strike, especially when literature entered the room. And strike she would if anyone had the audacity to talk to a neighbor while someone else was reciting the literary exercise that always opened the day's grammar session, whether a poem by Henry Wadsworth Longfellow or Edgar Allan Poe, or a speech by John Calhoun or Daniel Webster, or, in anticipation of a holiday, a long prose passage by James Fenimore Cooper read by the lady herself.

I suppose Miss Cunningham chose to put Jeanie Grant next to me in the back of the room because I rarely spoke to anyone in that class and generally kept a very low profile, partly out of a fear that I would be called to the blackboard to reveal my German "r" in some word I was as likely to misspell as not, and partly out of an honest effort, when it came to some of the literary exercises, to see if I couldn't actually like the poetry of Longfellow since my father seemed to, without reservation. Poe was easy because his words appeared to dance, the others we recited not so easy, but I did my best with all of them until Jeannie Grant began to distract me. Jeanie had come to Gordon from somewhere out west well after the school year had started, and rumor had it that she was a year behind where she normally should have been, which made her one of the oldest in the class, while I, at thirteen, was one of the youngest. She didn't actually speak to me when she moved back there next to me, in fact she seemed totally unaware of my presence for days, and if I found her attractive, it was mostly because she had beautiful athletic legs that she kept crossing and uncrossing and full breasts that she made no attempt to hide by what she wore, as did some of the younger girls in the room.

The thing that distracted me almost as much as her looks was the way she spent much of every English class drawing pictures on the left pages of her notebook, terrific sketches of houses surrounded by gardens and trees, sometimes with mountains in the background, and portraits of boys and girls that actually looked like boys and girls, whether holding hands or dancing or sitting side by side on a bench. Since I could barely draw a decent stick figure standing upright let alone human beings sitting down somewhere, I was much impressed. And maybe she saw something of that one afternoon when she finally caught me gazing over at what she was sketching and then quickly at her legs as she crossed them under her tartan skirt.

This was the afternoon before the start of the Easter holidays during a reading by Miss Cunningham of a passage from James Fenimore Cooper's *The Last of the Mohicans.* As I remember, it was a passage that had the unfortunate captive Cora stopping on a ledge of rocks overhanging a deep precipice and telling her evil captor, the Indian Magua, "Kill me if thou wilt, detestable Huron, I will go no farther," to which Magua, drawing his knife, replies, with what Cooper describes as a look in which conflicting passions fiercely contended, "Woman! Choose: the wigwam or the knife of Le Subtil!" It was that line that had made me turn my attention toward Jeanie.

"What are you looking at?" she asked me almost inaudibly as she held her notebook against her blouse. It wasn't really a question, and she was looking straight into my eyes, with just the beginning of a smile.

"Nothing," I said.

"You don't look like it's nothing."

I turned away. I could now see that Miss Cunningham had her eyes on us and was in cobra striking mode.

"I'll tell you later," I whispered, without moving my lips.

And I did, more or less. I waited for her in the corridor after class, and when she walked by sort of half pretending not to see me, with her books held by both arms crossed under her breasts, I eased over beside her and told her, lying in my teeth, that I hadn't meant to stare at her, only at her drawings, which I thought really neat stuff.

"Well those are just doodles," she said. "I've got better stuff than that at home. Some real drawings. Not that they're anything special."

"I'd like to see them sometime. I mean, if you could bring them to school someday."

Jeanie shook her head. "I don't think I want to do that. I mean, I don't really want to show them around. But you can see them at home sometime if you want."

"I'd like that," I said. "I mean it."

"Well here then."

She carefully handed me her books and notebook to carry for her as though passing me her nursing infant, and then she made me stand by her locker while she picked up another book and a beige cardigan she had stashed away in there. She didn't say anything when she handed me the extra book to carry, but I got the message that this meant she wanted me to walk her home right then and there, though she ended up holding on to her notebook and cardigan after I picked up what I needed from my own locker for homework during the holidays.

When we crossed Wisconsin Avenue and headed down 32nd toward Q Street, Jeanie actually stopped and shifted what she was carrying so that she could hook her arm through mine, a thing nobody had ever done before. It felt good, but I don't think she understood that, probably thought it embarrassed me, because she took her arm away the minute we came to Q Street even though nobody was in sight. And when we reached the house where she lived and headed up the stairs to her apartment, she stopped halfway up and studied me: "It's all right, you don't have to look so worried. There's nobody home. My mother doesn't get off work until supper time."

She had her own room up there, a nice size, with an easy chair opposite the bed and a window with a desk in front of it beside a bookcase with deep shelves where she kept her turntable and a batch of records along with the folders that had her drawings in them. She said she sometimes sketched at the desk but mostly in the easy chair, with a board on her lap, and that is where she had me sit while she showed me some of what she had in the large folders, each tied by a ribbon. She'd untie the ribbon, kneeling there on the floor beside me, and she'd choose this or that drawing to show me, rejecting a lot of them with a dismissive lift of her shoulder. What she showed me were landscapes I didn't recognize and portraits of this or that boy or girl I didn't know, both kinds maybe imaginary, yet they seemed to me so expert, even so beautiful, that I didn't know what to say to her, so I just sat there shaking my head as I looked at one after the other.

"What's the matter?" she finally said. "It's all right if you don't like them. I don't like most of them myself."

"No. They're terrific. Really. I just don't know what to say."

That made her smile. "Well, you don't have to say anything. Besides, most of them aren't even finished yet."

With that she closed the folder she'd been flipping through and took the pile of them back to the bookcase.

"Maybe someday I'll even sketch you," she said with her back turned.

"That'd be neat," I said. "I'd really like that."

"Would you?" she said, smiling again. "We'll see. I don't always sketch living people."

She went over to her stack of records and picked the top one to study.

"Have you heard the new Artie Shaw?" she asked without looking at me. "'Dancing in the Dark'?"

"Yea, I know that one. But I only heard it once. With some friends."

"Would you like to hear it again?"

"Sure. That'd be nice."

She put the record on the turntable, and when the music started she stepped back and then turned to stand there looking at me.

"So are you just going to sit there?" she said. "Or don't you know how to dance slow?"

"Sure," I said. "Nothing great. I go in mostly for catting. I mean, with the faster stuff. But sure, I can give it a try."

She just stood there waiting. When I got up and went over to her she had moved to the space between the desk and easy chair, and she came in against me with her cheek against mine in a way that gave me a sweet shiver. She was the kind of partner who made you feel that she knew your moves before you made them, and even though she was shorter than me, we fit so well together and she stayed in so tight against me that it didn't much matter that we had so little room in which to maneuver. My face must have been flushed but I could still feel her cheek warm against mine, and before we came to the end of the record I was having trouble concentrating on the music. She noticed that but she didn't say anything and she didn't let go, and then I felt her lips brush against my neck. I was sure that's what it was, but when I tried to kiss her, she turned her head away. She still didn't let go, and then she whispered against my ear, "Only if you really want to do it."

"I want to," I said quietly, a bit hoarsely.

She let go then and looked at me.

"Do you know how?" she asked. "And I don't mean just kissing."

"Well, I...

"I thought so," she said. "So I guess I'll have to help you."

She took me by the hand and led me over to the bed. She didn't get undressed all the way, just her skirt and panties, so I followed her lead. When we sat down beside each other on the edge of the bed, she still wouldn't let me kiss her. Then she lay back and told me in the simplest way what I was supposed to do. Though it was familiar enough in my head, it wasn't familiar anywhere else, and the newness of it kept me from responding as I should have until she helped me to get there, and even after both of us were ready and I was where she wanted me to be, I found I couldn't let go completely. From one point of view that was probably a good thing, but not from mine and maybe not from Jeanie's either, though she didn't say anything, and she let me kiss her as well as I knew how before I eased myself off of her.

We lay there side by side half-naked, neither of us looking down, and we talked for quite a long time, she doing most of the talking—all about her father taking off one day without any warning, which is what had cost her a year of school while she and her mother traveled from one place to another until the nursing job turned up in Washington, and though she said his leaving that way didn't really bother her much any-more because he had been a jerk most of the time and sometimes worse, she said it in a way that showed she was still bitter. And she also said that she was learning to live with the bad nerves her mother brought home most nights from her work at the hospital, because her mother at least allowed her to have all the privacy she wanted in her own room and even have friends up there whenever she chose to, which was just often enough to keep her from getting too lonely. I told her a bit about myself too, especially about my arrival in this country after living abroad a while and my problems adjusting to the school I'd first gone to across the city, but I didn't get very far into that before she moved suddenly to the edge of the bed and stood up with her back turned to put on her panties and skirt.

"You'd better get going now," she said over her shoulder. "I want to work a bit on my sketching before mother comes home and makes me cook our supper. I mean since you think what I've been doing is so terrific."

"I do," I said. "Really. And I wouldn't mind staying around a while to watch you work. I'd really like to see how you do it."

"No. I can't work with anyone watching. It's a thing I have."

So I had no choice but to get dressed myself and take off. At the door she let me kiss her again, but not for long, and as I stood there, she ran a finger down my cheek, smiled at me, then held the door open for me to go.

I didn't see Jeanie Grant during the holiday break. Since we'd exchanged phone numbers, I pretended to myself that if she really wanted to see me, maybe let me sit in that easy chair to have my portrait drawn, she could call me anytime. And of course I could have called her anytime too, but since I couldn't get some things straightened out in my mind, I didn't know what I wanted to say to her. I suppose I was suffering from what James Fenimor Cooper would call conflicting passions fiercely contending, the one roused by images of her bed and what we did there, the other roused by a misty apparition of Sir Galahad sitting in the chair Siege Perilous with the strength of ten because his heart was pure. Also, for the first time in weeks, I daydreamed about Lisa and some of the private things we used to talk about together in our hayloft hideout, and that kind of dreaming didn't help to settle my mind.

I'd kept up a little bit with what was going on in Greece through the

Cacheris family, hearing stories about the valiant challenge to Mussolini's invasion that the Greek forces had put up on the Albania front, but there had been no word from Lisa or the other friends I'd left behind in Salonika almost two years previously, and the public news was usually out of date by the time it reached me. What got me worried that spring came from the one Greek establishment beyond the northern margin of our neighborhood, a narrow imitation of a diner that had a soft-drink bar along one wall and booths along the other. I used to drop in there once in a while to practice my Greek and pick up any solid news or even rumors about what was going on over there that didn't make it into the rare article on Greece that my father came across in the Washington papers and discussed with my mother over supper.

The owner of "J's Café" always sat in the next to last booth, I imagine so that he could keep an eye on the kitchen beyond the swinging doors behind him and the spread of the room in front of him but also on the cash register and its attendant part way along the wall behind the bar. The owner's name in Greek was Yerassimos, but he'd changed that to Jerry soon after he came over from Kalamata in the Peloponnese as a teenager and then had to change his name again when the war came along because someone pointed out to him that Germans were called Jerry, at which point he became Jay, or J for short. He had a moustache that was turning gray but was even thicker than his thick black hair. We always spoke in Greek, his still fairly good despite his years of mixing it with broken English, mine already fading a bit. At least I felt my tongue stiffening over some words that afternoon towards the end of the Easter holidays in *1941*.

"How's it going, compatriot?" I said, easing down in the booth opposite Mr. J.

"Not good, my friend. Things look bad over there. The Germans have come across the border from Yugoslavia and are pushing us south so that we may have to end up in Crete."

"In Crete?"

"I heard it on the radio. But don't worry, we'll eat them up like cabbage in the end. I mean to say, I hate the Germans. And they used to be our friends."

"What's happening in Macedonia?"

"Macedonia? Macedonia's gone. Salonika's gone. A few days ago."

"What do you mean, gone?"

"Overrun. Occupied. What can I say? The last I heard, our army and the British army were already south of Larissa."

"My God."

"You said it right. My God."

"I have friends up there," I said. "Good friends. And we left everything behind when we left."

"Still, you're lucky. And I'm lucky. What can I say? Fuck the Germans. God protect the Greeks. But we're here now, you and me, in the best country in the world, what more can I say?"

That evening before we gathered for supper I asked my father if it was true that the German army was occupying Salonika. My father glanced up at my mother who was bringing him a glass of iced tea, then asked me where I'd heard that, and when I told him where, he wiped his mouth with his paper napkin, then took a sip of iced tea.

"I'm afraid it's true," he said.

"Well why didn't somebody tell me?"

"We didn't want you to worry," my mother said.

"But what's going to happen to the Farm School and our house and all the people over there?"

"The Farm School is American property," my father said. "The Germans may not bother it. At least for a while."

"So that means the war over there is just going to get worse and we're not going back anytime soon, is that it?"

My father lowered his head and took another sip.

"Well however long it goes on, I don't think we'll be going back until it's over. Not as a family. That wouldn't make sense even if they'd let us. Which they won't."

"And what about after the war?"

My father studied his glass. "No way of knowing in the Foreign Service. But I wouldn't count on it."

I stood there looking at my father and mother, and then I went upstairs and lay on my bed. I don't know where my brothers were. Budge was off somewhere with his high school crowd, none of whom he ever brought home, so it was almost as though he was living another life outside the family, and Bob was working with his usual private intensity on some project at the Stoddert Elementary School down on Calvert Street. Anyway, I didn't much feel like talking to anybody at that point. Even after two years away, I still thought of that Farm School house, surrounded by sweet peas and with a patio lawn in its center, as our family home, and though I was beginning to feel that I was just as American as anybody else in our Alban Towers neighborhood, it hadn't sunk in that it could be some years before we got back to the Farm School and everything we'd left behind over there. Now it suddenly came to me that we might not get back there at all, at least not to that house and the kind of life we'd known there.

I didn't go down to supper. I just lay there for a long time thinking, drawing images in my mind—the broad yellow fields of Macedonia, the gray-green vineyards on the slope behind the Farm School, the stony soccer field that could flay your knees, Lisa as midwife pulling out a baby with a "hlup"—images that were breaking my heart. I turned them off by beginning a letter to Lisa in my mind, telling her what I'd been up to these two years—most of what I'd been up to—and asking her to let me know if she and the others in our old neighborhood might be safe after all since it was American property. Then it came to me that this letter was a ridiculous idea. What chance in the world was there of a letter reaching a city occupied by the German army? Then I thought of writing the principal of the German School, who would surely be free to receive mail, asking him to pass on a letter to somebody at the American Farm School. That brought up a picture of the bald-headed principal throwing his head back in violent laughter: "So, my American friend, you think because you have a German grandfather who isn't really German you can use me as your messenger boy to get through our victorious army?" I lay there in misery, heightened now by a sense of my own helpless foolishness.

My mother came upstairs looking for me. She stood there beside my bed.

"Aren't you coming down for supper?"

"I'm not hungry."

"Are you sick?"

She leaned over and felt my forehead.

"I'm all right," I lied. "I'm just not hungry."

"Well, your brothers are back and we're all sitting at the table. You might have come down to tell us why you've suddenly lost your appetite and won't be joining us for supper."

I gazed at the ceiling. Mr. J's face came into focus there.

"What can I say? The Germans have occupied Salonika. Who knows when they'll go away so that we can get back there."

My mother touched my forehead again.

"Can I give you a bit of advice?" she finally said. "There are some things in the world that none of us can control no matter how much we may want to. Those are things we shouldn't spend much time worrying about. If we can possibly help it."

It was grand advice, and I've repeated it to myself to calm my nerves I don't know how many times since, but it did little good to dispel my sense of futility that particular day. I gave my mother what must have seemed a forlorn look. When she reached down again to give my cheek a little caress, I turned my head away.

By the end of the Easter break, I had myself under control again. It had come to me in a mostly unarticulated way that it was no great service to anybody for a person living in the best and safest country in the world to go around brooding about his feelings of loss while others less lucky were in danger of losing the roof over their heads and maybe their lives. I resolved that from now on I would concentrate on my school work, while at the same time working to improve my sense of responsibility to something other than myself. This resolve made it easier for me to accept what struck me as a kind of friendly indifference on the part of Jeanie Grant when we met up again in English class. She always said "Hi" with a little smile, the sort of smile that said to me "I know something you and I know that nobody else knows but I'm not telling." Yet nothing I did really seemed to touch her any longer, not the way I still looked at her every now and then when I couldn't help it or at what she was now drawing in some margin of the page in front of her, not even my occasional effort at casual talk in the corridor outside, where she would simply hover a moment to listen to me, smile or not, say a word or two, and move on. It was as though what had happened between us in her place was just another doodle stored away in the notebook of her mind.

That helped my new regime. I gradually stopped worrying about what Jeanie might or might not think of me. I did my best to fight my way through the boredom of mathematics in school, and at home I read Twain's *The Prince and the Pauper*, Dumas's *The Man in the Iron Mask*, and Dickens' *Nicholas Nickelby* and *Great Expectations*, all with full concentration and sometimes with more than a little pleasure. Dickens in particular gave me a new way of escaping what was bothering me in the real world, a more plausible way than what Miss Cunningham offered us in English class.

When I was old enough to look back on that spring and the summer that followed with more or less amused detachment, the strongest image I ended up with had little to do with my tormented adolescent conscience and much more to do with the way I viewed the evident lack of conscience in Jeanie Grant. For some time after we had both turned our attention elsewhere, I had seen her apparently casual sensuality as heartless and a degree offensive, especially when I learned from locker room talk during my second year in high school that she was considered the only easy lay in my class, in fact, one of the few in our high school who simply loved to do it when in the mood, did it as well as you could want and asked nothing special in return, moved on to the next encounter without romantic complications. In the big-band puritan romanticism of the 1940s, that was generally taken to be sinful indulgence, at least before marriage. In time—Jeanie's time well ahead of mine or that of most other men in my generation—it became equal opportunity liberation. That is where I was able, finally, to let it rest.

SEVEN

Most people during and beyond adolescence will record indelibly just where they were at a moment of somber historical significance such as the beginning of a war or the assassination of a president or a terrorist attack close to home. I remember lucidly that on Sunday, December 7, 1941, during the first news reports of the Japanese bombing of the American fleet at Pearl Harbor, most of the Alban Towers faithful of both sexes were not at home listening to the radio but in the basement of their Woodley Road hideout listening avidly to the newest hot recordings, Benny Goodman's "Bewitched, Bothered, and Bewildered" and the Ink Spots' "Do I Worry?" and "I Don't Want to Set the World on Fire." Just how the world outside their play-land had changed did not begin to sink in until the next day, when the talk in school and on the street revealed a new kind of excitement as the older boys spoke of signing up as soon as they turned seventeen to follow what several of their older brothers had decided to do that morning, and some of us gathered again that afternoon to listen to the news bulletins on the radio before returning to the phonograph and the latest Ray Eberle and Frank Sinatra.

The mood at home was appropriately serious. Though neither my mother nor my father had much to say about the attack on Pearl Harbor or the declaration of war by Congress the next day, they stayed beside the radio with the even more determined concentration than they would normally give to Henry Aldridge and to Fibber McGee and Molly, the two radio programs that sometimes brought the family together in the evening for communal laughter and casual comment. I remember that all of us crowded around the radio to hear President Roosevelt's message to the nation two days after Pearl Harbor, and though I can't recall what he had to say except for a phrase or two—"We Americans are not destroyers but builders" and "We are going to win the war and we are going to win the peace that follows"—the speech clearly moved my father, who sat there, lips compressed, head sometimes nodding, his face finally show-ing pride of a kind that seemed on the edge of tears. This made some-thing like pride rush through me as well. And in the weeks following, I felt what everyone else my age and older appeared to feel: the still unde-fined anticipation of important things about to happen, dangerous but exhilarating things, a feeling that remained unspoken but that colored our days both in the school corridors and beyond.

As winter moved into spring, some things did happen that were to have their influence on the way we lived, though nothing that could rouse the sensations of glory and sympathy and dread that came with reading in the newspapers—a sudden passion—about our forces engaged with the Japanese enemy in the Philippines. For one, my father's State Department assignment now came under a new title, The Special War Problems Division, and his work at the office intensified so that he not only arrived home late night after night but rarely had a weekend free, which meant that the rest of us in the family hardly saw him and therefore came less and less under his authority. For another, when rationing on the home front began to include not only rubber, sugar, and other things for the table but gas for cars, wartime adventure for some members of the pre-draft-age generation gradually moved underground.

In those days you could get a driver's license in Washington, D.C. at the age of sixteen, and if you could persuade your parents to give you a portion of their gas ration, it might provide you with a year or two of special pleasures—travel to outlying amusement parks, privacy for dat-ing—before those with a car who were moved by patriotism had to give up that version of the easy life for Navy or Marine Corps boot camp. There was nobody in the Alban Towers crew old enough to have a car until three new characters drifted into the neighborhood one late spring day from upper Foggy Bottom, the two Lee brothers, Dwight and Kermit, and their sometime buddy Lincoln Riggs, always called Riggs. The Lee brothers, sons of the Chief of Staff to one of the important southern Senators, lived in a renovated Federal house, and they could afford to go to a private school in another part of the city. Exactly where Riggs lived nobody in our crew ever found out, and he claimed to be "in transit educationally," which meant that he'd dropped out of one school and hadn't yet settled into another, nor was likely to. Though considered a mathematical genius by his buddies, he made it clear that he found school both tedious and beneath him, along with much else in ordinary life. Dwight Lee, who was easily old enough to drive—his brother a year or so younger—had a certain access to the family car, but he had now been restricted by his parents to a very small portion of their gas ration, and this he considered a challenge both to his pride as a Clark Gable look-alike on the make and to his spirit of independence as a future politician.

It turned out that this group of Foggy Bottom newcomers had come up to the Alban Towers in search of volunteers for what they called a sure-fire deal for making some cash while at the same time freeing the Lee brothers, and maybe others in their situation, from the tyranny of their parents when it came to use of the family car. Riggs, smarter if a bit younger than Dwight Lee, was the one who assumed the role of organizer and spokesman, I suppose in training to be Dwight's campaign manager. He got Kermit to round up whoever had gathered outside the Alban Towers Drug Store to pitch nickels and dimes against the steps under the arch, then, with his buddies standing casually behind him, squatted in front of the four or five of us who had enough curiosity to linger there long enough to hear what this newly-arrived character had to say.

"I don't even want to tell you how much we can make on this deal," he said. "There's no limit."

"How many hours will we have to put in?" somebody behind me asked.

"Hours? You think I'm talking about manual labor. I'm talking about a deal, my friend, you know, a business operation. But you've got to be really interested. I don't give out information on a deal of this kind just for charitable purposes."

He looked us over, squatting there like a basketball coach. Nobody said anything. Riggs lowered his voice.

"So here's the deal. We have a car courtesy of Dwight here, we don't have enough gas. So the first thing we do is fill the tank as full as we can. Dwight and I will take care of that initially. Our startup contribution until the cash begins to flow in."

"I thought the problem was rationing?" the guy behind me said. "So how do you fill the tank?"

Riggs smirked tolerantly. "One problem is rationing, my friend. But a siphon hose and a two-gallon can will take care of that for a start and some cash after that, I assure you. And if you think siphoning gas is unpatriotic in time of war, let me also assure you that our hose only enters the tanks of the very rich who can afford a donation to the needy, whether Packards, De Sotos, you name it. May I continue?"

Nobody said anything.

"So after we have the gas we fill the car with up to five people, counting Dwight here as the driver, and we drop off each of the partners at a grocery store, A&P, Sanitary, whatever we come across, Northwest, Northeast, Arlington, Alexandria, wherever, one region at a time. The guy dropped off goes in the store and picks up an item, something in there they've got overpriced like Tabasco sauce or something foreign, fancy, but small enough so that you can handle it quickly, slip it in your pocket and get out of there. Choice of item up to you. Then you get picked up by Dwight after he's dropped off everybody else in that round and you move on to another store where they haven't spotted you, and there you turn in your item for a cash refund on behalf of your mother, who sent you out for ketchup or barbecue sauce rather than Tabasco sauce or whatever item you're holding in your hand. Get it? Simple. Quick. Payback immediate. A sure thing if the guy behind the counter has any heart, and even if he doesn't. I mean there's a law regarding refunds in this city. I can guarantee that. I've checked it out up on Capitol Hill. Only you don't stick around the store if there's an argument, you just get out of there and we try the next store down the road. Am I making myself understood?"

"So what happens to the money?" somebody else asked. "We keep what we collect or you keep it for us?"

"You guys still don't get it, do you? We pool the money. This is America. Everybody has an equal share in the operation, so we distribute it in equal parts, with an extra share for the driver because he takes the greater risk and has to work harder and provides the car besides."

"So how do we get rid of all this stolen money?" the same guy asks.

"What do you mean stolen?" Riggs says. "You an anarchist or something? Or just stupid? This is straight business. All these stores give you a cash refund on anything you turn back in, at least those belonging to a chain. And you do with the money what you want once its yours by distribution. Buy a present for your girlfriend. Take a trip. Buy a bicycle. How the fuck do I know what you're going to do with the money?"

I didn't have a girlfriend and I couldn't think of where I might want to take a trip at that point and I had no real use for a bicycle, but I kept my mouth shut. And when the steps began to clear, I was one of the two who still sat there waiting to hear what Riggs had to say about the next step in his operation. The other kid who stayed I barely knew because he had moved into the neighborhood only recently when his father, originally from Italy, had taken over a snazzy kitchen in some mansion on Mass Avenue. The kid went by the name of Dago, which he took to be cause for pride.

"So only two of you are interested in this deal?" Riggs said, clearly disappointed. "Well at least that makes for one full car load. We'll just have to make several rounds with the same partners."

I hadn't said I was interested, but I hadn't said I wasn't interested either, and though I hadn't made up my mind what I was going to do, it began to be made up for me because I didn't move away when I could have. Why I didn't was not a thing I had words to explain to myself at the time. It wasn't exactly that I felt under pressure to prove myself as the youngest of the five gathered there or that I felt intimidated by the newcomers. It was mostly an unfamiliar feeling of excitement, an anticipation of risk-taking in a climate that now seemed open to risk-taking, maybe a way of proving to yourself that you still had guts now that you had a suspicion your heart was too malleable and pleasure-seeking ever to be what they called pure.

The next afternoon we gathered on the Alban Towers steps to initiate the first round of the grocery store deal. The Lee brothers and Riggs reported that they had made a successful foray into a residential area near the Georgetown reservoir and had managed to fill their two-gallon can not once but twice, the second time out of the tank of a vintage Packard just a minute or two ahead of the arrival of a 7th Precinct squad car at the far end of the street, obviously alerted by some local resident not in sympathy with their Robin Hood mode of solving their rationing problem. That day and the next the grocery store deal worked smoothly, all rounds carried out in Northwest Washington. I concentrated on Tabasco sauce until Riggs told us that too much of the same good thing might get us in trouble if a sudden shortage were reported in the two major supermarket chains we were working, at which point I switched to imported items such as chutney out of England and mustard out of France. But when we crossed over into Northeast Washington on the third day, we began to run into trouble here and there. The eyes of the black managers were sharper, so sometimes you had to give up as you cruised the aisles—when there were aisles—and come out empty handed, and there were other times, especially in the smaller stores, you'd get a serious argument on coming in to mosey up to the checkout counter for a refund.

"Boy. I do not know where you got this here mustard, but you surely did not get this here mustard in here."

"That's right. My mother got it."

"Your mother? Your mother been in here?"

"That's right. A few days ago. And I really need this refund to take home to her, because she's going to—"

"If your mother been in here to get this mustard, she done made it up herself and brought it in here in this jar, cause this here mustard say it come from the other side of the sea."

"I must've got the wrong store."

"You surely did. And the wrong side of town. So you better get your ass over yonder where it belongs."

It was during the second week that I pulled out of the grocery store deal. I told Riggs and the Lee brothers that I'd collected all the cash I needed for the time being and anyway would be heading out of the city for places elsewhere as soon as school was over at the end of the month, a total fabrication at that point. They weren't at all happy about this move of mine, a sign of disloyalty that immediately put me under general suspicion, though even they had begun to run thin on both store options and safe places to siphon gas and were now thinking of moving on to more distant virgin territory in Arlington or Alexandria or even Baltimore, depending on where enough cash might come in to make for purchasing gas coupons from an unnamed source they had in mind.

The truth was that the thrill of it all had faded for me, replaced by a kind of lingering dread, not only the fear of being caught, which was increasingly there, but the bad feeling that now came with putting money in my pocket by way of illegal gas and stealing imported mustard when there was a war on and when I didn't really need the money in the first place. I even decided that I didn't want lucre of that kind hanging around in the secret hiding place I'd made for it under the spare bed in the basement, so I took the money and went downtown to a place I'd scouted out for the right style and spent the best part of my cash in hand to buy myself a pair of burgundy pegged pants that really belonged with a zoot suit jacket and that billowed out at the knees and had cuffs that came close to hugging my ankles. And then I bought a gold-plated chain that stretched from my belt down my right thigh and back to my side pocket in a gorgeous great loop.

It was the first pair of pants I'd bought entirely on my own—no trip by streetcar with my mother down to Hecht's Department Store to try on this or that pair of dull-colored corduroy slacks, no jaunt by car with my father to the giant clothing store on the outskirts of town that gave Foreign Service personnel a special discount and that could turn my father manic to the point of his buying half a dozen of every item he came across that he chose for himself and for the rest of us, as though we were headed for a very long tour in some African desert or arctic tundra. Buying a pair of pants on my own was clearly a liberating experience, but buying a pegged pair that color was some kind of revolutionary act. At least so it came to seem when I went sauntering home wearing those pants, one hand twirling the gold chain near the key ring I'd bought to weight it down in my pocket, the other holding my fading corduroys.

I found my mother sitting in an easy chair in the living room darning socks. She looked up as I stood in the door, and I could tell from the expression on her face that I might as well have been a guerrilla holding a live grenade. Then her face relaxed, and for a moment I thought she was actually going to laugh.

"Well," she said. "You look fit to kill. Where did you borrow that outfit?"

"I didn't borrow it. I bought it."

"You bought it? With what money, my dear?"

"My allowance," I said. "I've been saving it up. And from some work I've been doing after school."

"I didn't know you've been working after school. Where have you been working?"

"Different places. Washing cars here and there down in Georgetown. Carrying stuff home for people from the supermarket. That's why I've been coming home late some nights."

"Why didn't you tell us that's why you've been coming home late? Your father and I have really been wondering about that. But we didn't want to interfere with what we thought was your, well, your new social life."

"I don't really have a social life to speak of," I said. "The point is, I didn't want anybody to worry about me so I didn't say anything. I mean Georgetown can be rough territory sometimes. But I know how to take care of myself down there."

My mother was still studying me, then she turned back to her darning. "I'm sure you do," she said. "But I wouldn't wear that outfit around the house if I were you. It may raise more questions than you want to answer."

Of course she had my father in mind, and I'm sure she told him about my new outfit at some point when he was in a relaxed mood, because he never spoke to me about that directly. What he did speak to me about directly was an idea he and my mother had formulated about how I might spend the better part of the summer ahead, an idea I was pretty sure was meant to separate me from whatever I was up to in Georgetown and elsewhere that was now leading me at the age of fourteen and a half into wearing those pegged pants and gold chain.

The idea was for me to spend a month or so as a hired hand on my grandparents' farm in upstate New York. My father would provide the blue overalls and heavy boots and any other special clothing I might need. My grandfather, who had diligently worked the land that he'd inherited as one of sixteen children and that he'd vastly expanded during his long farming life, had now left the world he knew for what he hoped, as a Jehovah's Witness convert, was a future paradise on earth. It would now be up to my grandmother to decide how many cows I was to milk and what other chores I was to perform for my wage of fifty cents a day, plus anything else I could put away in my spare time, such as picking raspberries to be transported to the local market in Wellsville for ten cents a box.

All of this had been arranged behind my back by what must have been an awkward phone conversation with my well-meaning and now lonely though still tough-minded grandmother, known in the family as Grandma Vossler. And if in the secret recesses of my heart I resented this imposed financial arrangement, along with the obvious effort to get me quickly dressed in something less dramatic than burgundy pegged pants, I was fairly relieved to have a way of soon escaping where I was at the moment. The vision of those broad yellow hay fields and green grazing meadows that belonged to the dairy portion of my grandfather's thousand-acre farm on the highest hill in Allegheny County, N.Y., merged with the still recurring memories of the Farm School cow barn and the grazing sheep meadows of Mt. Hortiati. This was food not only for nostalgia but for the possibility of a return to nature that I figured might cleanse my imagination of the capital city and some of its ways that I was now ready to leave behind me just as soon as I could.

⁕　⁕　⁕

The week after school was out, I climbed aboard a train in Union Station that had an Erie Railroad connection aimed toward Buffalo. I was wearing a slightly stained gabardine suit that had come to me a few days earlier as a hand-me-down from Budge, who was now getting newly outfitted by my father's Foreign Service discount store in anticipation of his attending Princeton in the fall to study engineering. As soon as the train cleared the city and headed into the open toward Baltimore, I felt immense relief, as though I'd just walked out of reform school a free man. And that feeling stayed with me during the long train ride across the border into New York state and west to Elmira and Wellsville, and from there by car up the steep climb toward Alma Hill. That took me past the gray, sway-backed remnant of the farm house in which my mother was born on the lower farm where our mixed herd of Guernsey and Holstein cows was now grazing and on up to the middle farm where the road separated the newest of our three barns from the white cottage that was home to Grandma Vossler, waiting to receive her gabardine-suited grandson at the head of the front path lined by raspberry bushes and crab apple trees.

Grandma Vossler was a stout woman with a generous face and nose, eyes that sometimes brightened with dry humor or irony, fairly tall for her generation, especially if you measured her beside her lean, rather pinch-faced husband, who, by the time I became conscious of him, was already bent from hard work in the fields and on the marginal oil "lease" beyond the upper farm. That lease had kept him in hope and debt all of his mature life as he drilled one dubious well after another on the outer edge of the famous Bradford oil field, and at the time of his death the previous fall, all but a few of the wells had been through the various modes available for draining a well dry and were now capped.

Grandma Vossler, though never as limber or handsome as my mother, had the kind of strong body and tireless will that kept her alive into her late nineties and that was clearly the source of my mother's early athletic talent as a YWCA basketball star, while her father's malleable mind and otherworldly inquisitiveness were the likely source of her intellectual vitality. It had never occurred to Grandma Vossler not to go on running the farm at full throttle after my grandfather's death, though her remnant portion of the "lease" on Alma Hill was turned over to my mother's brother, Adolph Vossler, known in the family as Uncle Duffy, who kept that family hope and dying income alive as best he could with less gambling instinct and more rationality than his father had shown—until Parkinson's disease cut his active life untimely short some years before all but one of the remaining uncapped wells went completely dry.

Grandma Vossler gave me a hefty hug. "So. The city boy has come to help us poor folk upstate make it through the haying. That's good. Only you'd better save this suit you're wearing for a trip into town. It won't make it through the morning in this godforsaken place."

"I've got overalls. New ones."

"That's good. Only don't count on them staying new very long. Life up here doesn't let anything stay new very long."

"That's all right. I don't mind wearing them out. I wouldn't have much use for them back in the city anyway."

"I bet you wouldn't. But maybe we can fatten you up a bit so they won't fit you for long anyway. And maybe put some muscle on you. I'd better warn you that the work here is hard."

"I'm not afraid of hard work, Grandma. Not when it comes to farming."

"That's what your grandfather used to say. Even after this place bent him nearly double. But I'm afraid good sense doesn't run strong on our side of the family."

She tried to help me carry my suitcase as we headed up to the cottage, but I eased it away from her. She sighed, wiped her hands on her black skirt, moved up ahead as though to show me the way.

To keep the farm running, Grandma Vossler had hired two black helpers, a father and son named Raymond and Alvin Rawlins, and installed them with their wives and occasional visiting relatives in the cream-colored house across from the third barn. Father and son were amiable if rather formal companions—always expecting the full Christian name, never Ray or Al—and deeply religious, though that didn't show in their everyday talk, only on weekends when the cream-colored house became a gathering place for preaching and hymn-singing, the first mostly inaudible, the second wondrously resonant and enticing. I was never invited to take part in those gatherings, and even after I got to know Raymond and Alvin to the point where I thought of them almost as family, I was too shy to ask permission to visit the cream-colored house of a weekend and had to settle for listening to that full-throated singing through the tiny open window of my attic room in the cottage, which was given me by Grandma Vossler as my private domain, shared at times by a resilient tabby mouser.

The routine of work on the farm was excruciating at the start—up for the 5:30 milking in the lower barn, quick breakfast of warm un-pasteurized milk and thick porridge in Grandma Vossler's kitchen, across to the barn opposite to help hitch the team of reluctant horses to the hay wagon, a rattling ride up the hill to the broad hay field above the cream-colored house or the field above that, then pitching wagon load after wagon load of hay that had to be unloaded in one or another barn until lunch time and more hay pitching until the late afternoon milking, which followed our rounding up the herd in the meadows beyond the lower barn, then raspberry picking or potato digging or egg gathering as time and spirit allowed, then supper, then bed, finally bed, sometimes even before dark.

If Raymond and Alvin hadn't been generous beyond justice during the early days of what then seemed to me, even with Farm School nostalgia, a kind of servitude, I'm fairly sure I would have found some way of fleeing Alma Hill for other pastures God knows where, if not for dreaded Foggy Bottom. But from the start, Raymond appeared fully aware of my soft hands and sometimes fickle will and took these silently into account. When it came to the milking, he made sure that I worked my way gradually from stripping a few cows to milking two or three and finally on to my expected quota of six and seven as my hands grew in strength and endurance and as some pleasure came into my relationship with a cow's udder. In the hay field, whenever the wagon load became high enough to strain my capacity for pitching a weight of hay that seemed the equal of my own, he would motion me to climb up to the top of the load to help in its shaping as best I could, while Alvin took over the full chore of pitching the hay up there as high as a fully grown man could reach.

Every now and then during the first two weeks, Raymond would ask to see my hands, touch them where there weren't blisters to see how the calluses were coming along. Sometimes he'd just shake his head in sympathy. One day he said: "You doin all right, mista Mike. You keep those blisters plastered up and you keep those gloves on during the day except for the milking and you put your salve on every night and you'll be just fine any day now." And he knew how to weave a break into the morning or afternoon's long labor on the wagon whenever it seemed that it was becoming too much for me, drawing up the horses to drink from the water barrel when I was the one who really needed water from the spigot at its side, stopping to sit for a moment under the shade of the wagon once it was loaded and again under the barn's shadow after it was unloaded. And much banter either about, or actually with, this or that cow as we worked our way down the stalls—all addressed by name, all bearing a special history—the dialogue not so much to make the cow relax and feel at home as to give me a chance to rest my fingers between one milking and another. I was lucky, too, that the practice hours I'd put in at the Farm School dairy still gave me a hold on the technique I needed, even if the years away from there devoted to basketball and football worked toward a different kind of touch and less strength in the fingers.

As the summer moved on its course and I became adjusted to the farm routine, there were good things in every day to make me grateful that my pegged pants and gold chain had earned me a rustication to Allegheny County, New York. For one, there was the landscape, those moments when Raymond would pull up the horses on the ridge above the upper barn and just sit there looking down at what he must have looked at a hundred times from that height since he brought his family out of nowhere to rescue Grandma Vossler's farm: the yellow and green hills, crossed by high forests here and there, tumbling down mile after mile to the plain that could carry your gaze, or anyway your imagination, as far as Bolivar and Olean to the west and Friendship and Belmont to the north. As with cool mountain water, it seemed you could taste the purity in the air at that height, and when the sun was low, the countryside spread before you would begin to take on a pastel shading that softened the summer's sharper tones and made you conscious of a deepening quiet. And there were trips with Uncle Duffy for a change of pace to the "lease" above the upper farm, dense forest land punctuated by great sharp-angled rock formations shaping abstract monuments and sudden clearings where the working oil pumps, like giant long-necked birds dipping their bills to peck into the earth and rise again in a slow rhythm, would fill the forest—and in the stillness of night, the hills beyond—with the ghostly honking sound of their endless labor.

There were also trips you could take for the pure pleasure of leaving the wagon behind and riding for a while in a pickup truck to carry the huge milk containers to the local cheese factory, where you could always count on picking up a tasting sample of what was surely the best cheddar that portion of the new world had to offer. And on Saturdays there were the trips into the Wellsville market with Grandma Vossler in her latest Ford, younger companion to the Model T and Model A that were still rusting away behind the upper barn, Raymond or Alvin driving, all of us dressed up in our weekend best. And once we'd turned in the produce we'd brought to market, all of us were free to spend our weekly earnings as we thought best for the hour or two before we headed back for the afternoon milking.

Grandma Vossler would always take me to the local diner so that she could treat me to a chocolate milkshake and then disappear to wander by herself down Main Street to chat with this or that old acquaintance and maybe buy something that caught her eye, while I moved to the back booth to chat with the Greek owner and his family in whatever mix of our two languages came to us in a given sentence, mine increasingly turning toward southern American. What news of "the old country" I could pick up in this way was chilling even if it came by way of a long and ragged grapevine between the Greek-American communities in New York and Chicago. The message was simply that thousands on thousands of Greeks in the cities had died of starvation the previous winter and spring and were dying still. That message remained constant through the rest of my days in Allegheny County.

I could never quite tuck this news away during the weekends, but by Monday evening, after the long workday's dying, thoughts of what my friends at the Farm School in Salonika might be going through had been mostly sweated out of me, and anticipation of another Grandma Vossler supper was the main thing on my mind: German cucumber salad and new potatoes in gravy and thicker pork chops than you ever came across farther east, followed by berries in cream and a pie filled with something choice from her gallery of homemade preserves. The plates were always heaping, and Grandma Vossler never had to tell me, as my parents often did, that I should remember the starving Armenians and leave nothing uneaten on my plate—exactly how that would help the Armenians I never quite figured out—nor did Grandma Vossler have to tell me that I would never make it into the Foreign Service, according to what was apparently my parents' plan, if I didn't improve the way I handled my knife, fork, and spoon. On Alma Hill my plate was always left as though I'd licked it clean, and how I used the available cutlery to get it all down in my raging hunger was a thing between me and what inner spirit moved me.

Grandma Vossler, who ate according to her own chosen rhythm, was there only to make sure I got up from the table thoroughly bloated, my brain awash with her tales of the hardship she and my grandfather had to face during the cold winters of his forest clearing and oil gambling years, when they could barely scrape together enough cash to send their two children to college in Alfred, New York, and maybe enough to provide some extra gas for a day's outing to Olean in one direction or Hornell in the other. The anecdotes were always matter of fact, usually farm talk about failed crops one year and failed wells another and hard times during the Depression when loans were scarce and credit tight and income paltry, the talk almost in monotone and touched by a quiet melancholy or heightened for a moment by a flash of irony about the unfair politics of it all. And then she would end her telling with a sigh and rise to stand there straight as she could, her thick hands ironing out her apron, as though ready yet again for the next challenge from fate. I remember that one time after I'd been a good listener for some days she stood up to look out the window at the dying sun and said, as much to herself as to me, that maybe my grandfather knew what he was doing after all.

"Most people around here thought he was half crazy for spending his life always in debt in order to pile one more chore on top of another. But I think he had a plan, and that was making sure his two children didn't end up as uneducated as their parents. So when your mother and Duffy would come home tired to their bones from climbing all the way up to the school house on top of Alma Hill from the lower farm and back again, he bought this place half way up to make it easier for them, and a bit later to make it easier still he bought the school house itself up on the hill and had it moved down yonder where the Rawlins are now camped out."

Granda Vossler smiled to herself, still gazing out the window.

"And when the wells first started coming in, he made sure there was enough put aside in the satchel by his bed to pay for their college, and he bought one car after another to get them safely up to Alfred and safely back whatever bitter weather might come our way."

She turned to look at me, and if the tears were close, she wasn't going to let me see them.

"You know, when you add it all up, ours was a better life than we would have had elsewhere. We were never hungry. We always had a car. Your mother got to go to Constantinople and see the world from there. Your grandfather got religion and died expecting paradise. Just think what might have happened to him and the rest of us if his father and mine had stayed in Germany."

The summer had turned toward August when Grandma Vossler came out one morning to find us in the middle barn where we were loading feed into the bins for fall storage. She had a message for me. My mother had phoned from Washington to ask her if I could be spared from work on the farm for the rest of the month and the month thereafter, because my father was about to go off on another business trip and wanted to speak to me before he left, and besides, she thought I might need some extra time to get ready for my transition to high school in September. I had no idea what my mother had in mind for this transition, which had seemed to me nothing more complicated than moving a few blocks deeper into Georgetown from the merely functional brick and gray stone building on Wisconsin avenue called Gordon Junior High to the beautiful white neo-classical temple-like building called Western

High School, where there were intracity sports, a cadet corps, fraternities and sororities, large halls for dancing, and who knows what other prospects for advanced gratification of one kind or another.

My father wanting to speak to me was more ominous. It usually was in those days. For a start, I didn't know what to make of his having been on a business trip, with another on its way. He never spoke to his sons about exactly what business at the State Department occupied him, and after the declaration of war, it became easy to think of him working under some kind of secrecy code, because we rarely overheard him talking to my mother about this or that foreign policy issue as we sometimes had in the past. Whatever was on his mind, I'd become too attached to my daily work on the farm to want to go home just yet, but I couldn't find any way to challenge what my parents had apparently decided for me, especially after Grandma Vossler said she'd told my mother that of course she could manage without me if she had to, though I'd done good work for her so far and though she'd miss my company at lunch and supper.

All that left me to do on Alma Hill before Uncle Duffy picked me up to take me to the train the next morning was a farewell tour of the lower barn to say goodbye to my favorite cows, a shy if long handshake with Raymond and Alvin, and a hug of Grandma Vossler that filled my arms. I told myself I was fine, ready for the return, face tanned, body stronger, mind clear of any particular craving. But when I'd retreated to my attic room after the farewell supper the previous evening, completely to my surprise I felt the tears come when I looked out my widow toward the upper farm and the lease, where the distant sound of pumping wells, as though echoing my mood, seemed the most melancholy sound in the world, the forest's bodiless heart.

* * *

What my father wanted to say to me appeared to have been carefully rehearsed. And as I think back on it, the expression on his face that evening invokes the cliché, "This is going to hurt me more than it's going to hurt you," which my father sometimes declared, never convincingly to my mind, on lowering my underpants to spank me with his bare hand during his paddling days. But I can believe that the parental obligation of discussing my apparent delinquency in having ordered through the mails, the previous year, a copy of Marie Stopes' *Married Love* may well have embarrassed him more than it embarrassed me. He had never discussed sex with either me or, as far as I know, with my brothers, and given his reticence about showing affection in public, I never really connected him to the subject even after our occasional maid in Washington revealed my parents' fairly routine Sunday pleasures. In any case, what he now had to say to me seemed to assume that I was already too deeply into the terrain of sexual recreation to need detailed guidance about the lay of the land in that territory.

We went up to my father's room after dinner the first evening I was back on Fulton Street, as it turned out the night before he was scheduled to travel out west on whatever unexplained mission was sending him in that direction. My father explained dryly, not looking directly at me, that after my mother found a copy of "Dr. Stopes's manual" in its mail envelope under the mattress of my bed, he had traced the purchase back to its source only to discover that I'd got hold of the book by way of an order form I had cut out of what he called a girlie magazine and had mailed in after actually putting a check mark in the box next to my signature so as to confirm that I was twenty-one years old. That was an act of dishonesty, my father said, that could have had legal consequences, but his decision not to sue the publisher or the magazine for corrupting a minor permitted the question to be dropped in the end. What he was not ready to drop was the issue of my reading a book like that and bringing a magazine like that into the house.

"Well I may be a minor," I said, "but by the time that book got to me a year ago, it didn't tell me much I didn't know already."

"I haven't read it and I don't plan to," my father said. "But if you have to be twenty-one years old to read it, then it isn't the kind of book meant for your eyes."

"I mean some of it is pretty corny stuff. Like gathering rosemary and lavender is a way to get started with your wife. Which I admit may not be a bad idea, only where are you supposed to find things like that in the middle of a city?"

"Well whatever you may think of that book, you shouldn't be ordering anything from a magazine of that kind even if it is sent through the United States mails. That magazine had other things you could order too. Have you ordered other things?"

"Like what?"

"Condoms, for example. Rubbers."

"Why would I order rubbers from that magazine?"

My father seemed not to know what to say to that. We were sitting side by side on his bed, and he now stood up to look out the front window steadily, uncomfortably, as though someone was down there stealing a car.

"I haven't ordered any rubbers," I said quietly to his back. "I swear."

"Well you might be tempted to. The point is, that kind of thing is not safe. You don't know what you're getting. If you want to order rubbers, you do it through me. Is that understood?"

The image of my placing an order of that kind with my father as I might have another pair of overalls made me struggle to keep a serious face and tone, but I finally managed to say somberly that it was understood, that I thanked him for the offer, that I would surely keep it in mind. This was the end of our private session, the first and last conversation I had with him on the subject of sex. My father didn't even turn around as I got up to leave. As he stood there gazing out the window, he seemed much preoccupied by weightier matters, so I simply slipped out without another word.

I think I now know what so preoccupied him as he prepared himself for that trip out west. Among the papers in his archive there is a small spiral notebook with "Progress" printed on its orange cover, and the reverse of the cover identifies the notebook, in my father's block letters, as the property of James H. Keeley, Jr., c/o Department of State, Washington, D.C. The first page, again in block letters, outlines the categories the bearer will use to record the authorities consulted and duties performed under the general heading "Schedule For Camp Inspection Reports." In the eighty-odd pages that follow, the notebook offers penned-in details of my father's inspection visits—as representative of the Internees Section of the Special War Problems Division, usually accompanied by a representative of the War Relocation Authority—to camps identified either as Assembly Center or Detention Station or simply Project, these in or near Missoula, Portland, Tule Lake, San Francisco, Santa Anita, Salt Lake City, and Denver, among the camp visits identified by dates that specify the summer of 1942.

In the same archive folder there is a second much larger notebook, dated May 27, 1944, and authored by one Graham H. Stuart of the War Records File, that binds together a carbon copy description of the history, regulations, and administrative structure relevant to this and other functions of the Special War Problems Division. You learn from several pages in this document that the situation of the Japanese in the United States during the spring of 1942 was complicated "by the fact that it was felt necessary for the safety of the country to consider the entire western coast as a potential combat zone and to exclude all persons of Japanese or part-Japanese ancestry and individually objectionable European enemy aliens from this area." And further on you learn that most of the Japanese in the United States, more than 100,000, were inhabitants of this zone, and about sixty-three percent were American-born and therefore citizens. The document adds: "Nevertheless, the emergency was such that it was not thought feasible to permit even loyal Japanese to remain there." So all Japanese, aliens and American-born, were to be gathered into ten relocation centers established on public lands under the War Relocation Authority created by President Roosevelt on March 18, 1942, the largest of these at Tule Lake, California, which eventually had 16,807 residents, and no center with less than 6,000.

The orange notebook called "Progress" records, in my father's careful, painfully detailed script, the crowded, depressing, or inappropriate facilities at one camp after another during his summer 1942 inspection tour, for example, at the Portland Assembly Center:

> 12 acres under one roof . . . Cubicles large enough to accommodate 2-12 with average of 50 sq. ft. per person as sleeping quarters . . . No laundry facilities.

Keeley residence
(Hastings House)
American Farm School,
Salonika

The milk wagon, Panayotis, and the author.

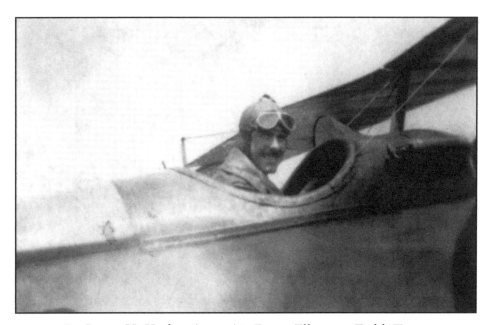

Lt. James H. Keeley, Army Air Force, Ellington Field, Texas

Consul James H. Keeley
and the house trailer.

Mike, Nartouie, and Bob on Kastania Mountain.

King George II of Greece visits the American Farm School

Mt. Pelion: morning calisthenics on the beach

The Keeley boys
at Vrnjacka Banja

Christmas pageant at the German School

The sack race

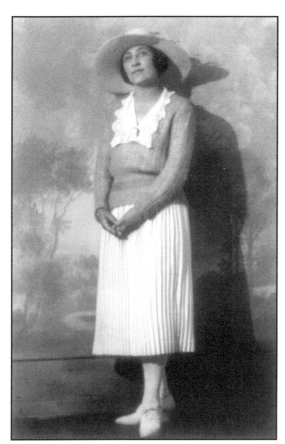

Mathilde Vossler Keeley
as a young mother

Sailboat racing at Camp Cory on Keuka Lake

The author contemplating open country to the west

Tunneling through a
giant redwood in
California

Lunch stop by a stream

The Vossler family of Alma Hill

Pitching hay on the Alma Hill farm

Western High School

A company of the Western High Cadet Corps

The spring dance

The Princeton University
Chapel, c. 1945

The Princeton sun dial
in wartime

The author as
Seaman Second Class

Father and son on leave.

California Congressman to Speak

Congressman Richard W. Nixon of California will address the Republican Club of Princeton University at a meeting in Whig Hall on Tuesday evening at 8 o'clock, to which the public is invited.

Mr. Nixon who is serving his first term in Congress, is an active supporter of former Governor Harold E. Stassen for the Presidency in 1948. He is a Navy veteran.

Congressman Richard "W." Nixon comes to Princeton

Athens: awaiting the postwar return

Rep. "Heartily," a "hot Somali," is petitioned to "Save Somaliland"

Farm School students rehearse for Greek Independence Day

"My teacher" earns a goat at auction

Mary Stathatos-Kyris
Keeley

George Seferis
and the author on the
poet's terrace in Athens

The author
as first novelist

Hospital: 250 beds but some of buildings poorly laid out. 1 Caucasian doctor from the Navaho Indian Reservation, 8 Japanese doctors. Bldg badly arranged according to hospital needs.

And the Poston Project:

Quarters: Crowded due to large number of colonists received before adequate living quarters available. This had in some cases necessitated putting four married couples in a 20 x 25 ft. cubicle.

Then at the Salt Lake Detention Station:

County jail building, red brick, 3 stories, barred windows, surrounded by cement . . . Forbidding appearance. . . . Can be approached only through main entrance to jail through double or treble grilled doors.

And at the Denver camp:

Army steel cots . . . inside a grilled enclosure . . . In an adjoining cage in the same room are ordinary Post prisoners—in for AWOL + other infractions of military regime. Clear air but still very much a *jail.*

The orange notebook gives most attention to the huge Tule Lake Project which, we learn, had 9,167 "colonists" as of July 6, 1942, presumably mostly American citizens of Japanese origin, with another 6000 expected in daily lots of 500 "beginning about July 9th." Among the catalogued entries outlining camp facilities in exasperating detail, with comments on what is provided, what permitted, and what forbidden, are the following:

Adult Education: Elementary and High School education still unprovided. *Lavatories:* One men's shower and lavatory per block of *17* residence bldgs. *Laundry:* There is no mechanical equipment. *Mail:* Japanese writing is forbidden. *Library:* Japanese books are proscribed, except if translation of English books.

And finally, a full account of the Mess Hall produce from a *2700* acre farm that provided each "colonist" with *3350* to *4000* calories a day at *$0.40* per person.

When I first looked through the orange notebook more than half a century after its record of this grotesque moment in American history, I was dismayed—no, stronger than that, offended—both by the implications of the data provided and by the punctilious, bureaucratic style of my father's recording. Of course he wasn't responsible for this policy that took American citizens, along with enemy aliens, from their homes and relocated them indefinitely, really incarcerated them, in such strictly confined quarters under rigid censorship, however amply supplied by local agriculture during years of national rationing. And of course as a government inspector he was only following orders, doing his duty as a civil servant in wartime, even if I heard myself saying so with nervous recollection of justifications offered by those who served America's enemies in concentration camps abroad that proved to be much more unhealthy for interned foreigners and finally fatal for so many millions of foreigners and citizens alike. But granted that my father was merely serving his government's dubious decrees in time of war, how could he so coolly and relentlessly record all those relocation camp details without anywhere revealing his discomfort about what he was up to? How could he go on and on without at some point throwing his pen away in disgust?

It took a second and third reading to convince me that it was exactly the specificity and wealth of detail in those reports that showed where my father's purpose lay, where his pulse beat. The reports were meant to be translated into official evidence not only of what was being done but of what needed to be done. How could anybody read his commentary on the Portland Assembly Center's quarters without laundry facilities and its poorly laid out hospital or the Poston Project's *20 x 25* cubicles for four married couples or the Denver camp's grilled cage for sleeping on steel cots, and perhaps most of all, the Tule Lake Project's parsimonious schools, lavatories, laundry facilities, and its second-language mail and censored library—how could anybody confront item after item of that kind in the inspector's report without hearing the plea for drastic improvement that colored so much of it, even if one passed quickly over signal remarks such as "But in any event there will still be crowding," or "Badly arranged according to hospital needs" or "Clear air but still a *jail.*" The detail was essential for demonstrating what was not there as well as what was, the tone professional but slanted when necessary, the evidence for what was missing not quite allowed to speak for itself.

There is nothing in the archive to show whether or not the warning signals in the orange notebook were heard in Washington, D.C. during the summer of 1942, but there are several passages in Graham H. Stuart's larger typewritten notebook that suggest they were not sufficiently heard in the longer run. You learn from this document that there was a problem for the authorities a year and a half later at the Tule Lake Center. As was the case at other camps that were mainly for Japanese "evacuees" who were American citizens, the "colonists" at Tule Lake were not treated as enemy alien internees and therefore, ironically, were not subject to the protection of the Geneva Conventions. Nevertheless, the document reports, Japanese evacuees at other centers were permitted many more liberties than those granted to alien internees. Tule Lake was an exception. Why? Another passage tells the revealing tale: of all relocation centers, this one "has become the most difficult to handle and on two occasions in January, 1944, the Spanish Embassy in charge of Japanese interests in the United States has filed complaints in connection with the following incidents. As a result of a riot on November 4, 1943 the military authorities were forced to intervene to protect the administrative staff and to maintain order. Six individuals were placed under temporary arrest and the unruly element segregated. Although more closely restricted, the segregated group were not harshly treated and their food was the same as supplied to the others. A hunger strike was entirely voluntary since sufficient food was always available."

Those "colonists" who rose up in the Tule Lake Center during the fall of *1943*, whether citizens or aliens, had clearly become American enough by that time to have assimilated a lesson or two from the American tradition of civil disobedience in their pursuit of happiness in unhappy times. The authorities, on the other hand, appeared ready to move in another direction, after labeling the rebels "pro-Japanese." The section of the typed document on "Civilian Internees" concludes: "Incidentally, the segregation of the pro-Japanese evacuee group in the Tule Lake Center has brought about a condition such that this Section is considering, in conjunction with War, Justice, and the Relocation Authority, as to whether it may not evolve into an internment camp." That ominous development would at least have brought the Center, perhaps paradoxically, under the protection of the Geneva Conventions.

EIGHT

While Washington, D.C. adjusted to wartime necessity, Western High School in Georgetown remained a grand playground for the aspiring young not yet ready for war, though it took some months for me, as a newcomer, to figure out the established hierarchy among the competitive games it offered and the accepted boundaries of play. It turned out that a definable class system governed social progress at the school, but this had little to do with class as it was often defined in the world outside the nation's capital. The occupation or income of one's parents was irrelevant since these remained generally unspecified and undeclared in the high school corridors, as did the date of your family's arrival in the U.S., whether your name was Stoddart or O'Connor or Castro or Chin.

What counted in the high school social system, for boys and girls alike, was how good-looking you were, how casual about that and all other attributes, how famous in non-academic enterprise from sports to dancing, and most of all, whether you belonged to a fraternity or sorority. The Washington high school version of the selection process that has been standard in colleges and universities for generations was not complicated by what schools you or your father or your grandfather may have attended or what special standing they may have had in this or that elite community. You normally earned a bid to enter the exclusive Western High system by how relatively good-looking, casual, athletic, or otherwise non-academically distinguished you were or showed promise of becoming. You could also gain some standing in the system as a male if you were less than good-looking but had extraordinary early success on the football field or basketball court or if you had some gift of charm to go along with extreme casualness, the kind that earned you the attention of boys and girls a class above yours. And sometimes you rose in the system by pure accident.

There were, of course, other systems to satisfy the less superficial or the less fortunate if still ambitious, such as the cadet corps that competed in drill and demeanor with other cadet corps in the city and that provided the possibility of promotion from private to non-commissioned officer to sabered officer with access to the Officers' Club. And there were any number of clubs for enhancing academic enterprise: History, Chemistry, Constitution, Debate, Gluck Auf, En Avant, El Ciculo Espanol, Cog, and a club exclusively for what the yearbook described as "Western's literary maidens who mull over modern literature and its moods and modes." There were also non-academic clubs for actors, band players, bowlers, chess players, journalists, riflers, and singers. As the war progressed, a Victory Corps was established to encourage students to take an active part in the war effort. Finally, there was an honor society for those who had made the honor roll five times, though the social advantage of that society remained highly dubious. When it came to opportunity and advancement in what proved to be the keenest area of competition with what were considered the greatest of possible rewards, the territory given over to dancing, dating, love-making, and ultimately going steady, with a pearl-studded pin to serve as a badge of faith, it was membership in fraternities and sororities that counted as nothing else, whether Hi-Y, DeMolay, Sigma Tau Lambda, Sigma Delta, and their sister sororities, unlisted in the yearbook but well known to all with hope, whether the beautiful, the merely ordinary, or the unjustly damned.

I don't remember exactly why I chose to join the Western High cadet corps in the fall of 1942, a decision that in retrospect seems to have hung curiously between my blossoming impulse toward better self-discipline and an equally strong impulse toward self-reliant liberation. It may have been a further effort to escape the lingering shadow of the adventure in delinquency that I'd tried to shed when I went off to the yellow fields of Alma Hill for the summer. It was clear from your first days at Western High that the cadet corps was taken very seriously by some—even some fraternity boys—but for reasons that were not entirely obvious at the time. One reason may have been the presence in that school of a number of sons of the military serving in the government, some hoping to head for West Point. Another reason, forcefully aired by cadet recruiters soon after your first days at the school, was that joining the cadet corps in anticipation of your future service in the armed forces now became both a practical and a patriotic choice in time of war. I suspect that the most persuasive reason was the look of the uniforms that appeared in the school corridors on drill days: for privates and non-coms, navy blue caps, jackets, and trousers, with golden brass buttons everywhere and a neat white belt across the waist, and for officers, golden hatbands and epaulets and leather belts across the chest and waist to hold a silver sword. If you had no strong hope of wearing a football, basketball, or baseball uniform, dressing as a cadet with the prospect of all that golden brass and maybe a silver sword somewhere down the road surely worked to nurture the self-esteem of some and the competitive instinct of others.

In any case, I gave the corps several seasons of hard work in the late afternoon learning to make my feet move at another's sharp orders in patterns contrary to the practiced ease of a pegged-pants zoot-suited dancer—by the right flank MARCH, by the left flank MARCH, right oblique MARCH, left oblique MARCH, to the rear MARCH—and eventually mastering the intricate manual of arms with a wooden imitation of a rifle that seemed to have its own innate rhythm. After the first city-wide competition in which my short-legged Company G came in fourth among our four Western High companies, I decided the military life could wait until I was old enough to play soldier or sailor for real.

What proved to be my long-term reward for drilling of that kind were the several friendships I made among those who were senior to me in the corps and took me under their wing. There was Brian Childers, son of Brigadier General Childers, who was marked for a career in the Air Force not because he harbored nascent military genes by way of his father but because he heard music traveling at all times through the air, especially, he said, in soaring flight, high above the earth beyond the veil of clouds, though he never let on if this otherworldly access to music was tested or just imagined. He was the only one I came across in that school who could talk about poetry without embarrassment, and he was the first to teach me how to listen to Beethoven and Brahms and Wagner. In his senior year he ended up the best officer in the corps and the most popular—without showing that he cared one way or another. And most of all, there was Roger Saleeby, who had come to Washington out of the deep south, six foot four, loose-limbed, very casual in bearing and attitude, slouching to cover his height except when on parade, Marlon Brando in his features though with a distinct olive skin.

Given his size, exactly how our paths crossed beginning at opposite ends of the afternoon drill I can't recall, but at some point we discovered that we had a Syrian connection—his father's roots in Damascus and my residence there from birth to the age of three—and that connection had led to further dialogue about his father as an immigrant business man and my father as a diplomat who had once served in his father's hometown. One day after a long drill session on the dead-end street behind the school, Roger invited me to come over to his place on Connecticut Avenue to meet his parents and to try out some of his mother's taboule and other Syrian delicacies that she, a tall belle from Alabama, had learned over the years to please her Near Eastern husband. The senior Saleebys, in time almost as warm-hearted toward me as toward their son, became my second family, the food, the talk, the attitude recalling in delicious detail my life in Greece among the refugee families from Anatolia and the generosity of their ways.

Roger Saleeby soon became my closest friend, ready on any excuse to take off into open country north or south of Washington to find farm land and forest trails and a hilly landscape, anything that might bring back childhood images of the green fields we'd both put behind us in moving to a wartime city. And for a while we had another companion for excursions out of town, a quick-witted eccentric classmate of Saleeby's named Frank Connolly, short and neckless but fast on his feet, with a like interest in escaping from the city and its discontents. An unspoken rule during our excursions was never to speak about high school business, academic, extra-curricular, whatever, once we were clear of the city line, and though each of us was privately bent on earning our way into college and who knows where beyond by keeping up our grades—Saleeby ended up an atomic scientist out of Princeton and Harvard and Connolly an Ivy League linguist—it was necessary for the moment to pretend to each other and everyone else that school was of no serious concern in our young lives. It also proved necessary to speak in a made-up language, a shared code, as though that gave authenticity to our gesture of revolt against routine and convention.

It was Frank who invented much of the language that eventually shaped dialogue not only in our circle of friends and relatives but in most other corners of Western High School and from there into a communal future that lasted well beyond the end of the war. In the Connolly-Saleeby lingo, you greeted people by saying "What's your story?" and instead of "Let's take off," you said "Leave us fold." You didn't outwit or seduce people, whether through subterfuge or persuasion, you "eefed" them. And "eefing" became a mode of conduct that was cause for admiration so long as it remained within relatively legal bounds, whether that meant eefing your way free into a movie theater by an exit door or into sexual regions normally prohibited on a first or even second date during those puritan years. In the Connolly-Saleeby lingo, if you couldn't "fight" something, it meant you couldn't stand it, and if you were challenged to "deny" something, it meant you couldn't deny it, while "claiming" something was expressing an undeniable truth. Unacceptable things or people were "false" or "miserable," acceptable things or people were "desirous," and a serious outing was "a deal," while a minor outing was "a count." To make a mess of some action or intention was to "clobber it." So, in the Connolly-Saleeby lingo, you might challenge somebody in the know to deny that he couldn't fight another miserable count like the one in progress unless he was ready to claim that it could now be turned into a desirous deal by the prospect of eefing some false authority figure, or on a more personal note, a reluctant date, before he himself could be eefed by being recognized too quickly for his miserable eefiness, in which case the deal was clobbered.

That first year there were a number of desirous out-of-town deals, including trips to Manassas and Fredricksburg to the south and as far as Gettysburg to the north, all approved and even modestly financed at home on the excuse that we were studying Civil War battles in school, only a minor lie since Connolly was a Civil War buff who, it turned out, had his eye at that time on West Point. We didn't in any case confine ourselves to battlefields but traveled farther on as time allowed into open territory, in the case of Fredericksburg as far as the Blue Ridge Mountains, where we followed the main trails and side trails up and down that high wooded country until we began to run out of time and money. Again short of cash in Gettysburg, Saleeby pulled off a major eef by arranging for a single room with an outsize bed and a fire escape that made it possible for the three of us to share a miserable night in what must have been the grubbiest hotel south of Philadelphia.

But the truth is that our subversive efforts to create an underground life in the open air did not really challenge what we knew to be the beating heart of the high school society that we would manage to leave behind only for the moment. That heart was nurtured by the fraternity and sorority system and its privileged access to the bright and the beautiful in the game of love. If that game became a crucial preoccupation—how many in the school could say that it hadn't at some point?—and if you weren't a star athlete or simply above it all for your own reasons, joining a fraternity or sorority became the golden avenue to possibilities, as not being asked to join became the cruelest of rejections for those who cared, if only a degree more cruel than what pledges had to go through to be accepted by their fraternity brothers or sorority sisters. Even Saleeby and Connolly had both joined separate fraternities in their first year, and in the course of my first year, I pledged a third, nominated by Brian Childers. He'd succeeded on my behalf only after a senior group of his fraternity brothers received his assurance—and mine—that I was no longer involved with what they called the mangy Riggs-Lee crew and their brand of juvenile delinquency. How they'd uncovered that phase of my hidden life I thought completely buried remained a fraternity secret.

The fraternity was Hi-Y, the smallest but to some minds the classiest of the school's four, made up of a mix of athletes, class officers, serious students, less than serious students and cutups who were considered to be hotshot lovers or flashy dancers, all more or less popular in their fashion and all presumably the kind of person a pledge might choose to emulate if he could eventually rise that high. There was also one sadist in the fraternity who was put in charge of seeing that pledges, called "goats," were properly mistreated during the qualification "goating" period and who was the chief wielder of the four-foot-long wooden paddles one inch thick that were the instruments of punishment for demerits at the weekly meetings of the fraternity that included a soul-searching group therapy session among the members and a blistering review of a goat's progress toward his final Hell Week and initiation night.

The purpose of goating was simple: testing a pledge's passion for joining the fraternity by humiliating him day in and day out for six weeks during which time he was ordered by any member he came across to do menial or disgusting or salacious work in his out-of-school hours—polishing the brass buttons and insignia of the few cadets in the fraternity, cleaning the men's room floor with a toothbrush, interrupting some unknown sorority sister's lunch by transporting the kind of personal message that would make her turn crimson. And then you waited out the week to be ordered on Saturday night to bend and grab your ankles so that you could be beaten just below the coccyx—if you were lucky—with a paddle five or six or more times for demerits earned by having failed to perform this or that assigned chore to the point of a purely imaginary perfection, the paddle sometimes breaking into splinters if aimed well and with sufficient force.

The sadist in charge, presumably chosen because of his heft and heartlessness, would come at the goat from a running start halfway across the room, swing the paddle with his gathered force, and then have another go until the beaten goat either refused to take any more or swallowed his pride and pain enough to admit to the gathered brothers that he was the lowest of the low and hardly fit to be a goat at all. I recall only one goat who was too proud to go on and just walked out of the room without a word never to return, and another who was required to quit goating because he was caught twice on a Saturday night with padding in his pants. But as was true of other regions in the animal kingdom, violence and humiliation in the fraternity system were generally accepted as the necessary price to be paid for the anticipated sweet rutting down the road.

"All right, goat. Bend over and grab you ankles. And now that you're down there, lick my shoes. You're really going to lick my shoes? How disgusting. Don't you have any pride? Two demerits for being so disgusting as to try to lick my filthy shoes. No, don't get up yet, we've just begun. I want you to start reciting the Gettysburg Address, and every time you hesitate or make a mistake, you better brace yourself because I'm standing here ready to give you a WHACK—O bless the Lord, the paddle broke right in half, but you were a good goat after all and remembered to bring along two more, so let me hear it—four score and what? Louder, disgusting goat, you dare mock the Gettysburg Address and honest Abe Lincoln by reciting his famous speech under your breath? WHACK. Are you ready to show respect for the great men of your country? Now lets hear it again, Four score and... No, you don't tell me you've worked off all your demerits because you've just earned yourself two more demerits for being much too eager to avoid reciting the Gettysburg Address, you miserable filthy unpatriotic goat WHACK..."

And so on into the miserable night.

I got through Hell Week without any major problem because it turned out to be like any other week for a goat except that the chores were doubled and the humiliation focused more on embarrassing yourself with members of our sister sorority, Zeta Beta Psi, by having to find a sister who was willing to let you wear her bobby socks and long sweater or drink milk out of her moccasin shoes or leave the full lipstick image of a kiss on your cheek in front of a member of the faculty—and triple demerits if your persuasion failed. In the end, the number of demerits didn't matter, because Initiation Night at the end of the week was a free-for-all, with all but the most reticent members of the fraternity ready to take their turn with the paddle as suited their whim. I was ordered to wear bathing trunks and nothing else under a disposable pair of pants and to bring a large blindfold along with my three paddles to a vacant lot on 37th Street behind the high school at least half an hour before dark on that April evening of an unusually warm spring.

I arrived at that vacant lot when the sun was out of sight and the dying glow of dusk right for my mood, especially after I'd managed to raid my father's liquor cabinet for two long swigs of sweet vermouth before leaving home in my bathing trunks and my oldest corduroys. I stood there waiting in the middle of the lot for more long minutes than I cared to estimate, working up my courage with thoughts about the still nameless sorority sister who had been generous and gutsy enough to plant that kiss on my cheek in front of our large unsmiling mathematics teacher, Miss Wanamaker. When the fraternity sadist suddenly appeared out of nowhere, he took my paddles from me without a word and laid them down beside me, then tied the blindfold around my head tight enough to hurt. I could hear the rustle of others gathering around, some low talk, a muffled laugh, and then the sadist's booming voice: "All right now, miserable goat, we're going to play a little game of blind-man's buff. When you hear a voice calling 'goat,' we want you to find that voice and tell us which of our brothers it is, and if you're too stupid to recognize who your brothers are by now, you bend over immediately and assume the position, hands on your ankles, ass in the air. Got that, goat?" And then a few feet away I heard a screeching "Goat, here goat, that's a good goat, come get me stupid goat." And when I lunged, there was of course nothing there. And then another phony voice: "Here goat, over here." And another lunge into air. And another voice. Then the sadist: "If you can't catch the voice, miserable goat, at least tell us which brother it belongs to. Is it Leeth? Or Chidlaw. Or Gillette? Or Hite? Or Webster? No, you idiot goat. It isn't any of those, so you don't even know who your brothers are by this time. Disgusting. So you'd better assume the position. Quick, now. No more playing games."

The first time I assumed the position, with the SMACK of the paddle I fell flat on my face. And then again the second time. "What's the matter with you, goat? Why do you keep falling down? Is there something wrong with your legs? Now assume the position and hold it." But I couldn't. The sadist picked me up and grasped me by the shoulders. "Aha. What's this, miserable goat? What do I smell on your stinking breath? You've been drinking wine, have you, you filthy goat, is that what's wrong with you? Then we'll have to sober you up fast, because there is still a long night ahead." So when I next assumed the position, he stood there holding me so that I wouldn't fall over while one after another of my future brothers took his turn with a paddle, some more proficient than others, some eventually breaking the paddle, but all proficient enough. I don't know how many swats it took to convince them that I was thoroughly sober and how many more for good measure, but it was enough to make it impossible for me to sit down or even stand up straight when they pushed me into the back of somebody's car and drove me off blindfolded God knows where. And it took that long ride into oblivion to bring my voice back to normal.

We ended up on a dirt road somewhere because I could smell the dust come up from the wheels as the car came to a stop. Two of my future brothers took me by the arms to help me up a small hill and then let go of me in a place open enough for me to feel a breeze on my exposed forehead. I don't know how many were still there with me, but a new voice I didn't recognize now told me that I was about to be offered my farewell dinner as a goat. "Can you please tell us what you'd like for dinner?" the voice said. I couldn't tell them what I'd like. "Then we'll have to serve you up what little we have on hand." Somebody opened my belt and the cord on my bathing trunks and I suddenly felt a cold and sticky trickle spreading over my private parts and then I smelled some kind of rancid oil. "You've kept us so long tonight that we've decided to start your dinner with breakfast, so here is some grape nuts cereal to go along with your molasses and salad dressing." I felt handful after handful of grape nuts ground into my pubic hair. "And now some canned peaches to ease it all down." I felt the clammy peaches where no peaches had a right to go. "And finally the main course so you don't go hungry on the long trip home." Something heavy, something wet and slippery and ice-cold, come in on top of the peaches, but I could only guess what it was from the vague fishy smell of it. Then I heard car doors slamming and the sound of the car moving out. While I waited there for some new surprise, I heard what was clearly a bird call in the distance behind me, one that didn't sound phony. Then pure silence.

I took the blindfold off and stood there adjusting my eyes to the darkness. I was at the edge of a fallow field surrounded by trees and no signs of life anywhere. Perversely, I was suddenly euphoric. I pulled the fish out of my trunks by its tail and flung it as far as I could into the wilderness behind me. Then I took off the trunks and flung them after the fish. I tried to clean myself by using tufts of dry grass from the ground around me, but much of the molasses and honey and whatever else they'd used to glue my farewell meal inside my trunks remained tenaciously there, now with new blades of grass stuck to it. I was afraid I'd end up ripping off skin and hair trying to get myself cleaner, so I pulled up my corduroys carefully and walked out to the road, slowly, awkwardly, shaking my head yet beaming.

I found myself on a highway either in Maryland or Virginia, without the sun to guide me toward east or west and the constellations mostly behind clouds. I decided to start walking until I found a house that seemed hospitable enough to let me make a phone call, but within the first mile, a pick-up truck came along and stopped when I raised my thumb. The driver, about my father's age, said he was headed toward Arlington but could let me off at Key Bridge if that would do, then went silent until he apparently couldn't resist telling me that I didn't look real good, he was sorry to say, and didn't smell too good either. I explained that I'd been in a fight with some guys I thought my friends who'd ended up leaving me stranded on the highway, but I was actually feeling all right at that moment, really pretty good under the circumstances. I walked home from Key Bridge up through Georgetown, cutting into the back streets when I could, avoiding the high school, the night walkers, and any illuminated evidence of the world of normal human beings. I found my mother and father waiting up for me in the living room. They tried to look cheerful.

"How'd it go?" my father asked.

"All right," I said. "I'm all right. Just a little dirty."

"What did they do to you?" my father asked.

"Not much," I said. "I'm fine."

And then something came over me, something beyond embarrassment or even intimacy, some impulse to show my parents what my fraternity brothers had done, I suppose as a badge of honor. So I turned and lowered my corduroys.

"That's what they did," I said.

I heard my mother gasp. I pulled up my pants and turned to see the same expression on my father's face that I'd seen when the Salonika doctor stretched my broken arm.

"Jesus, it's black," my father said. "They must have broken every blood vessel there."

My mother got up and came over to smooth the sticky hair off my forehead. She looked on the edge of tears. Then she took my hand and led me upstairs, and she kept hold of my hand as she drew the bath water. She didn't let go until the tub was half full. Then the two of them left me to myself. Neither of them asked if I really thought it was worth letting people do that to me, and for a while I didn't ask myself. But before the year was out, I'd fallen in love with a member of our sister sorority, and by that time, with my pearl-framed fraternity pin on her sweater to signal our loyalty to each other and to the conventions we then shared, any such question seemed beside the point.

Her name was Mary Ann. I first met her when I went over one day during lunch hour to thank the girl from Zeta Beta Psi for being a good enough sport to plant that kiss on my cheek in front of Miss Wanamaker during my Hell Week. Mary Ann was sitting beside this sorority sister, and it was the way Mary Ann looked at me as I stood there, slouching casually, that not only caught my eye but caught it in a way that wouldn't let go. She had a directness in her look, nothing made up in it, and at the same time the turn of her mouth, lips full and broad, gave you a sense of sadness that didn't quite disappear even when she was smiling, as though she was carrying a secret darkness inside her that she couldn't keep entirely hidden. I didn't realize it at the time, but those features, at least their apparent relevance for mystery, were inspired as much by my recent reading in nineteenth century novels as they were by the reality in front of me. Anyway, they made her otherwise rather ordinary face strike me as exceptional, especially framed as it was by thick auburn hair that fell into lush curls on both sides of her head, the side opposite her part marked by a silver barrette. She was relatively short but didn't really seem so, because, though she wore the same long sweaters and skirts and sometimes the jumpers that were popular that year and the next, what she wore showed style and shading of a kind that eventually got her voted the best dressed girl in our class. But I didn't notice any of that at first. What I noticed were those eyes and that mouth and the new sensation that they began to bring into my days from that first encounter through the rest of the warm spring.

I had no hope of following through quickly on what I'd begun to feel that first day, I was still much too shy for that, especially when I'd run into Mary Ann here and there and get a nod and an ambiguous smile that was just the kind to make me think she was now willing to recognize me as a member of her brother fraternity but that was as far as she would go. I asked around to see what I could find out about her that might give me a clue as to how to approach her for a date at some point down the road. What I picked up from my fraternity brothers for a start was that she seemed to be one of those sorority girls who kept mostly to herself and didn't get much involved in the usual courting games other sisters chose to engage in.

That I liked—in a way. The rumor was that she'd had a boyfriend the previous year, a senior at Western who was now in the Marines and stationed nobody knew where, this doomed relationship having given her a special aura when she first entered Western. But in any case she now seemed more interested in spending her time outside school studying fashion design, which I learned was where she hoped to end up professionally some day. I also learned that early on she'd joined the school's "literary maidens" called Moderns, which meant at the very least that she sometimes read books for pleasure. That seemed a kind of opening.

After some further strictly confidential dialogue about Mary Ann with my fraternity brothers who knew her best, I decided to try the poetry route for a start. I leafed through the worn anthology that I'd picked up on the deck of the SS *Exachorda* until I found a poem by Robert Browning that wasn't exactly perfect for the message I had in mind but might nevertheless serve for an approach: "Nay but you, who do not love her, /Is she not pure gold, my mistress? /Holds earth aught—speak the truth—above her? /Aught like this tress, see, and this tress, /And this last fairest tress of all, /So fair, see, ere I let it fall?" Etc.

I signed the poem "By Robert Browning from Anonymous" and put it in an envelope addressed to her home a few blocks north of the high school, and I waited while I built up enough courage to let her know in some appropriate way who this "Anonymous" was. I didn't have to wait long before the problem was taken out of my hands. It was less than a week later when I ran into her across the street from the high school at the soda and sandwich place that our fraternity sometimes used for casual gatherings after school hours. Mary Ann was there at a table with a girl I'd never seen before, and she gave me a very curious look when she spotted me standing inside the doorway: no sadness in it, something much closer to irony. She got up and came right over to me.

"Can we talk?" she said quietly.

"Sure," I said. "Right now? Here?"

"I just want to make sure of one thing. I hope you don't go around talking to your Hi-Y buddies about my being your mistress with tresses you love to hold in your hand."

It wasn't really an accusation because that lovely mouth of hers didn't quite let it be, at least not as I saw it, but it wasn't exactly friendly either.

"Now why would I do a thing like that?" I said.

Mary Ann studied me. "I don't know. I suppose as a kind of fraternity joke. Like sending that kind of love poem to somebody you don't really know at all and signing it 'Anonymous' to give the boys a laugh."

"It wasn't a joke," I heard my voice saying. "And nobody in the fraternity knows about that poem."

"Well somebody knows something. How else would I know who sent it? And I don't think that kind of thing is really funny at all."

"I didn't mean it to be funny," I said.

The irony came back into her smile. "Then what did you possibly mean it to be?"

"I don't know," I said. "Can we please go somewhere else to talk? So I can try to explain without all these people around?"

She must have seen something desperate in my face, anyway something that softened her a bit.

"All right, you can walk me home. But don't think I'm going to let you stay around for more than a minute once we get there. Is that understood?"

This was the way the golden days of that spring began to take form, though the afternoon's little lesson in betrayal by whoever it was among my fraternity brothers who'd let the confidential truth about my private feelings leak out was only the least of such lessons taught in the extracurricular course covering cultural conventions at Western High School during the Second World War. When it came to what I assumed people called first love, I was not only as illiterate as all other newcomers to the territory, but I didn't know where to turn to get a better understanding of what I'd begun to feel so suddenly and what I could do about it, a feeling different from other short-lived childhood attractions but also so much less substantial than the kind of bond I'd felt with Lisa those many years ago, though for the moment more intense, irrational, unmanageable. And no Lisa there to give me advice, even if I could have explained what surely would have seemed to her rather strange customs and modes of behavior for young people supposedly grown up enough to think of being in love. What would Lisa have said, from her Greek Macedonian perspective, about student lovers conspicuously holding hands and nuzzling in public with this or that partner of the month, and pinning, then unpinning, fraternity pins as though they were wilting corsages, and going steady sometimes as unsteadily as the changing seasons? And what would she have made of my manic persistence in keeping after Mary Ann however dim the prospects appeared of my getting anywhere beyond her tolerant willingness, one or two days a week, to let me walk her home while I talked my head off in a fairly sanitized way about where I'd been and what I'd done and where I hoped to go in my still confused image of possibilities?

During those first weeks Mary Ann rarely said anything, just studied me now and then with a look that hovered somewhere between mild amusement and restrained irony. Maybe the only reason she tolerated me at all was an unarticulated recognition that my relentless pursuit was somehow flattering to her and a fairly harmless way to get through an afternoon so long as it remained all talk. And that is what it remained day after day.

It was Charles Dickens and my slowly emerging, untutored literary vision of the ways of the world that finally helped me to vault ahead, Dickens' *Great Expectations* specifically. That was a book I'd read avidly the previous summer, and though it was still much in my mind, I decided to take a copy out of the local library to carry with my other books as I walked Mary Ann home yet again, my hope being that she, as one of the Western High School "Moderns," would be grandly impressed by such literary seriousness. That meant I had to give the book another quick reading over the best part of a weekend, and this convinced me that it was truly the greatest thing I'd ever read—not by any stretch of sympathy the story of my life as it was or might become, but here and there perfect for my mood at that moment. And my image of Pip as an outsider trying to work his way into a society that was foreign to his marsh and forge upbringing seemed at least partially relevant to mine.

As the gods sometimes arrange things, it turned out that Mary Ann had not only read the novel earlier that year but had pretty much liked it as much as I did, even if we didn't agree about certain essential things in it. That just became an excuse for a conversation that finally got me inside her house to meet her parents briefly and into a man-to-woman debate with her that carried me forward deliciously into dinner time. Her father, a retired civil servant, was working on his stamp collection at the dining table, and her mother, an accomplished amateur seamstress who made most of her daughter's clothes, was at her sewing machine in a corner of the living room. That left the kitchen table free for Mary Ann and me, and after the curiously formal introductions to her parents and a bit of uncomfortable if smile-rich small talk, Mary Ann took my hand and led me down the hallway to the kitchen, already scoring points on her side of the debate about whether Estella or Pip was the larger sufferer or the larger betrayer.

"I mean what Miss Havisham did to Pip was nothing compared to what she did to Estella," Mary Ann said.

"What did she do to Estella that Estella didn't do to herself?"

"For one thing, she ruined her for marriage. Look at how her marriage turned out."

"That was Miss Havisham's fault? That was her stupid husband's fault."

"But she married him because of Miss Havisham. She couldn't help herself."

Mary Ann was now sitting at the head of the kitchen table, and I had pulled up a chair to sit as close as I could get to her, even if it was at an angle. Our books were stacked there between us. I decided I would pick up *Great Expectations* and leaf through it soberly to cover a sudden flush of insight that told me I hadn't read it carefully enough to know what the hell I was talking about.

"Anyway," I said, without looking up from the book, "whatever Miss Havisham may have done to Estella doesn't really excuse the cruel way she went along with Miss Havisham's using her to betray Pip all that time."

"If you're going to talk about betrayal," Mary Ann said, "what about the way Pip treated Joe and Biddy? And Magwitch when he first came back to London and…"

"Well at least he learned how to behave in the end."

"So did Estella. Why else would she want to marry Pip in the end?"

I looked over at her. "Because he was madly in love with her. He never gave up on that for a minute."

That made Mary Ann smile, unnervingly. "You're such a romantic," she said. "Anyway, I'm not sure they end up getting married. When we read that book in our Moderns group, one of the girls who thinks she's hot stuff reported that Charles Dickens had written another end to his story in which Estella gets married again to a doctor in the country and disappears."

"I don't believe that," I said. "The story couldn't end that way."

"Well that's what this girl said. And she read something she'd copied out in the library to prove it."

"I don't believe her. Just listen to this. You wouldn't want to change a single word."

I was on the last page in the book and I read: "I took her hand in mine, and we went out of the ruined place; and, as the morning mists had risen long ago when I first left the forge, so, the evening mists were rising now, and in all the broad expanse of tranquil light they showed to me, I saw no shadow of another parting from her."

Mary Ann sat there gazing at me. Then she suddenly reached over and touched my cheek.

"Yes, you're a terrible romantic," she said.

And before I could answer her, she leaned forward and kissed me on the mouth, just a quick touch of a kiss, but enough, God knows, enough for a beginning.

It was almost a month later that Mary Ann agreed to go with me to the end-of-the-year dance at Western. We had been out on two dates by then, both times ending up at Sam Tehan's bar near Georgetown University, where a splinter group from Western called the Back Booth Boys, made up of friends belonging to different fraternities but sharing a slanted attitude toward conventional high school life, came together regularly to drink beer and keep outsiders at bay by speaking in the Connolly-Saleeby code lingo that had not yet conquered the whole school. We were all underage, but each of us had a draft card to show that we weren't, either purchased from one of the dispossessed on M Street or picked out of the US mails by those of us who supplemented our meager allowance through temporary work at the main Post Office downtown during the heavy sorting seasons. When we brought a date into Sam's, the girl had to get away with pretending to be older than she was or drink from her date's glass, rarely an issue in either case given Tehan's tolerant staff, especially in those days, when the waitresses figured that not long down the line, the boys would be in uniform somewhere out of town and their girls elsewhere on somebody else's arm.

Mary Ann proved to be less than a devoted beer drinker, just game for a sip every now and then, a thing that did not sit well with some of the Back Booth Boys but stood for a sign of class with others. When I walked her home by a long, slow route after the first date, she let me kiss her goodnight, a bit stiffly and tentatively, but she held on to my arm for an extra second in a way that told me it was all right, I wasn't to give up yet, but I wasn't to be in a great rush either. During the second date she actually had a glass of beer to herself, and when I took her home, much too late to hope that she might ask me to come inside for a few minutes, she let me sit down beside her on the front steps so that we could listen to the almost voiceless night sounds from the vacant lot across the street and study a patch of open sky. I listened for a long while and when I finally turned to tell her I don't know what, she put a finger to her lips to silence me, those gorgeous brooding lips, then drew me gently in to the sweet taste of her open kiss and then another after that.

It was the dance that finally sealed the fate of my expectations that spring. Since this happened to be the first formal dance I'd been to at the school, I had to check out the preliminary rituals with a fraternity brother I trusted to get all of it more or less right: the gardenia corsage picked up too early but kept fresh on a dampened washcloth under my bed, my new gabardine suit from Hecht's cleared by my mother of forgotten labels and sewn-up pockets as I strained at the bit to get out the front door, then waiting respectfully until Mary Ann's parents could watch me pin the corsage against her collarbone as though I was wearing hockey gloves, then stepping back to tell her how really beautiful she looked in the burgundy dress her mother had made for the occasion—the uncomplicated truth there—then raising my crooked arm to offer room for Mary Ann's as we descended the front steps a little out of step, finally waving goodbye with a broad honeymoon smile aimed at her sober-faced parents still standing sculptured in the doorway as we turned the first corner.

The dance itself proved easy, at least after the moment of mixed terror and pride on entering that clean well-lighted gym, Mary Ann still on my arm, to face the gaze of chaperones, the banter of fraternity brothers and sorority sisters, the indifference of all the seasoned dancers who had clearly been there with this or that partner so many times before. Once we were into the dance though, thanks to Beverly Garfield and my training course in her Woodley Road basement, Mary Ann and I "catted" more or less gracefully through the slower versions of the local Lindy, and when it came to the really slow numbers, we gradually eased into each other as close as we could get and moved in tune as though this was where we'd been living together since that almost motionless rhythm was brought into our neighborhood for the secret delectation of chaperoned lovers.

When Mary Ann agreed to be my date for the Houseparty weekend that followed, I decided that would be the right time to propose that we go steady. The weekend was organized exclusively for the fraternity and sorority crowd in rented cottages at Colonial Beach on the Potomac south of Washington, the sexes assigned to separate quarters at least for the early morning hours, the rest of the time devoted to a freewheeling assault on food and drink and rational behavior, along with the more serious pastime of searching out prospects for one or more after-dark date. Though all of my roving fraternity brothers and all of Mary Ann's clinging sorority sisters were there for constant distraction during our first day by the shore, I managed to find ways to keep her if not to myself at least beside me most of the time, and when the sun came down low behind us to cast long shadows across the sand, we finally settled into a section of the beach taken over by couples snuggling up for intimacy some distance from the increasingly raucous drinking and cavorting of the unattached. It was then that I brought out the silver box that had my fraternity pin in it, laid out on thick white tissue paper. I handed the box to Mary Ann. She opened it, stared at the pin, looked at me, looked at the pin again, then handed the box back to me.

"That's sweet," she said. "Really. The sweetest thing. But I just can't. It's too soon."

"Well it's not too soon for me," I said. "How long will it take not to be too soon?"

"I don't know, "she said. "We'll just have to wait and see."

I handed the box back to her. "You keep it. Until you make up your mind that you can wear it. I don't plan to wear it myself and I'm not giving it to anybody else."

She was looking at me with that sad downturn of her mouth, which beyond reason and prospect had first touched my heart.

"You mustn't say things like that," she said. "It makes me feel guilty."

"Well I don't want you to feel guilty. Why should you feel guilty?"

"I can't explain it," she said. "Please don't make me try."

I thought her face was about to break up, so I cupped my hands over hers, the one holding my silver box, but when I made a move to take the box back from her so that she'd feel better about the whole thing, she wouldn't release it, even after I held her close and kissed her and she'd put her arms around me to keep her balance. And then I felt her hand come down and slip the box back into my pocket.

"It's just too sudden," she said. "You keep it for now. Maybe by tomorrow or the next day it will be all right."

And tomorrow it was. She didn't tell me why, and we didn't make a ceremony out of it. Late in the afternoon she suggested we take a walk a ways down the beach, and once we were by ourselves, she simply asked me to take out my fraternity pin and pin it to her blouse where she pointed her finger, which—as I knew well enough already—was supposed to be more or less over her heart.

Once school was out, I told my mother and father that I'd signed up for a summer job that would keep me in the city and at home, but I didn't tell them why, and they didn't ask, I suppose content that I'd managed on my own to find what seemed like honest work that would keep me busy and out of trouble. The job was helping to clear the U.S. Botanical Gardens below the Capitol of dying plants and withering flowers and the Capitol grounds clean of picnic garbage and the discarded trophies of casual love. Through the summer months I worked three hours in the morning and three in the afternoon picking up messy things with a spiked stick and digging viscous fertilized earth with a trowel and transporting fetid vegetation over and yon under the guidance of the toothless, sex-starved head gardener ever ready with excessive goodwill and traveling hands. After work I would meet Mary Ann for a long walk in the clear air of Rock Creek Park or along the Potomac, and in the evenings after our separate suppers, we would get together again in her kitchen or on her front porch to look through this or that art book she'd taken out of the library and sometimes read in my poetry anthology, skipping any poem more than two pages long and limiting ourselves to two or three poems at a sitting, as though more would be a wasteful luxury. Mary Ann became my teacher in art, about which I knew nothing, and I became her conscience in poetry, about which she showed an unstable tolerance, at least at the start. There was nothing to keep this private after-hours classroom in motion except the impetus of exploration and discovery, which may be the reason it not only worked to carry each of us a ways into new territory but in my case began to chart a lasting passion.

The weekends—Saturday night, anyway—were given over to after-midnight vigils on the banks of the river or dimly-lit dancing parties in any living room that parents of a sorority sister or fraternity brother were casual enough, as they left town for the weekend, to make available. Mary Ann's parents apparently trusted her without reservation, so she was allowed to stay out as late as she pleased, and my mother, probably having figured out what I was up to from the evidence of lipstick on my shirts and handkerchiefs, chose to ignore the tense creaking sounds I made on crossing through her room in the small hours to my bed on the back porch. Mary Ann and I would sometimes drift home to her place just before the stars began to fade—sleepy-eyed, humming some tune by Fats Waller or the Mills Brothers or Dick Haymes that seemed right for our somnolent mood, then sit on the front porch steps until the first inescapable signs of daylight

As I look back on those weekends from the new millennium, what brings them up sharply in my memory is how relatively innocent they were. We never moved beyond those long sessions of cuddling and neck-ing, whether on somebody's couch or with other barely visible figures wrapped into each other or alone on some gently accommodating carpet of grass when the night was warm enough and the setting right. Not that I didn't sometimes hope for a sign that Mary Ann was ready for more, but when the sign didn't come, I suited myself to her rhythm and accept-ed what she was prepared to give without ever pressing to go farther, and that included talk about where we might or might not be headed. I sup-pose her reluctance to talk about her feelings, our feelings, should have been a signal of trouble down the road, but I was too content with what we had that summer to think along those lines. All that was unspoken between us simply remained unspoken into the first months of the new school year. We walked the corridors of Western High as a couple seri-ous enough about each other to show openly that we were going steady like other couples bound by a pearl-framed fraternity pin, and though we didn't see as much of each other once school activities began to fill the hours of diminishing daylight, what free afternoons we had and weekend evenings were still only for each other—at least until

Christmas.

One thing I did that fall on my own time was work up a private record of the war in Europe now that it had taken an exciting turn for the Allies. I bought myself a map that included the whole of the continent, the Mediterranean, and a section of the North African coast, and I began to use that to mark the changing front line as it moved in our favor. The idea had come to me not long after I overheard my father talking to my mother about rumors of an Allied invasion into the belly of Europe by way of Greece, a momentous prospect, and even when the invasion actually shifted to Sicily, I decided to get into the action vicariously by plotting the progress of our advance on my map as best I could from newspaper reports and my father's occasional intelligence. This I did by way of an eraser and a pencil line newly drawn across Italy whenever the news was favorable enough to indicate significant movement north toward the Alps and what I hoped would be a victory forcing the Germans to withdraw from Yugoslavia and Greece next door.

I also remember that these were days of unusual stress for my father, though I couldn't be sure exactly why. One day he was on a high and offering my mother a glass of vermouth after bringing home news that his division in the State Department had arranged an exchange of civilian internees by way of a ship called the SS *Gripsholm* and that Charlie and Ann House of the American Farm School, who had refused to leave Greece when the Germans invaded the country, would be arriving in the States on board that ship after being released from their separate internment camps in the heart of Germany. Yet not many days later I came home from a fraternity meeting to find my father sitting at the dining room table with his head in his hands and my mother standing behind him with her hands on his shoulders. He didn't look up when I came in, but as I hovered there on my way upstairs, confused by what I saw, he let his hands drop and I could make out that he he'd been crying, was still crying silently, a thing that I'd never seen him do before and that I couldn't bear to watch. I heard him say, under his breath, "What can I do about it? There's nothing I can do about it. Nothing at all. That's the trouble."

I never learned what it was that he couldn't do anything about. The detention camps here? The internment camps over there? The failure of the U. S. to take in enough fleeing refugees? The complications of arranging prisoner exchanges with the enemy? The bureaucratic arrogance or insensitivity of his superiors? Whatever the wartime secrets behind his distress and whatever the burden of his unhappy responsibilities in the Special War Problems Division, the painful truths that made him weep ended up buried with him, and this despite his pack-rat predilection for keeping on file every piece of personal or business correspondence of his mature years and every professional document of his long public career that didn't violate the laws of confidentiality. What I did learn from his archive was that one of his long absences from the office during those months had not been for the purpose of checking out detention centers but to take a leave for unspecified medical reasons, followed by a period of recovery from fatigue. In any case, whatever the hidden circumstances at the time, he was considered healthy enough by the fall of the following year to take up the dangerous assignment of U.S. Consul General at the liberated and then strategically vital Belgian port of Antwerp, which came under persistent attack from October 13, 1944 to March 30, 1945, by some 5,000 V-1 flying bombs and some 1,200 V-2 rocket bombs fired in desperation from Nazi Germany under Hitler's maniacal boast in his final days to make of Antwerp a city without a port or a port without a city.

As I think back on the fall and winter of 1943, I realize how far my life had drifted away from whatever center had once shaped a sense of family at home. Though I remained close to my younger brother and kept up with his friend Plato, he was now in Gordon Junior High and had his own circle of growing adolescents and his own challenges. Budge was at Princeton working his way through a hard program in engineering and attached to the family only by correspondence and holiday trips home. My father's preoccupation with the latest war problem sometimes kept him in the office on the weekends as well. And my mother was too burdened by her own problems or too tactful to become openly engaged with the post-puberty progress of her two sons still living at home. Whether on Fulton Street or farther downtown, I felt I was mostly on my own in those days, and though this suited my sense of myself, especially after I started going steady with Mary Ann, I was no great comfort to my parents during those difficult seasons and they were no great comfort to me when I felt things in my small corner of the world had begun to fall apart.

It began with Christmas, that most cruel of holidays. The first week in December I again signed up for part-time work sorting mail down at the main post office to earn enough to buy Mary Ann her present of a gold ankle bracelet with her name engraved on it and, irrationally, to pick up another draft card that didn't have me labeled 4-F like the one in my wallet. The work kept me from seeing Mary Ann during the weekend before Christmas, but since we were out of school until after New Year's, I had plenty of time to be with her after work during the weekdays before Christmas Eve. It was during one of those frosty weekday afternoons, the sun too low to be of any help, the two of us bundled up for a walk over to Dumbarton Oaks, that she told me she wouldn't be going out with me on Christmas Eve. We'd planned to look in on the service at the Washington Cathedral for a start and see what else might turn up, but now she told me that her folks wanted her to go with them to their own church in Georgetown and that was a thing, given the day, she couldn't really refuse. She didn't say which church in Georgetown or why she couldn't arrange for me to go along, and I was too surprised by the news, then too upset, to do anything but simply swallow it. She did promise to get me invited home Christmas Day afternoon for the special eggnog her mother always made for a gathering of relatives, but that didn't work to relieve the unease that had come with her pulling out of our Christmas Eve date suddenly like that.

There was no tradition in my family of going to church at Christmas or Easter or any other time as a family—least of all on Sunday mornings, private playtime for the older generation. My mother did come to hear me and brother Bob sing in a communal concert that brought us to the Washington Cathedral during our first year in the city while we were serving as choir boys on the other side of Connecticut Avenue, and I remember her saying with some feeling that both of us looked like angels up there with the others in our black and white gowns, an image no doubt enhanced by our profound soprano earnestness for the occasion.

But that was the first and last time I saw her in church. And if she'd known about the pre-puberty dirty talk and the much-thumbed porno comic strips that circulated in the choir stalls during rehearsals and even concerts, her angelic imagery would no doubt have risen like the smoke of incense to dissipate against the high stained-glass windows in that spectacular place.

Since I'd planned to revisit the Washington Cathedral with Mary Ann this particular Christmas Eve, that is where I went, even if I now had to do so by myself, and that is how I learned indelibly that there is very little in communal celebration as melancholy as singing all the old Christmas carols and listening to the exquisite music of a boy's and men's choir while you are standing or sitting among strangers and your girl is standing or sitting with someone else. It was during the afternoon of Christmas Day that I found out exactly who it was besides her parents that she'd been to church with on Christmas Eve. This came out during the chirpy punch bowl gathering of unknown aunts and cousins at her place when I finally found a moment to take Mary Ann by the hand and lead her over to a corner of the living room near the Christmas tree to give her the package with the gold ankle bracelet in it and maybe earn a quick kiss when she got it open.

What happened was that she looked at the bracelet, turned it over in her hand, looked at it again, then turned away suddenly to face the wall because tears had started streaming down her face. Then she excused herself and went upstairs, taking my present with her. I stood there waiting where I was, pretending to be fascinated by some of the Christmas tree decorations that must have been at least a half a century old because they were fading or efflorescent, and when Mary Ann came back down, her face made right again, she touched my arm and said "We have to talk," then signaled me to follow her to the foot of the stairs so that we could sit there privately on the second step.

"I wanted to tell you all last week but I just couldn't," she said. "Bradley's back in town on shore leave."

"Bradley?"

"So I had to see him. I mean he's been gone over six months and he only has ten days and then he goes back to sea or wherever for who knows how long."

"Who's Bradley?"

"I thought you knew. I thought everybody knew. The senior I was dating all last year before he joined the Marines."

"I didn't know it was some guy named Bradley. I just knew it was some guy."

Mary Ann now looked miserable, her face, her mouth—I couldn't look at her.

"It's all right," I said. "I—"

"It isn't all right. But I just can't help it."

The tears were streaming down her cheeks again, so I just sat there with my arm around her shoulder, and then I stood up and went over to gaze out the front door window at nothing because I couldn't any longer control what was happening to my face.

We saw each other during the week between Christmas and New Year's—twice, just in the afternoon. The first afternoon we talked about everything but what we should have talked about, and it was very pleasant, friendly, quite unsatisfactory. The second afternoon I asked her if she would be going with me to our fraternity-sorority party on New Year's Eve two days down the road, and she said of course, she was really looking forward to that and was already working on a new dress. This told me that Bradley would no longer be in town by New Year's Eve, maybe had cleared out already, though it hardly mattered at that point because her not talking about him, not saying a single word about what was really going on between the two of them and my not giving her the benefit of asking her, kept him there in front of us the whole time, from my point of view intolerably. And of course I began to read him into the whole history of our months together—her long reluctance to commit herself and her reticence once she'd made the commitment, as though holding back some part of her feeling was the one way she could still honor the thing she hadn't yet completely lost. And maybe didn't want to lose completely. Ever.

At the New Year's Eve party she was as close and affectionate when we danced as she used to be, so that nobody watching us would have suspected the new distance that was there between us, and at midnight, though neither of us could come up with anything special to say, we clung to each other as exclusively as others there who were going steady. It was after the party, walking home in the cold of that early January morning, that I finally spoke as I felt I had to.

"Is he gone?" I said.

"Bradley? Yes, he's gone."

"But he's not really gone, is he?"

Mary Ann stopped to look at me, long enough to make me turn away. "I don't know what to say," she said. "That's why I can't talk to you about it. So please don't make me."

"You don't have to say anything. I understand how you feel. It's the way I feel about you."

She was still looking at me, shaking her head now. Then she let her eyes drop. "You can't really understand, because it's a thing I don't understand myself. And it's not a thing I really want. Honestly. I just can't help myself."

I suddenly felt sorry for her, sorry for myself, hopeless about where we were and where we might go. And though we held on to each other long and close at her door and though she kissed me with as much tenderness as she'd ever shown, I knew it was over. Not that I had any intention of ending it myself. I was content to live with what there still was, to let the wounding play itself out as best it could, but I now knew that she wouldn't be content with that for long. Some intuition told me that the betrayer is sometimes more driven by the need for honesty than the betrayed, though it took me some years to acknowledge that you couldn't always be sure who was betraying whom in the game of love. Had Bradley betrayed Mary Ann by dropping her suddenly to join the Marines yet returning like that six or seven months later full of expectations? Besides betraying me in her fashion, had Mary Ann also betrayed her obviously strong feeling for Bradley by allowing herself to get involved with me? Had I betrayed my supposedly selfless and enduring feeling for her by not giving her the slightest benefit of the doubt the minute betrayal began to stalk our life together?

None of this occurred to me at the time. All that mattered to me then was that I knew I had lost her, and for a long time this changed my perception of love's possibilities. Though we went on seeing each other for a while, it didn't really surprise me when a few weeks into February, between my sixteenth birthday and Valentine's Day, I received a silver box in the mail that had no message in it except my fraternity pin laid out on a piece of burgundy velvet cloth between layers of pink tissue paper.

It was something over a year later, during my freshman year at Princeton, when I learned from a former fraternity brother visiting the campus that another fraternity brother of mine had already begun to date Mary Ann more or less secretly in the days before my fraternity pin arrived in the mail. And I learned some years later that yet another fraternity brother—the one considered the most handsome if less than the brightest in the class ahead of mine—had married her and had divorced her and had died still relatively young. I don't know if Mary Ann remarried, but I did hear that Bradley had come out of the Marines trailing some clouds of glory along with the G. I. Bill and had soon disappeared into New York City to become a blossoming entrepreneur.

If it is the fracturing of innocence that makes the failure of what is called first love the most wounding of such failures, it is also some remnant memory of that innocence which nourishes the image of what was there for a time and can never quite be again. What has remained in my mind is an image of honest feeling, maybe naïve, maybe too literary in its way, but a feeling that could hold its pure shape exactly because there was no sexual initiation of a kind that might have made it turn complex too soon. Though simple and uncomplicated and not as deep as love can be, the recollection of it never dissolved totally in the shadow of what came later that was more enduring. At the same time, I was never moved to try to see Mary Ann again once I'd left Western High and the neighborhood we'd explored together—that is, until I received an invitation to my fiftieth high school reunion. I decided, against my first impulse, to accept the invitation out of a certain nostalgia to catch up with the few members of my class I still remembered, most of all the girl whose features as I recalled them hadn't faded over the years. Just before I boarded the train for Washington, a message by fax arrived from the one Hi-Y fraternity brother I'd kept up with since graduation, the one who'd filled me in every now and then on Mary Ann's history and who'd agreed to help me look her up in Washington whether or not she showed up at the reunion. His message: Mary Ann was in the hospital dying of cancer, and though she appreciated my wanting to see her again after all this time, she asked that I not visit her there because she couldn't bear to have me see her in that condition. It was the saddest of messages I received that spring, but I took it to be one worthy of Estella's early disciple in romance, and reluctantly I honored it.

NINE

The late winter and spring of *1944* were ambivalent seasons for me. On the one hand, to avoid the barren afternoons I buried myself in school work inside and outside the classroom and in heavy free-lance reading, and then, to break that routine, I signed on as manager of the baseball team after failing to make the infield as either shortstop or second baseman because of my eccentric behavior with a bat. And I sought relief in another direction by spending my evenings smoking whatever cigarettes still circulated late in wartime and drinking draft beer with the Back Booth Boys in Sam Tehan's until it became easy, returning home mildly buzzed, to sleep the night away without dreams. I suppose it was inevitable that these stag beer-drinking sessions would finally lead to trouble, though given my earlier career as grocery store shoplifter, what happened the evening in question was surely a tempest in a teapot from the point of view of outsiders, if some kind of serious moral crisis from my father's point of view and a lesson in humiliation from mine.

This is what happened. The Back Booth Boys who had come together that evening—Roger Saleeby, Frank Connolly, Nick Wright, and myself—decided on leaving Tehan's to head down to M Street to look for Bobby Sellers, George Athey, and others of the crew who sometimes hung out in a bar closer to the border with Foggy Bottom. We never got that far. At the time no one of us was feeling any pain, but we weren't plastered either, and why we ended up trying to ride part way down M Street in an empty hand-cart we came across is a thing I likely couldn't have explained even then. All I remember is that the going was not easy despite six-foot-four Roger doing the pushing while the rest of us took turns riding in the thing, and the clatter it made along the bed of the streetcar tracks was enough to raise ghostly figures in some of the dimly lit windows we rolled our way past. At some point it also raised the Seventh Precinct. I was in the cart when it dipped and stopped suddenly enough to throw me to my knees, and then I felt a pair of arms come around me to turn me sideways and haul me out into the street. I thought it was Roger playing around but in fact it was a cop his height and heavier.

The others must have scattered when the cops came sidling up to the cart, but Roger and I ended up in the rear seat of a squad car heading back through Georgetown to the Seventh Precinct. Neither cop in the front seat said a word. I watched Roger ease his wallet out of his back pocket and calmly remove the draft card he had in there, then slide the card out of sight under his belt. I moved to do the same, but once I had my wallet in my lap, I had trouble getting the draft card out, the new one I'd jammed into a window slot to replace the one that had me 4F. The cop beside the driver suddenly whipped his flashlight around and flashed it at my lap.

"What you got there, boy?"

"Nothing," I said. "Just checking my cash. 'Cause I—"

"You think somebody's taken your cash? Like who? Or is it you who's taken somebody else's cash? Just hand that wallet up here and let's have a look."

I handed him the wallet. Saleeby said "Christ" under his breath and looked out the side window, I suppose to avoid looking any longer at his stupid friend. The cop was fingering what little cash I had in there, then focused on the window slot with the draft card in it.

"So whose wallet is this?" he asked me, without turning. "It sure isn't yours because this here draft card has you classified as a married man with children. You already married with children, boy? Or did you just happen to steal this wallet from somebody who is?"

"Well the wallet's mine but the draft card isn't."

"Now just how does that come to be?"

"It's a long story. I really don't think it would interest you."

"You hear that, Joe? He doesn't think it would interest us."

Joe was shaking his head. "I think we'd better hear your story. You'd be surprised how interested we are in stories. Though not the kind made up."

So I told them I'd bought the draft card from a guy I ran into on M Street. And I did that, I said, because I was hoping to use it one of these days to prove I was old enough to sign up for the Marines, only I didn't realize it made me out to be married with children, which was something I had in mind all right but not just at the moment with the war still on.

"That's very interesting," Joe said. "And I suppose another thing you have in mind is using it to by a beer now and then, right? You and your tall buddy there. Who looks old enough not to need it most of the time, right?"

I was about to say that neither I nor my buddy Roger really went in for drinking beer, but a glance at Roger told me I'd better just shut up. At the Seventh Precinct they interrogated us in separate rooms. Mine was small but brightly lit, and they let me sit in there on a bench alone for a good half hour, by which time I was very sober. The officer who came in to question me looked a generation older than the two who'd picked us up, and the first thing he tried to find out was where I'd used my confiscated draft card to buy beer. I told him it was a place on M Street I'd been in for the first time that night and couldn't for the life of me remember the name of or the exact location, and it turned out he didn't seem much concerned about that, I suppose because most places that served beer in that section of the District of Columbia had friendly relations with the police. What really concerned him was my involvement in what he called the car coasting racket, and he said my buddy next door had already admitted being involved in it and had put the finger on me as one of the original organizers of the operation, along with one Roy Whitman, who had taken a powder just as the FBI was ready to move in and nab him.

Unfortunately I knew the Roy Whitman that this gray-haired, forked-tongue officer was talking about. Whitman was an arrogant, spiffy zoot-suiter who had dropped out of school several years previously and who was given to coasting unlocked cars from Wisconsin Avenue down to Connecticut Avenue or Dupont Circle to impress a date or to save himself car fare or just for the hell of it. This personal welfare program created a considerable inconvenience for several police precincts in Northwest Washington that had to deal with one or another reportedly stolen car that was actually not stolen but eventually turned up parked many blocks from where its owner had last given it a resting place. Whitman used to hang out around Western in search of company, but I hadn't seen him in months.

I was certain that the officer was lying about what Roger may have told him in the next room—Saleeby was hardly the kind to try and save his skin by putting a buddy in jeopardy—so I simply denied any knowledge of Roy Whitman's whereabouts or this car coasting racket the officer had mentioned. And I went on denying it until another officer finally came in and said they'd now got hold of James Keeley, so the chief had agreed to release me in the custody of my father in view of his position as an official of the U. S. government, but I could be sure they'd be keeping an eye on me from now on—and he handed me my wallet with the cash still in it but not the draft card.

The news about James Keeley was not good news most ways you might look at it, and Roger, who was now waiting for me across the street from the precinct station, knew that as well as I did. He offered to come home with me for moral support, even though aware that his loose-limbed Southern bearing and his invented lingo did not earn him much favor at the Keeley residence. I told him not to worry, I'd make out all right, so he walked with me up Wisconsin Avenue to the corner of Fulton Street, then headed on over toward his place on Connecticut Avenue. My father was waiting for me in the front doorway. He looked the way he must have looked confronting one of his Army Air Corps training planes with its nose smashed into the ground and its tail in the air at a forty-five degree angle.

"So," he said. "The big-time drinker has made it home without falling on his face. The police managed to sober you up some, is that it?"

"Did they tell you I was a big-time drinker? When all I ever have is a few beers now and then?"

"Is that so? A few beers now and then all over town with somebody else's draft card. Well now, your mother and I would like you to give us the honor of drinking a few beers with us. Right here in your own home, where you don't have to use an illegal draft card and get yourself arrested in the middle of the night."

"I'm not really up for another beer," I said.

"Oh yes you are. You just come in here and sit at the dining room table in the safety of your own home and we'll see what kind of beer drinker you are."

My mother was standing there looking very unhappy, but she didn't say anything, so I couldn't be sure whether it was me or my father who was making her look like that—maybe both. When my father moved into the dining room, she didn't follow. He motioned me to sit at the head of the table as though pointing a saber. I sat down. My father disappeared into the kitchen and came back with a tall glass of beer.

"I'm really not up for it," I said. "I mean it."

"Not up for drinking with your family in your own home? Just drink your beer and don't give me any lip."

I took a swallow, and then another.

"Jesus," I said to nobody in particular. "It's a boilermaker."

"It's a what?"

"A boilermaker. There's a shot of whiskey in here. Maybe two."

"Well, you'll just have to live with that," my father said. "I only have six beers out there, and I'm sure that's not enough to show you what it really means to be a big-time drinker so you won't be tempted again to run amok in the streets and bring out the police to chase you down and take you in like a common criminal."

He stood there waiting with his hands on his hips, so I said to myself what the hell, I'll show him, and I finished the boilermaker.

"At least it's not a depth charge," I said, beginning to feel a little woozy. "You can break your front teeth on a depth charge if you're not careful. I mean the shot glass can come at your teeth WHACK, like that."

"I don't know what you're mumbling about," my father said. "And I'm not surprised."

He didn't wait to be enlightened either but went out to the kitchen again and came back with another boilermaker. I decided if that was the game he wanted to play, I'd play along and show him who knew how to drink and who didn't. During the third boilermaker, he wanted to know who else had been in on this drunken public disturbance besides Saleeby, about whom he knew from the police, and this Frank Connolly, who admitted having been there too after he'd called his father to check it out.

"You called General Connolly in the middle of the night?"

"I thought he'd be grateful to know what his son was up to before it ruined his chances of going to West Point. Isn't that where your friend wants to go? And I spoke to Mrs. Saleeby because Mr. Saleeby was out of town, I suppose in Lebanon or Syria or wherever he comes from. I thought it was time they knew that their son was leading my son into criminal activity before it goes any farther."

"You told her that? How could you do a thing like that? He wasn't doing any leading. If anybody was doing any leading, it was me."

"I suppose it's good of you to defend him, but I don't believe you for a minute. You may think your father is stupid, but I've had some experience judging people's character over the years. I know the Irish. I'm part Irish myself. And I've spent a lot of time in the Near East."

I was now getting very woozy and very depressed, but I went on drinking and my father went on lecturing. At one point he said that he was thinking about sending me to reform school instead of college, but that would depend on my behavior from now on and on the friends I decided to keep or not keep, beginning with Saleeby, who was obviously the kind of bad influence I should have learned by now to stay clear of.

"You can't send me to reform school," I said, very shaky now, very pissed and pissed off both. "Only the police can do that, I mean only the law or whatever sends people to reform school and you're not the law. You may think you're the law but you're not. I mean even though I may have been born abroad, I have my rights as a citizen of this country and I—"

I couldn't go on. The whole room was turning now, and my head was a fuzzy mess. I saw my mother come in, looking as though she couldn't make up her mind whether to laugh or wail about what was going on. I felt my stomach begin to heave, so I lurched toward the stairs and started climbing up mostly on my knees. I heard a scurrying at the top of the stairs but there was nothing there when I reached the top, and that was a good thing because, in a neat arc, I let loose whatever portion of the beer and whiskey hadn't yet made it into my blood stream, weaved around that disaster, then clawed my way toward the back porch. I don't remember what happened after that, but I eventually got a report from brother Bob, who'd been taking it all in from the top of the stairs before he had to back off. He said I got to my bed all right and sat there on the edge of it gazing into space, but when I finally bent over to take off my shoes, I ended up on the floor, then eased myself back on the bed by way of a slow roll that began head first from a kneeling position and that ended up with both head and feet hanging over the bed sideways but enough of the rest of me on it to allow me to stay put, and that is where I stayed while he went back to bed.

Somebody must have come up at some point to straighten me out, because I woke up the next morning lying flat in the right direction, still dressed but without shoes. My mother, looking only a touch less unhappy than when I'd last seen her, was standing there waiting to hand me a bucket and a mop and a message from my father. After cleaning up the mess I'd made, I was to stay confined at home during the coming week-end and I was grounded during the week following except for school hours. What was to happen after that remained to be considered as soon as my father returned from the official trip he'd set out on early that morning after hardly any sleep. My mother then said she'd made break-fast for me but maybe I'd prefer to skip breakfast and wait for lunch given that it was eleven o'clock. I thanked her and said I preferred to skip breakfast and maybe lunch too, so she put the bucket and mop down, put a hand to my forehead to see if I had a fever, gave her head a little shake and half smiled, then went her way.

I ran into Roger as school was letting out on Monday, and we went over to sit at a table across the street while he had a chocolate milkshake. I told him about my evening at home after the Seventh Precinct—what

I could remember of it.

"Your old man is really something," he said. "My mother's fit to be tied. So is Frank's father. I mean they're both really pissed off. Can you believe your old man got my mother out of bed to tell her that her son was some sort of ringleader of a gang of hoodlums? That's the word he used. Hoodlums. Meaning you and me, my friend."

"I can believe it. The old man was really pissed off himself."

"Well what right did he have to get my mother involved? She said it wasn't enough that he scared the hell out of her by calling at that hour and telling her that he'd talked the police into releasing her son down in Georgetown but went on to lecture her about her son's behavior and what parents had a duty to do about it until she finally told him to go to bed and cool down and then hung up on him."

"Well at least my old man got us released."

"He's a jerk. We were going to be released anyway. What could they hold us for? Rolling a cart down M Street? Drinking beer at Sam's? I bet Sam's been their buddy since long ago. And I bet Roy Whitman's half way to California by now."

"Well my old man may be a jerk to you, but he's doing serious work for the government in time of war. And that sometimes gets to him. Makes him a little crazy. I can tell."

"He's a jerk. That's all I can say."

"Well he doesn't think much of you either. As a matter of fact, he thinks I shouldn't have any more time for you."

"Is that what he thinks? Well, screw him."

"Maybe he's right. Maybe we should cool it for a while. I mean, until he gets over being so mad. The point is, for better or worse, the man's my father."

"Well if that's what you think, screw you too. No more time for me. Is that it?"

"I just think we ought to maybe cool it for a while. I can't go over to Sam's for a week or so anyway, and after that—"

Roger pushed his milkshake away and stood up suddenly.

"OK, buddy. If that's the way it is, I'll see you around."

"Sit down," I said.

"Not on your life. No sir. Not any longer. I'll just see you around, pal."

He turned and was gone. I had a lot of time to think during the week I was grounded, and what I ended up thinking was, if there's a jerk in my family, it's me first of all. It took another month before Roger would listen to me long enough to hear me tell him I'd been wrong to speak to him that way, to think that way, but by his graduation in June, he'd more or less forgiven me and we were again friendly enough to talk of rooming together if I eventually ended up at Princeton, where he was headed in the fall—and that's what happened. He never forgave my father, nor did his mother, and it took me some years as well, too many. Not that I ever quite forgave myself either. It was this moment across the street from Western High that taught me the school year's final lesson in betrayal and that outlined for me the one steadfast boundary between what was fair and unfair when it came to friendship, a boundary that I swore I would never again violate at a friend's expense, even when trying to defend the home territory. And another thing I learned in the soul-searching aftermath of that boilermaker party with my parents at home: I had stopped addressing either of them in the third person.

*　*　*

On one of the end pages of the orange notebook called "Progress" that my father kept during an early tour of the internment camps, there is a penciled note: "Things to do: Send to boys: *Chins up! Short Stories with Long Morals* by Mildred Seydell: "A way of thinking that will lead to happiness and success." I have found these very helpful and so I want to share them with you. Have typewriter repaired. Get laundry and leave key at Hotel...." Recovering this note from the James Hugh Keeley archive jogged my memory of those days in 1944 that I'd devoted to a new regime of self-discipline which I had hoped would bring me in line with the way an aspiring American adolescent, still not entirely free of foreign trappings and newly wounded in the heart, ought to shape his American life for the better. The Preface to Mildred Seydell's book—a copy of which I recently dug up in my local library—outlines The Long

Morals that back then seemed to offer me a way of clearing my sometimes clouded vision: "To achieve happiness isn't as difficult as you might think. I speak from experience. You merely have to learn to laugh at yourself, to have confidence in goodness, courage to work, and a sense to quit when it is time to play: a philosophy that in the depths of unhappiness will be the periscope to enable you to see the happiness above and ahead." At the time, I felt a need for that periscope, and if I didn't find laughing at myself easy enough, the rest seemed to me reasonable advice, especially since it hadn't come directly from my father but from a neutral third party that I took to have a motherly disposition not unlike my mother's or Mrs. Saleeby's.

An opportunity to put this advice to the test came in the form of an invitation to spend the summer as a counselor at Camp Cory. What better training ground for exercising confidence in goodness and courage in work, especially with the possibility of time out for play close by in a town called Hammondsport at the foot of Keuka Lake, where a lovely new sorority sister named Cindy Doyle was vacationing at her uncle's summer home? So I accepted the Camp Cory invitation. My sense of new possibilities in upstate New York was reinforced by the sudden arrival of Charlie and Ann House of the American Farm School as exchanged internees to be our house guests on Fulton Street for a spell. They brought with them recollections of a less complicated world across the sea, where pleasures had once been immediate, consequences always muted by a certain open generosity, and loyalties taken for granted. As expatriates who had never gone totally native, the two guests still carried their own kind of evangelical American faith that told them God would provide—Ann House especially, beaming with what my father once called, with a touch of irritation after a shared vacation in Yugoslavia, her cheerful belief that there was a happy valley waiting around every dangerous bend in the road even when you were about to be sent flying over a cliff by a deviant oncoming truck.

The Houses didn't have any recent news of our friends in Macedonia, Lisa and her family in particular, but they told us that they'd left Theo Litsas, our old Scout Master and Pelion Guide, in charge of the Farm School before they were transported to their separate internment camps.

They were convinced that Theo—especially with a German wife—would somehow work out an arrangement with the occupying forces to save the School from harm, and their optimism bore fruit. My father learned eventually from State Department sources that the Wehrmacht contingent stationed at the Farm School had wired the main school dormitory with the intention of blasting it heavenward by dynamite but that Theo Litsas had persuaded them at the last minute that an act of that kind against future Greek village children would bring down the vengeance of local gods they would do well not to challenge if they hoped to make it safely home to their Tyrolean wonderland. Theo must have had a special access to the grace of the prevailing gods, because that same September, not more than twenty kilometers from the Farm School, the Wehrmacht, in retaliation for the shooting of a German soldier, burned a village to the ground after sealing some seventy villagers, mostly women and children, into the local bakery and roasting them alive in order to save the ammunition it would have taken to shoot them in cold blood.

With a boost from the optimism of Charlie and Ann House, I left for the Finger Lakes on fate's upward cycle. It was long enough after D-Day for me and everyone else to be convinced that only a short ways down the road the Allies would be entering Paris, and not long after that, Berlin, and maybe even before this final German retreat would come the liberation of Greece and its neighbors. In our ignorance, nobody was ready to give thought or voice to the downward cycle that had already brought civil war of the harshest kind to that part of the world.

At Camp Cory I was put in charge of a cabin of ten campers, each only three or four years younger than me, more or less representing a cross-section of those signed up at their level, some rich and some poor, some ambitious, some lackadaisical, some difficult, a few overly friendly, a few sullen, at least one committed delinquent, one bedwetter, and one crybaby. The variety was exhilarating and unsettling by turns, and it took cunning, persuasion, group prayers, character review sessions, promises of reward for good conduct, and some latent threats of violence to keep the group from constantly unraveling at the margins. Mildred Seydell's confidence in goodness and the courage to work were amply tested in the first weeks, and by the end of the second session, I was more than hungry for some time to play on my own and in my own fashion. I got permission to take a day and night off so I could head down to the foot of Lake Keuka to visit Cindy Doyle at the lakeside cottage near Hammondsport that belonged to her uncle and his new wife.

Cindy was a year younger than me, in her first year at Western High, and she had come into the Hi-Y sister sorority late in the year, among the most popular of the recently pledged. We'd never been out on a date because by the time I got around to thinking about dating somebody new after Mary Ann and I broke up, the school year was almost over—and Cindy had been the first to get me thinking that way. One of the few times I actually got to speak to her while somebody else wasn't moving in to get her attention, she seemed very friendly, and along with the usual small talk about where we'd come from and where we might be going, we ended up talking a bit about our plans for the summer. That's when I found out she was going to be spending August with her aunt near the southern end of Lake Keuka, and that's when she told me to give her a call and maybe come over for a visit. I called on August 1.

Now, sitting there beside her on the swing chair eating a sandwich, I felt very comfortable. Part of it was just being in a home after weeks of camp life, but mostly it was Cindy's way of making me feel that it was important to her that I was there. She kept getting up to bring me things—more mayonnaise for my sandwich, a root beer, a slice of cake, a paper napkin that she used to reach over and wipe away a spot of what she said was orange icing on my cheek. And she talked easily, about how quickly she'd grown up coming to Washington from Albany, where her father had been in the State Legislature before taking a senior job in the Justice Department, even if she missed the slower pace of Albany sometimes, and about the problems she'd had adjusting to sorority life at Western. But what seemed new was the way she listened when you started talking, sitting slightly forward and looking straight at you, as though what you had to say was really interesting, more than it possibly could have been to someone so far removed from life at a camp for restless boys. I finally clammed up, and when I found I couldn't go on looking at her in the same innocently focused way she appeared to be looking at me, I suggested we might want to ask permission to rig the K-boat tied up at the dock and sail a ways up the lake if the idea appealed to her.

"We don't have to ask permission" she said. "The boat belongs to the family. And I'm a member of the family as much as my aunt is."

No more discussion. We carried the leftover lunch things out to the kitchen and took off for the boat house to pick up the jib stored away in the sail locker down there. I eased the sailboat into the dock and jumped aboard to let down the centerboard and put in the rudder, then moved to the bow to help Cindy raise the jib. We unfurled the mainsail, hauled it up, and I held the boat luffing into the light offshore breeze while Cindy pushed us off. As we pulled away from the dock, I bore off to angle out toward the middle of the lake in an easy broad reach. When I pointed up a bit and headed north, we passed Cindy's aunt floating on her back in the shallows a ways up-shore, and though we waved, she either didn't see us or pretended not to.

It was a clear afternoon, no sign of clouds anywhere, and the breeze was just right for sailing up the lake without much of a strain on the sheets or the kind of heeling that might keep you occupied leaning out for ballast, and we headed that way for a while just taking in the feel of the afternoon, the freedom of having nowhere particular to go and for the moment out of touch with time. I scanned the shore on the near side every now and then to see what there was to see, mostly cottages like Cindy's with boathouses and docks and a boat of one kind or another tied up close in or lying at anchor and sometimes a spread of forest heavy with underbrush and completely clear of anything man-made, where you could imagine birds crossing high in the trees and quick animals scurrying below but couldn't hear a thing out in the middle of that lake, which now seemed the quietest place in the world.

We'd been cruising along for some time when I asked Cindy if she wanted to take over the tiller for a while, and since she did, I moved up to sit farther forward, still holding the jib sheet, so I could have a broad look at the coast ahead on both sides of the lake. It was mostly open country. The breeze was even lighter now most of the time, and there were patches where the surface of the water showed no ruffling at all, though that never lasted. Every now and then, after gliding through one of those calm stretches, we would come into a little gust that would heel the boat enough to stir us out of our languor and make us pay attention again to where the sails were set. A ways farther along, straight ahead, you could see the steep bluff that divided Lake Keuka into two branches, and if you looked hard you could make out a lone building high up near the edge of the bluff that Cindy said she thought was some kind of chapel, though she couldn't say who put it there or when.

"It looks awfully isolated to me," I said. "Who would be likely to go to church up there? Except maybe a monk or two, if there are any around here. I mean I've seen monasteries that hang over the edge of cliffs above the sea like, well like, I don't know."

"I don't think you'll find any monks around here," Cindy said. "Maybe just people who like a view of nature from high up to go with their prayers."

"Well you'd have to be a pretty strong believer in something more than nature to go traipsing all the way up there when you've got a lake as peaceful as this right at your feet."

Cindy gave her shoulders a little shrug. "Maybe. I don't know. I used to be a pretty strong believer myself when I lived outside Albany, but it doesn't make as much sense to me anymore. Not since I moved to the nation's capital. You end up sometimes not knowing what to believe in down there."

"I'm having some of the same problem," I said. "I mean, I miss the countryside most of the time. And seeing things clearly the way you can sometimes when you're in open country."

"I know what you mean," Cindy said. "At least I think I do. You want to believe in the things you can see and feel. Things that make you feel free. And those are things you can't really talk about to anybody else. Not even to God. At least I can't any longer without thinking I'll spoil it if I do."

She wasn't looking at me now but somewhere out there in the space ahead, some private place out of sight, so I didn't say anything more. Before we finally came up close to the bluff, she said maybe I should take the tiller again so that we could come about and begin to head back, though she thought it might be nice to find a spot along the shore where we could drop anchor and have a swim. When I asked her what we would do for bathing suits, she looked at me without a touch of shyness and said, simply, "I guess what we're wearing. I mean underneath. If that's all right with you." It wasn't really a question I was meant to answer, so I didn't.

The spot I found was offshore from one of those sections of dense forest that was uninhabited except by wild life. I dropped anchor where it was shallow enough to give us plenty of chain to pay out if we needed to, then went to the stern to coil the stern line, and facing out to sea, took off my shorts and T-shirt, tucked them away in a corner back there, and stood up over the rudder in my skivvy shorts to take a belly dive off the stern that I hoped Cindy didn't see. I yelled to her to throw me the stern line, and I swam with that into the shallow water where I'd spotted a fallen tree trunk that just reached the water's edge and that looked heavy enough for holding the line. When I'd tied up there, I turned to see Cindy sitting on the gunwale in her panties and bra, leaning back slightly, just about to slip into the water. She looked gorgeous. She didn't catch me gazing at her this time but eased herself in and took off in a slow breast stroke, then flipped over and looked back to see where I was, then went on in an easy back stroke until I caught up with her.

I don't know how long we were in the water but it was a good spell. We swam side by side a long ways down the shore, keeping together most of the time but sometimes, when one of us would get a little ahead waiting for the other to catch up and then taking off again, like porpoises playing tag but never quite touching, until we were both out of breath so that we had to lie on our backs and float a while, gazing up at that clear blue expanse of nothing. The sun was softer than it had been but still as warm as you could want where you were naked to it, and now that we were close to the shore, you could sometimes hear a bird calling out from the forest to where we'd pulled up in the still water. We swam back the same way, still hugging the shore, keeping together most of the time but each letting the other go off on a tangent in a new stroke farther out or closer in if that was the moment's pleasure, then working it so that we came back together to tread water a bit or float beside each other for another long look at the sky and the slowly changing light.

When we got back to the boat, I hauled myself up and sat on the gunwale to give Cindy a hand, but she didn't need it, raising herself by her arms and slithering up on her belly to flip over so that she could sit beside me, her legs dangling over the side and lazily kicking the air, her arms stretched in front of her to cover some of where her wet underclothes clung to her skin. I reached down under the tiller and dug out my T-shirt and handed it to her.

"That's all right," she said. "You'll need that yourself. I'll just stretch out a bit and let the sun dry me off."

She flipped her legs around and went up to the bow and sat down on the forward deck, then lay back with her hands behind her head, eyes closed to the low sun. I waited a bit, then went up and lay down next to her.

When she opened her eyes and turned to look at me, I leaned over and kissed her. She lowered her arms and I felt her hand on the back of my neck holding my head where it was. I touched her face, ran my fingers over her face and down the side of her neck, and then the front of her neck, and as I raised my head to look at her, she brought it back with her hand so that I would kiss her again. When I moved my fingers down to the little hollow of her throat and started farther down, she gripped my hand and held it, her eyes still closed.

"You can touch me wherever you want," she said. "But I count on you to be gentle. Can I count on that?"

Again, I figured it wasn't really a question I was meant to answer, so I didn't except by freeing my hand from hers to touch two fingers to her lips. I was then as gentle as she wanted me to be.

The sun was low and turning red by the time we had sailed back within sight of the dock in front of the Doyle cottage, and as we cruised in closer we spotted Aunt Ellen—that turned out to be her name—crossing the lawn and skipping down the steps to wait for us on the dock. When I came around into the wind and luffed up beside the dock I told Cindy to throw her a line, and to my surprise Aunt Ellen caught it and kneeled to tie it to the end of the dock with a quick bowline knot. She said that she'd been worried when it took us so long getting back, because she didn't know if I had any idea how to handle a K-boat on that

lake, even if she trusted Cindy with it and even if the wind wasn't much
to speak of. That was all she said about our being gone since lunch, and
at supper, made up of the left-over potato salad and cold cuts, she was
quite pleasant and talkative, probably relieved that we were there alive to
listen to her tell about her exhausting volunteer work for the Red Cross
and the war bond drive and a new committee, of which she was the
recording secretary, that was trying to recruit qualified younger people
for her country club.

After supper, the three of us sitting in the living room's wicker furniture, we heard about Aunt Ellen's exciting work for some historic preser-
vation society in the Albany region that she thought Cindy ought to join
because it was a kind of moral obligation on the part of anybody who
had her family's long association with that city going back to great
grandparents and certain important early political figures I'd never heard
of. I don't know whether she was trying to impress me or discourage me,
but since one of my grandfathers was a first generation immigrant from
Germany and the other of unknown background in Ireland, I had no
ancestors I could bring to the table to fortify my credentials for spending time with her niece. And Aunt Ellen gave no sign of going to bed
early. At one point she picked up a book and excused herself to go sit
beside a standing lamp and read. Cindy, who'd been excruciatingly quiet,
suddenly stood up and said she was going out to look at the stars, and I
vaulted up to follow her.

We sat on the back steps of the porch and studied the stars for a
while, pointing out the constellations each of us knew. Cindy said that
the longer you looked up there the more it made you wonder how those
stars got there in the first place, and I said that was especially so if you
couldn't believe that something can just be created out of nothing the
way some people apparently did, or what was even more difficult, if you
couldn't believe that something had always been there without a beginning, not only in our galaxy but out there beyond anything we would ever
see, a thought that seemed to make Cindy shiver. When she shivered a
second time, I put my arm around her. She said she must have taken in
too much sun that afternoon because she was suddenly feeling very tired.
I felt as wide awake as I could be, but I didn't say so. I drew her to me

to give her a kiss, not the kind that really counted but enough, and that made her look at me in that straight head-on way of hers and take my face in her hands to kiss me gently, sweetly. "I guess this has to be good-night," she said, "much as I like being out here," and she stood up to go inside.

I stayed out there for a while gazing across the lake at the dark shore opposite. When I finally went inside, the lights in the living room were out, the upstairs was dark and silent, and there was only a pale light in the hallway outside the guest room. I got up in the morning just after daylight in order to make it back to camp to relieve my replacement counselor for the day off I'd promised him. The house was so quiet you could hear the trees outside rustling in the breeze that had begun to come gusting in off the lake. Nobody was up and it looked like nobody was likely to be up soon. I found some paper and a pencil in the table under the telephone, so I wrote out a note thanking Aunt Ellen for her warm hospitality, which was a slight strain on the truth, and another note thanking Cindy for the very best day I'd had that summer, which seemed to me the whole truth as far as it went. As I crossed the front lawn I found that I was smiling at myself—not laughing, just smiling, the best I could do that morning for Mildred Seydell.

The cycle of fate took a sudden downward turn soon after I got back to Camp Cory. The director of the senior camp called the counselors to a special meeting in the dining hall, and he told us that the rumors about an epidemic of infantile paralysis that may have already come our way were exaggerated but had a certain basis in fact. Cases of what was commonly called polio had increased along the East Coast as the summer lengthened, and there had already been sufficient cancellations for the camp session coming up to make it necessary to cut back on the number of cabins and counselors. He wanted volunteers willing to pull out at that point, and since most were ready and willing, we drew lots and I found myself packing to return to Fulton Street.

As soon as I had settled in back home my father called a family conference, which meant an announcement for the benefit of my brother Bob and me, since my mother already knew what he was going to say and Budge had now transferred to the Navy V-12 unit at Cornell on a full-time basis. My father wanted us to know that he would soon be leaving for the port of Antwerp in Belgium as the American Consul General, that port, recently captured by the Allies, being an essential point of entry for supplies to the advancing American and British armies. He had no idea how long this assignment would last, but he would probably not be allowed to bring the family over until the war ended, and even though things were now going well for our side, there was no way of knowing when that might be. In the meanwhile, he wanted us to take good care of our mother and not to give her cause for worry while he was gone. He also wanted us to work hard in school because he couldn't be sure what might lie ahead for our education once we went abroad again, given the current situation throughout Europe. In my case he recommended that I take whatever extra course might be needed to assure that I qualified for a high school diploma in mid-year rather than June, a prospect that he had already checked out with the principal on my behalf, and this would make it possible for me to do some studying on my own, especially if in a foreign setting, until I matured a bit and had a chance to settle on where I might go to college, assuming I was still interested in going to college and still interested in eventually trying to join the Foreign Service, as I had once seemed to be. End of conference.

It's true that I'd thought about going into the Foreign Service now and then and had actually asked my father at one point to bring home a sample copy of the Foreign Service written exam, what ended up striking me as horrific, terrifying, covering history and economics and statistics and even styles of furniture among quoted passages about other things you'd never thought about and had to answer questions about without hesitation or you'd never make it to the end of those passages under the designated time constraints. The sample test was discouraging at the time, but I figured by my graduation from college, if it was a decent college, I ought to have learned enough to breeze through whatever they might come up with to test my capacity for serving my country oversees, where I'd already spent more time than most my age. What was more discouraging than the test was my persistent failure, according to both my mother and my father, to develop the kind of table manners and physical posture and ways of speaking that were appropriate for a Foreign Service

Officer. Admonitions such as "You'll never get into the Foreign Service
if you go around eating spaghetti that way and slouching like a hunchback," or "You'll never get into the Foreign Service if you use that disgusting word to describe somebody else's opinion" became the kind of
refrain at home that, though thoroughly justified, was thoroughly dispir-
iting. But again, I convinced myself that with further education, I would
learn in time how to eat and walk and talk in ways appropriate for somebody representing the United States government abroad should that be
the route I finally chose to take. I was not entirely comfortable about my
father's nudging me, with the principal's help, to start heading in that
direction so early, but I ended up taking the extra course in typing that
he'd suggested—my mother had urged Latin—and thereby graduated
with the Class of February, 1945, the month I turned seventeen.

The advantage of mid-year graduation, once you became serious
about applying for college and once you were transformed into what in
those days they labeled a miserable grind, was the restricted competition:
very few classmates at mid-year were there because they were getting
ahead of themselves, many others were there because they were making
up for time lost due to sloth or indifference or having failed too many
courses. I also had the advantage of no longer being in love, which gave
me the extra space I needed outside the classroom to improve my record
in extra-curricular activities and student politics, which I was told some
of the better colleges considered only a degree less important than good
grades. I ran for office in the newly created Student Council and ended
up third, which made me secretary, though without ever having to write
or type anything. And when it came to the election of class officers, I
ended up fourth, the slot for treasurer, which would surely have been
considered an abomination if the record of my Alban Towers days had
become public at any point.

I did have several dates with Cindy during that fall semester, but they
were not very satisfactory for either of us. It was as though the city raised
a heavy gray cloud over the easy accommodation we'd made to each other
in the bright light of our day on Keuka Lake. First came the lack of
comfort and grace that went with necking and petting in the tight back
seat of her father's garaged Hudson, her choice for home privacy. More

important was her feeling that my likely departure from Washington at the end of that semester made what we were doing a kind of sporadic pickup game that couldn't lead anywhere. This was matched by my feeling that she was using my possible going away as an excuse to date anybody else in the senior class she found halfway interesting, as she had in fact begun to do soon after we were back in school. And it didn't really help that we were both right. Nor did it help for me to discover that Mary Ann was now pinned to another of my fraternity brothers.

With Saleeby and Connolly gone, I wasn't any longer tempted to spend much time at Sam Tehan's, which meant more of a chance for reading on my own, everything from a surprising first and only book by my paternal grandfather, *Democracy or Despotism in the American Capital*, to Thackeray's *Vanity Fair*. However undisciplined, this new devotion to things of the mind, along with my mid-year advantage in odds and my restricted social life, helped my academic performance, so that by the end of the semester I was chosen to be valedictorian for the February graduation. My father's hope of bringing his family to join him in Antwerp was doomed, as the fall and winter progressed, by both the flying rockets raining down on that port city and by the Battle of the Bulge that slowed the Allied advance in Europe. This made the need to enter college urgent, since neither of my parents appeared happy about my being let loose in the nation's capital that spring while we waited out the end of the war against Germany. The prospect of going to college apparently touched such a small portion of any mid-year high school class that faculty advice about where you might go wasn't considered necessary, but I'd been told by someone who had a State Department connection that there were two colleges with especially strong Foreign Service programs, and they happened to be the only two colleges about which I had even modest knowledge: Georgetown and Princeton. Georgetown had serious disadvantages. Aside from being too close to home, it was too close for comfort to the 7th Precinct, Sam Tehans, and streets familiar to me from a life I was ready to put behind me—at least for a while. That left Princeton, in any case famous from my point of view as the one American university I had heard of during my days in Greece and the first choice of both Budge and Roger Saleeby.

I turned to my mother for advice about how you got into Princeton. She considered the question grimly, no doubt depressed by the news from Antwerp but trying somehow to be positive. Her suggestion was that I go to Princeton and consult the Admissions Office about what one needed to do to be considered for admission into their accelerated program this spring and maybe arrange a personal interview on the spot now that time was running out both for getting into any college immediately and for our hope of going abroad soon. I understood her to mean that, given the desperate circumstances, my best and maybe only chance was using my wits somehow to talk my way into the place. So I followed her advice and took the train to Princeton Junction, New Jersey, a stop on the main line north that I'd noted with only a touch of curiosity during my trip to Wellsville, New York, those many months earlier.

I was more attentive this time, in fact focused with expectation on the passing landscape the minute the train headed north of Philadelphia. That was not fulfilling for the most part, dreary countryside when you could see it, spotted by faceless factories, whether working or abandoned, and crummy track-side housing that made you sorry people had to live that way. And when you finally came out to a view of the Delaware River, you found it spanned suddenly by a bridge that was scaffolding for a giant sign bringing unwanted industrial news: TRENTON MAKES THE WORLD TAKES. But at Princeton Junction, with a quaint hut-like station and a single-car connecting train called The Dinky, things became human again, and once you were on that train, the landscape opened out into a spread of unspoiled fields bordered in the distance by a tree-lined lake and beyond that the gothic towers of the university. Crossing that lake into dense winter forest gave you the feel of entering undiscovered country, and when you stepped off the Dinky for the walk to the top of the campus, you passed between buildings in so many new styles—along with all the imitation gothic, huge Venetian-like facades, Greek-style temples, colonial mansions, a grand ivy-covered administration building with a belltower, and beyond that even a kind of cathedral—you seemed, at least for the length of that walk, to have wandered into a sudden Neverland.

I decided not to go looking for my buddy Roger Saleeby until I knew where I stood about getting myself admitted into this vaguely intimidating new world. My plan was to park myself for as long as it took outside the office of Dean Radcliffe Heermance, described by the people in security I consulted as the ranking member of the admissions staff on campus—maybe the only member. From the window of the small room his secretary occupied, I watched a platoon of uniformed cadets march past, presumably on their way to class somewhere. As far as I could see, there were so few civilian students on campus that it could have been the middle of the Christmas vacation break. Since I'd arrived in Princeton with only my high school transcript, the secretary—a sweet-looking, grandmotherly type—asked me to fill out an application form as best I could, skipping the required essay and anything else I couldn't come up with on the spot. When I was done, she took the application form and the high-school transcript into Dean Heermance's office at the far end of the hallway outside.

I waited, looking out the window again. The lawn in front of the ivy-covered building that the secretary called Nassau Hall was just beginning to show through the latest snowfall, and black squirrels were scurrying around here and there to see what they might scrounge. When the secretary came back, she told me to be good enough to take a seat on the bench in the hallway, the Dean would be with me shortly. The Dean in fact made me wait well over forty-five minutes, during which time I mulled over what I ought to say to him under these difficult circumstances and decided I should impress on him how important it was that I be admitted to Princeton as soon as possible so that I could get a bit of college under my belt before either going overseas with my family or joining the U. S. Navy, one or the other of which I planned to do in the fall, immediately after my accelerated freshman year. On second thought, I decided to drop the mention of possibly going overseas, an idea that suddenly seemed counterproductive as well as remote. On third thought, that decision unsettled me.

Dean Heermance, standing behind a vast desk in a large, wood-paneled office, was short, stout, late-middle-aged, with a straight-backed posture that at first suggested long military service, though he was dressed in the standard academic uniform of his day: tweed jacket, pipe in pocket, gray flannel pants. He glanced at me, started shuffling through some papers on his desk without really looking at them, then glanced up again.

"So, young man, you want to come to Princeton. Now just why do you want to do that? And at this particular moment?"

"Because it's Princeton," I said. "I mean, because it's the place I want to get some college under my belt before I join the U. S. Navy. Sir."

"Well may I ask why you don't get some naval service under your belt before you try going to college? I see from your papers here that you just turned seventeen two weeks ago."

"I don't think I'm quite ready for the U. S. Navy, sir."

"But you're ready for Princeton, is that it?"

"Yes sir."

"How so?"

"Well, my academic program has taken off recently. Really taken off. Which is why I ended up being valedictorian of my class."

"That is certainly to your credit. Most of those who are admit to Princeton are valedictorians of their class. Even in wartime. But there are classes and classes, schools and schools. That is why we also look at your College Board scores for a comparative evaluation. I don't see any such scores in your file here."

"College Board scores? Well, I hadn't yet decided to go to college when they gave those College Board tests, whenever it was. As I remember I was only a junior at the time and barely sixteen. Then my father was called overseas in the State Department, I mean in the Foreign Service, and I decided, you know, with a war going on..."

"Well let me ask you something else. To fill in your background a bit. I see that your mother's maiden name is Vossler. Is that a Jewish name?"

"Jewish? No, it's German. Actually, Norwegian originally, according to my grandmother. It means 'hunter' or something like that."

"Ah, Norwegian hunter. Fine. That's settled. Not that members of the Jewish faith aren't welcome at Princeton, but of course within reason. Any athletic credentials?"

"I grew up playing soccer, so I'm pretty good at that. And I was manager of the baseball team at Western High when we won the league."

"Well athletics aren't as important these days as they will be when the war is over, so I guess we can let that pass. Do I understand that your brother is in the Class of '46 at Princeton?"

"Was at Princeton. He transferred to Cornell. To the Navy program there. Because there was no Navy program here at the time."

"Good. Any other Princeton connection in your background? I'm just trying to build a case for you when there isn't much to go on here without the College Boards. I mean we're happy to have as many qualified freshman as we can get these days, but even in wartime one has to keep up one's standards and expectations. For your benefit as well as ours."

"Well my father went to Princeton. In a way."

"What way was that?"

"My mother told me he graduated from the School of Military Aeronautics housed at Princeton University during the First World War."

"Well, now we have something to work with. That would make him at least a bastard son of Princeton, wouldn't you say? What, what?"

Dean Heermance was smiling broadly at his joke. I tried to smile too. Then he picked up the folder that had my papers in it, scribbled something on the front of it, and handed it to me.

"You take this in to Miss Calhoun and tell her to make sure to note that on the basis of your partial qualifications I'm admitting you in the category of Special Student, though I don't want you to think that makes you anything special. Miss Calhoun can fill you in on how to sign up for a dormitory room. But since I'm making you an exceptional case, I don't want you deciding to go off and join the Navy tomorrow or the next day. Is that agreed?"

"Yes sir."

Dean Heermance was still smiling. "And stop calling me sir. You're not in the service yet. You're just in the greatest university in the world. As you'll probably discover too late to do you all the good it should. Now go off and do your best to become a legitimate son of Princeton so that I end up at least partially justified in what I've done for you today".

When I came out into the clear winter air, I felt euphoric. It was mid-afternoon by then, and the light was still sharp and clean, giving to some of what it touched an enamel glow. There were many tall trees and two old colonial mansions in front of Nassau Hall touched by that light, as well as the façade of the building itself, and beyond that to one side, the brown library building with towers of different kinds and arches and fancy windows, all in some other style. Just as I began to feel a bit out of place in that much rich architecture, I came across an open space separating the art museum and two dormitories that had a display of snow sculpture—snowmen and snowwomen posed as though gamboling in a dance, some wearing cardboard hats, others makeshift masks—a beautiful construction by unknown hands that brought me back to where I felt I might learn to belong.

One of those dormitories was Saleeby's. I had his address from his mother, a corner room on the ground floor of North Dod. When I knocked on the door I heard "Come on in if you have to." I found him slouched over a desk under the front window, working on something with his slide rule.

"Jesus," he said. "What are you doing here?"

"Getting myself admitted to this university," I said. "I think they took me in because they're desperate for civilians who aren't draft bait and because it turns out my father is considered a bastard son of Princeton."

"Well they've got some of that right anyway," Saleeby said. "When are they letting you in?"

"Two weeks down the road. For the third semester. I'm on my way to sign up for a room."

Saleeby stood up and stretched. He looked taller than I remembered. And older. But he also looked relaxed, content to see me.

"Well, I'll mosey over there with you," he said. "Maybe we can fix it so you move in here eventually, assuming I can get my roommate Wilcox to go along with the idea. Or maybe there's room across the way with the ex-Marine over there, even if he's a wild man out of control sometimes. Or upstairs with Dengler and the trumpet he likes play at five in the morning. Or maybe with Merwin and the horse he tethers out front sometimes. I mean to tell you, we've got a miserable motley crew in this entry and the next, half geniuses and half madmen game for anything."

"Well I'm pretty much game for anything these days. After I get through signing up over there, maybe you can fix me up with a date and pick one up for yourself so we can have ourselves a small celebration. On me, naturally."

"A date? Saleeby said. Where do you think you are? This is Princeton, New Jersey."

"I don't mean anything serious. A coed friend of a friend, whatever you can arrange on the spot."

"Coed? You must be out of your mind. There are no coeds here. There are hardly any women period. The place is a monastery. Which is probably just as well, because they work your balls off most of the time."

"So what do you do for, you know, female companionship? I mean, how can there be no women in a university as famous as this?"

Saleeby shook his head. "Man, where have you been? Well, I guess I know where you've been. Anyway, this isn't high school and it isn't Foggy Bottom. There are things you thought you knew but don't know at all and things you know but find you have to learn all over again. You'll see soon enough. But women—forget it."

TEN

At the start of the *1945* spring semester, the university was somberly confronting the final months of war in Europe and the probability of a costly invasion of Japan that might take another year and maybe two. Uniformed units of the V-*12* still dominated the campus, and the modest selection of civilian undergraduates were either younger than the expected average and still awaiting their call to service or were considerably older than the average, veterans discharged early for one reason or another and now trying to make up for lost time. For those in the V-*12*, the posture was all business and no horseplay, as it was for the returning veterans. For the seventeen year-olds, the posture was presenting the best possible front in the face of an unfamiliar and sometimes intimidating intellectual theater, especially for those arriving from the sandlot league of public high schools rather than the privileged league of well-established prep schools. The faculty was still depleted by those who had gone off to war, and the three-semester accelerated program called for more devotion than usual on the part of those still teaching, as did their having to cope with a mix of the very young, the very experienced, and sometimes the only partially qualified, whether admitted to the university by the U. S. Navy or by Dean Heermance. The abundant days that arrived with the G. I. Bill and a broad selection of returning veterans, maturely ambitious and intolerant of silliness, were still a year or more away.

That spring the curriculum continued to be more limited than in normal seasons but on the whole as rigorous and demanding as ever, good grades exceedingly sparse, the Gentleman's 3 (Princeton's equivalent of the Gentleman's C) still a respectable average, failing grades of 6 not so rare as they became, the ultimate humiliation of a 7, meaning "flagrant neglect," still a lively threat that had not yet been absorbed into the more conventional F of later years. But outside the classroom, the post-First World War aura made familiar by F. Scott Fitzgerald was in serious decline. The times were too sober, the relevance of college ritual under serious suspicion, the sense of life in transit still a prevailing inhibition against carefree excess. The annual "cane spree" tug of war between the freshman and sophomore classes had to be suspended out of lack of spirited participants, and at least one rah-rah sophomore, who made the mistake of trying to force an ex-Marine to wear the traditional dinky cap that identified freshmen, was sighted backing off and running for his life ahead of a swinging length of tire chain that the Marine wielded whenever he felt it necessary to dissuade somebody foolish enough to think his private war against potential enemies was over.

During those lean months, even full professors were recruited to serve as freshmen advisors. Mine turned out to be so distinguished, so grand and quietly self-assured—Alpheus Thomas Mason, soon to publish a seven-hundred-page biography entitled *Brandeis: A Free Man's Life*—that I simply sat still opposite him and did my best to speak as little as possible for fear of revealing my profound ignorance of what a university had to offer a former back-booth cowboy with an adopted southern accent and an academic past largely devoid of anything relevant to the particular present and future now before him. Professor Mason, learning that I hoped to enter the University's Woodrow Wilson School of Public and International Affairs in my junior year, asked for a start about my background in politics, economics, history, and foreign languages, and when I revealed zero education in the first two, Muzzey's *A History of Our Country* for the third, and, in the case of foreign languages, a little French, a little Spanish, and a mostly lost speaking knowledge of German and Modern Greek, Professor Mason stood up to gaze out of his window toward the deserts of vast eternity apparently encroaching upon him, and told me the obvious, that I had much work ahead of me, much work, yes indeed.

Except for beginning German, my "gut" course, the schedule we arranged proved demanding, sometimes exhausting, sometimes exhilarating: politics and French for the diplomatic future, "Christian Ethics and Modern Society" presumably for spiritual inspiration, 18th Century English merely for fun (despite Professor Mason's "dubiety" about that). One of the silent rewards for my dogged notetaking at lectures the following weeks and my slow reading into the small hours of the night proved to be the discovery of how much pleasure most of the heavy thinkers in my schedule seemed to take in the clash of ideas and their efforts to express this precisely and sometimes even lyrically. My remnant notes, the spelling atrocious, show that in the case of political theory, I didn't survive with much enthusiasm beyond Plato, Aristotle, and Cicero into medieval and post-medieval theories (by the time we arrived at Rousseau, my note-taking had reverted to a sandlot mode: "He went nuts in England and returned to France. While nuts, he wrote his Confessions"). But the course in ethics and society—mysteriously, profoundly—uprooted most of the southern prejudices I'd adopted in the nation's capital, while at the same time planting the seeds of a lasting suspicion of capitalist greed and a more sophisticated understanding of personal liberty and social change than my days in Georgetown had inspired, now nourished by Tawney's *The Acquisitve Society* and Niebuhr's *The Children of Light and the Children of Darkness.* And in the 18th century English course, I found myself slowly dragged from easy romanticism toward an appreciation of satire and irony and double-edged humor by way of Swift, Pope, Fielding, Stern, and Dr. Johnson.

The essential help given this passage into new ways of seeing and feeling came from certain teachers who had mastered the art of making what was complex or obscure or subtly beautiful both accessible and entertaining. I remember especially Robert Kilburn Root's talent for turning himself, as he sat behind the lecture table, into a stooped, cramped, rat-faced image of Alexander Pope mocking the world's foolishness from his grotto as he read lines from the "Rape of the Lock" with a little wink to signal the poet's wit at the end:

> Then flashed the living lightning from her eyes,
> And screams of horror rend the affrighted skies.
> Not louder shrieks to pitying heaven are cast,
> When husbands or when lapdogs breathe their last.

Then, emerging from his imitation grotto and standing tall and stately to gaze at the heavens, Root would take on the soft voice of the lyrical Pope to end the day's lecture as though the hunchback had suddenly been transformed into the eternal lover by the power of his own verse:

> When those fair suns shall set, as set they must,
> And all those tresses shall be laid in dust,
> This Lock the Muse shall consecrate to fame,
> And midst the stars inscribe Belinda's name.

In those days of accelerated study, there was little time outside the classroom and the long hours of reading in the dorm for communal play, and no time—or money or opportunity—for romance of any kind, at least not for an entering freshman on a tight budget and a taxing schedule. Between lectures and classes, a break for exercise, and night reading, those of us who came to the university on a tuition scholarship were required as part of our student aid package to work as waiters in the undergraduate dining halls, another kind of challenge, even if the energy involved was minimal once you learned to stack an even spread of piled dishes and flatware on an oval tray half your height and balance the tray on one hand and one shoulder as you wove your way between tables of hungry undergraduates sometimes leaning back unaware of your passing or in too much of a hurry to get in or out of their chosen perch. And there was some relief from the isolation and bleary-eyed intensity of keeping up with classroom assignments in the one outdoor activity I managed to introduce into my springtime monasticism: varsity soccer.

As Dean Heermance had hinted, soccer was not yet a very serious athletic enterprise at Princeton, and during wartime the pool of fairly skilled soccer players had almost run dry. That spring the front line could claim a talented young Englishman, a Canadian, two reasonably efficient prep school players, and for a while, a slow if determined high school graduate with pre-war experience on the overgrown soccer fields of Greek Macedonia. The halfbacks and fullbacks were made up mostly of surplus junior varsity football players who had been quickly trained, more or less, to keep their hands to themselves and to kick a ball shaped like a watermelon instead of a cantaloupe. Jimmy Reed, the tough if diminutive soccer coach, could sometimes be heard yelling at one or another of his recently recruited backs: "For God's sake, if you can't learn to kick the ball straight, at least learn to kick your opponent without broadcasting it to the referee." Coach Reed decided that even though I was right-footed, my best position was outside left, where I might make up for my lack of speed by plausible ball handling. I can't remember if I ever scored a goal—I think not—or how long it took for me to move down the bench into the second-string contingent, but by the end of the season, I had decided that the soccer touch was a thing I had sacrificed by giving myself wholeheartedly to the primary American sports of basketball, touch football, and baseball, a rationalization that fit in neatly with my increasing devotion to American history, literature, and politics, the guiding impulse of my academic life in the years immediately ahead and one further step toward trying to make myself a full-blooded American, whatever remnant of nostalgia still governed my secret heart.

My first break from the grinding adjustment to Princeton that spring came with a quick trip to Washington for Easter. The mood at home on Fulton Street seemed brighter than it had been in many months. Brother Bob was doing very well in his first year at Western High: excellent grades, pledged to Hi-Y with his best friend Plato, and, rumor had it, dating the prettiest girl in their class. Brother Budge was closing in successfully on his commission as a Navy Ensign and his bachelor's degree in mechanical engineering. Our mother was more relaxed than I had ever seen her, I suppose partly because she had only one son out of three to care for at close quarters but most of all because she was now receiving uninterrupted mail from Belgium. The word she passed on from our father was that the rocket attack on Antwerp had finally ended, and though he didn't expect that "the family"—meaning my mother and

Bob—would be able to join him immediately, that prospect now appeared to be within sight.

The correspondence in my father's archive also reveals that at this time he was taking steps to see to it that the "loyal alien" members of his staff in Antwerp be awarded the Medal of Merit for their service to the United States from October, 1944 to March, 1945, during which period, according his official request, these faithful employees "refused to quit the city and calmly carried out their assigned duties in a most efficient manner, escaping death miraculously as bombs and rockets repeatedly fell around the Consular premises," while at the start of the same six-month period, after only a few days on duty, "three American members of the staff quit Antwerp, refusing to serve there while the bombing continued." My father's obituary records that he himself was awarded the Medal of Freedom by President Truman "for his contribution to keeping up the morale of the people of Antwerp, Belgium, while serving there as Consul General during the siege of that city"—an award his second son learned about only when he spotted the medal on his father's dresser in a Doylestown, Pennsylvania, retirement home during his father's eighty-ninth and final year.

The other Easter news that reached Fulton Street came by way of a phone call from Charlie and Anne House, now on Long Island awaiting their return to Greece: the German army had cleared out of Salonika the previous October, a few weeks after burning down the village on the mountain behind the Farm School, and in the six months since, though staff morale was low because wages were insufficient to pay for proper food and clothing, and though there was still political turmoil in the country, the School had managed to bind most of the wounds the occupying forces had caused before their departure, including some of the damage from the bomb they'd planted at the last minute in the main classroom building. The dormitory building was under renovation, as were the German barracks the occupiers had left behind as their crude memorial. The word I received about Lisa and her family was sparse and only a bit reassuring. Charlie House reported that as far as he knew they'd survived the Occupation and were healthy, but Lisa and her older sister had long since left the School when their parents moved to town in keeping with normal practice after their father had reached retirement age some years previously, so exactly where they might be now he couldn't say. The news that Lisa appeared to have survived the city's war years of famine and all the rest brought much relief, but her family's move to town from a relative oasis early in the Occupation seemed odd, since those were hardly normal times. And was she still in the city? How could one get in touch with the family, with her, these days? Charlie House didn't know.

A later break from routine that spring, one that brought everyone outside into the headiest of May evenings, was the celebration of V-E Day in New York City. I went in with Roger Saleeby and his roommate Vox Wilcox, neither a heavy drinker as you'd rate college drinkers in those days, but all of us high enough on beer and euphoria to be as uninhibited in noise and gesture as most others on the scene once we hit the crowds near Times Square and swarmed with them wherever the rhythm of jubilation took us, all strangers turned brothers and sisters in that long night of rejoicing. For a while the only hiatus in the drifting seaswell of celebrants occurred whenever we came across a soldier or sailor or Marine, these always given space to be honored by applause and sometimes the gift of a kiss from one or another new sister in the crowd. And as the evening cruised toward midnight, need or restlessness or casual opportunity began to fragment the crowd into small groups or linked couples that would break away heading in one direction or another toward a bar or restaurant, and sometimes those in uniform who had discovered a partner in a moment of shared elation could be seen easing their way toward any alcove or vestibule or dead end alleyway that might offer enough privacy for some quick loving. Those of us without partners or prospects finally gave in to fatigue, and on the long ride back to Princeton Junction and the Dinky, we hardly said a word to each other, I suppose a bit depressed in the afterglow of history that others of our generation had more cause to celebrate than underage or deferred college students—even if we still saw a long trek to Tokyo down the road.

It took another short break to visit Grandma Vossler on Alma Hill before I could enter with enough enthusiasm into the summer term. She saw right away that something was eating at me, because I was too absorbed in what was on my mind to give her welcome home dinner of cucumber salad and roast pork and pile of mashed potatoes the attention I used to.

"Is it a girl?" she asked to break into my silence.

"A girl?"

"I mean the thing that's making you sit there without a word picking at your plate like a fussy chicken."

"There's no girl," I said. "Not in Princeton. I'm just wondering if it's really right for me to be sitting on my fat bottom in that university while there's still a war to be fought."

"Your bottom isn't fat enough as far as I'm concerned. In truth you're so thin I doubt they'd take you in the service until you put on some more flesh. What do they feed you in that place anyway?"

"The food's all right. I just get too busy to eat sometimes. The point is, with the war finished in Europe, there's only Japan left. But that could be tough, and I'd like to get into that before it's over."

"Would you? Is that what they're teaching you in that university? Seventeen years old and a whole life ahead of you but you're in a hurry to end it before you've fairly begun to grow up."

"I just think I owe it to my country."

"Your country will be fine without you giving up your education before you've given it more than half a year. If you're needed, there will be time for you to join later, don't you worry."

I wasn't entirely convinced by Grandma Vossler's commitment to saving my education and my skin, but she planted enough question in my mind about what was sensible at that point to get me back to Princeton for the summer term, though I did so with the full expectation of joining the Navy at the end of my freshman year in October, well before the draft would take away my freedom of choice—and my chance to prove, by volunteering for active duty, that I'd finally become as much an American patriot as any other American my age. I breezed through July, fully concentrating on my work inside and outside the classroom, and then things began to shift out of focus, so that I ended the academic year having sadly drifted into the Gentleman 3 category, as I learned when I added up the final grades that were posted for all to see on bulletin boards in the grand rotunda of Alexander Hall—a cruel, invasive administrative procedure of those days that was eventually abandoned. To my surprise, I discovered that, along with the expected 1 in German, I did best in English, a beguiling diversion that I hadn't taken all that seriously, and in economics, which I'd hated, while doing worse in the more essential Foreign Service subjects of politics and history. But at the time I didn't dwell on this curious development. I had more pressing things on my mind.

On August 6 of that summer, news arrived on campus and spread quickly to all of us who happened to be in our dorms, a radio coming alive on every floor in every entry. President Truman was heard announcing that a single bomb equal to 20,000 tons of TNT and 2,000 times more powerful than the largest bomb yet used in the history of warfare had been dropped by an American Air Force plane on the Japanese city of Hiroshima, destroying much of it. A later bulletin from Guam confirmed that 4.1 miles of the city's 7 miles had been obliterated: "A large part of Hiroshima simply dissolved into a vast cloud of dust. . . . What had been a city going about its business on a sunny morning went up in a mountain of dust-filled smoke, black at the base and towering into a plume of white to 40,000 feet." The news was stunning, impossible to take in fully, cause for both jubilation and some anxiety, though at that moment in the course of the war, not a moral issue that any one I ran into thought open to debate. I went looking for Saleeby and Wilcox to see what they made of it.

Saleeby was pacing the room, shoulders hunched, all excitement. "I told you guys who spend your time worrying about Mayans in Mexico and Greeks in the Mediterranean. We're the greatest country on earth when it comes to science. And I bet you some of our people in this here neighborhood were involved in making that bomb. You'll see."

"Why do you always make fun of Mayans?" Wilcox said. "You don't know anything about Mayans and the kind of civilization they built while this country was still grazing ground for buffaloes and wild Indians."

"The point is," I said, "what's this bomb going to do about the war?"

"What's it going to do?" Saleeby said. "If we drop a slew more, it'll bury Japan in the sea."

"We've got an invasion force over there waiting," Wilcox said. "They can't go dropping a slew of bombs like that all over the place. Besides, what would be the point of invading a desert?"

"We've been dropping tons of bombs over there for weeks anyway," Saleeby said. "This will just hurry it up a bit."

"So how much do you figure this will to hurry it up?" I said.

"Who knows?" Saleeby said. "Should be over in six months. Nine months maybe. The Japs will fight from any hole they can climb into. They're all Kamikaze types."

"Well if it's only going to take six months," I said, "I'd better get a move on or the whole thing will be over before I get a decent piece of it."

Both of them looked at me as though I'd said something odd.

"You planning on joining up, is that it?" Saleeby said.

"I've been thinking about it. Before I become draft bait."

"Well I'm already draft bait," Saleeby said. "So I figure I'll just sit tight and see what happens."

"And I'm sitting tight too," Wilcox said. "Since things haven't turned bad enough yet for them to draft a diabetic."

The next morning I cut classes and took the train into Trenton to the naval recruiting station there. It turned out that I wasn't the only one in that region of New Jersey who had the bright idea of joining the war effort the day after the first atom bomb was dropped on Japan, but I eventually made my way down the line of those waiting to be interviewed by the recruiting officer, who seemed completely unimpressed by my being a college student explaining my motivation and was much more interested in what machinery and tools I'd used working on a farm. I was finally checked out by a medical officer, who suggested I was on the light side for my height (5 foot 11 1/2 inches, 128 pounds) and therefore ought to put some weight on in the days ahead, but he had no other comment on what he apparently considered a barely satisfactory body for an able-bodied apprentice seaman, as my rank would be designated once I was called to active duty. Neither the recruiting officer nor the medical officer had a clue as to when that might be. I returned to Princeton to wait, very pleased with myself for what I'd done and hardly in the right mood to concentrate on school work more than was necessary to get by respectably in view of my going off to war any day now, finally as American in my sense of myself as I possibly could be.

The day after this trip to Trenton, Russia declared war on Japan, and the day after that a second, even more powerful atom bomb was dropped on Nagasaki, and the day after that a report went out that the Japanese were ready to accept the Potsdam Conference terms of surrender on condition that the Emperor retain his sovereignty, if lose his status as a living god. As I continued to bide my time, I tuned in to the radio whenever there was a free moment, read as best I could, started packing up my books and notebooks from the previous semester. The war went on, with regular bombings, kamikaze responses, further talk about the desperate fighting that might be needed before the bitter end. Then, on August 14, one week after the first bomb was dropped and five days after the second, Japan surrendered unconditionally. On V-J Day, with class exercises suspended, I went into New York City again with Saleeby and Wilcox and a few others, but I remember nothing in particular about that occasion beyond the general uninhibited exuberance and my intense disappointment at not yet being in uniform. The summer term ended on October 20, and on November 3, just under two months after I'd signed up in the Naval Reserve, I reported for duty at Camp Perry, Virginia.

My final days in Princeton were careless. Part of me felt liberated by my imminent crossing into a new life and another part of me felt like an exiled archer who'd missed his target, as a Greek poet once put it. During my last week in the dining halls, distracted by rowdy noise and movement, I slipped on the stairs going down to the lower level while balancing a tray piled high with dirty plates and saucers, lost the dishes and tray down the stairs in one grand sweeping release, a spectacular farewell to that chore which resounded through the corridors as though a small plane had crashed into the dining hall. A cheer rose the way it might for a marathon victor entering the stadium. Ten months later, in the final distribution of mail before my discharge aboard the carrier Tarawa off the California coast, I received a bill for $145 from the Princeton Boarding Department "for damage to University property from the dining hall kitchen, to be paid in full before your re-entry to the university can be entertained." I watched the bill float down from the flight deck into the Pacific Ocean as though an errant palm leaf caught in a puff of wind.

The barracks I was assigned to in Camp Perry, formerly a training base for naval engineers called Seabees, had the feel not so much of a temporary construction that was gradually wearing itself out as of a building that had never been finished in the first place: the floor, walls, and roof did not appear to have been made to fit into each other because there were gaps everywhere that were clearly not caused by the ravages of time but by failed measurements and missed connections. When we first settled into the barracks, the air inside was sharply clean because of the access these pervasive slivers of light provided to the world of nature outside, but as the season drifted toward late November, the need for heat from the two belly stoves at either end of the room, fed by buckets of kerosene, soon filled the place with a dense mephitic smell that even a rich selection of body odors had trouble penetrating. There were times when you found yourself lying in your bunk in a fairly contorted position in order to get your nose up against one of those slits of light for a long taste of fresh air, that is, relatively long since the contrast between the cold outside and the heat inside had a crippling effect not only on your olfactory responses but eventually on your capacity to breathe. And the bunks were too narrow, the mattress too lumpish, the mattress cover—the so-called fart sack—too crinkling to permit long-term contortion or much more freedom than the full-length stretch imposed by the imaginary collar around your neck and the board under your back. I came across a letter in my father's archive addressed to my mother and dated November 29, 1945, in which he says, with reference to his middle son in boot camp: "This is the bed he made for himself, and will probably be the making of him." Ah, dear departed father, if you had only known how close that bed came to unmaking your son through despair at the start of his naval career, you would have been less sanguine about what makes and unmakes a seventeen-year-old apprentice seaman almost six feet tall weighing 128 pounds, apparently bearing some indelible stigmata of a college freshman but still passionate about open space.

It was both luck and my proficiency in manual of arms drills, thanks to my season in the Western High cadet corps, that eventually saved my underweight and aching body from being undone by some of the menial chores and longer marches and even rifle range exercises that were the essential training in boot camp. Though the petty officer in charge of our company, like most regular navy types, was ready with much irony and little sympathy for any recruit who'd actually been to college, he had a position to fill that called for a degree of literacy: company mailman. And fortune came my way when the Lieutenant JG in charge of our petty officer spotted me one day helping another recruit work his way through the manual of arms and suggested I be assigned to help other recruits who still found moving a rifle around sharply in that stiff, angular way some kind of mystery. His suggestion stuck in the petty officer's craw. Making recruits master the manual of arms was his territory, and I suppose to keep me in my place and to solve his mailman problem at the same time, this suddenly became my major assignment to the end of my boot camp days. And to show me that I was not to take this new assignment lightly, he brought out *The Bluejackets' Manual* and read me a paragraph under the heading WORDS OF ADVICE FOR APPRENTICE SEAMEN:

> You may be homesick and lonesome for a while. We all were. You are starting a new life, with new surroundings and new friends. Grin and bear it as we all did. No man ever succeeded by hanging on to his mother's apron strings all his life. But right here, do this: Write home often and ask them to write to you often. A letter from home will buck you up more than anything else.

What neither the petty officer nor *The Bluejackets' Manual* knew how to tell you was that serving as mailman in boot camp could sometimes break your heart or stab your conscience. It wasn't only the pain, well-documented in one or another war movie, of facing the sadness, or frustration, or even anger of those who waited and waited for a letter that never came or those who received from your hand a Dear John letter that seemed to end any prospect of happiness in their new life before it had fairly begun. And it wasn't only the arduous struggle to work your way through illiteracy and sandlot English and bad spelling—your own included—while helping someone to write that first or second or third unanswered letter home. It was most of all what letters of that kind said about the life left behind on the other side of the tall fence that sur-rounded our camp and how increasingly tenuous our link to it was becoming. For example:

Dear Mom,
I am writing you with the help of our mailman to tell you again that I haven't stolen a thing since arriving in this terrble place I don't know how may days now gone by. You may not believe what I am telling you, you always had trouble believ-ing me, but our mailman can testify to the truth of it. And he will verify that we had to give up all our civilian clothes and most of our possession on coming here and we haven't yet had liberty or shore leave to go into town to buy anything even if we had money for it. So there is nothing in here worth stealing anyway. I just wanted you to know that I am keeping my promise to you and to the judge who sent me here instead of reform school and that it wasn't a mistake but a new lease on life.

A lot of love.,
Jerome

And another I remember fairly well:

Dearest Nancy,
Sweetheart. I have been in this barracks three weeks now and there hasn't been a moment lying in my bunk when I haven't thought of you. And that hasn't always been easy with the smell in here and the swabjockey next to me snoring most of the time and making other noises. Anyway, I told you I would be faithful to you come hell or high water and that is what I have been all these days. I haven't had a thought for anybody

else, honestly, and when I say anybody else, you know who I mean. So I have kept up my end of our personal engagement and I know you will have too. That's so, isn't it? Please don't wait any longer to write and tell me that it's so.

Your Norbert

It soon became clear to me that the mailman in a boot camp company not only had an easy work schedule given his need to traipse over to the base post office to deposit and pick up mail twice a day more or less at times of his own choosing, but his role as ghost writer and confidant earned him a standing with many that was only a degree below that of the company chaplain. The disadvantage, along with the ripening of so much intimately revealed pain, turned out to be some of the dubious companions that this kind of celebrity brought with it, not so much those who too freely unburdened themselves to you as those who subtly came on to you for some benefit your position might bring them, whether as a witness to their honesty or a pawn to their dishonesty, for example, the letters I was cajoled into writing for those trying to avoid outstanding fines or unpaid alimony on the grounds that they were now legitimately beyond the reach of the law because they were honorably serving their country.

✦ ✦ ✦

With the end of boot camp and my promotion from Apprentice Seaman to Seaman Second Class came a ten-day leave before I was to report to Norfolk, Virginia, and my assignment to the fleet. I spent that leave in Washington, even though the house on Fulton Street was no longer ours. Budge was now a commissioned officer on a fast attack destroyer, and my mother and younger brother Bob, after moving to Antwerp during the summer, were now on their way to Athens, where my father had just been assigned to the American Mission for Observing the Greek Elections. At that moment he was in Washington for consultation and had rented an efficiency apartment on Connecticut Avenue to accommodate the two of us in the family temporarily in town.

It was not an ideal arrangement for a senior Foreign Sevice officer still recuperating from months under the threat of rocket bombs and a liberated swabjockey just released from a fenced-in camp and eager to roam freely in his new Navy blues and to taste the world of possibilities in his old neighborhood. During those days—and for some years thereafter—my father did not rest easily when his eyes were closed either at night or during the day. However quietly I might cross his room to the bathroom—he slept in the apartment's single bedroom, I on the living-room couch—the poor man would wake up startled and rise up in bed to stare at me as though I was facing him suddenly with a submachine gun.

I truly felt sorry for him at those moments, but at the same time, during waking hours he seemed unable to take in the fact that I was now eighteen years old and used to being on my own, so that in those close quarters he got on my nerves probably not much less than I got on his. He was obviously no longer used to having another body around in such proximity, because my mode of life clearly disturbed him at moments, whether it was my way of letting my toilet articles have their own casual space in relief from the discipline of storing everything I owned neatly for possible inspection, or whether it was the irregular hours I kept in my pursuit of some of the pleasures in the company of others—the few Back Booth Boys still around—that three dry months in a boot camp barracks had prohibited.

But these were not things I knew how to justify to my father, nor could I complain openly about his time-consuming punctiliousness after taking over the bathroom for his morning ablutions, with his toilet articles and unguents laid out neatly around the sink and on the top of the toilet bowl for a series of rituals that included, after a long shower, winding a broad waist band around his middle-aged spread and standing in front of the mirror to apply a hair net to his thinning hair once he'd washed it a second time in the sink with special soaps and treated it with ointments, then meticulously, surgeon-like, unwrapping, setting up, wiping, dipping, delicately employing, and finally cleaning and wrapping up all his shaving and manicure paraphernalia. Our ten days together, instead of offering a chance to find out what we might come to respect and maybe even like in each other, ended up adding to the tension and distance that had grown out of my drink-at-home evening with him on Fulton Street those many months ago.

Yet there were a few moments when we were actually able to cross the great divide that had come between us, though only indirectly, by way of two persistent gestures on his part—I can't think of a better term—that stayed with my father almost to his dying days. One of these was to show certain documents and letters that he'd been working on with some passion to whichever son happened to be on hand at the moment—not to get advice, since the material came forth after it had been made public by him one way or another, nor for extended discussion, since there rarely appeared to be need for that, but to demonstrate his commitment to some cause that roused his sense of justice, his patriotism, or his image of righteous behavior. By the time he became Minister to Syria in 1948, the documentation had begun to focus almost exclusively on the Arab-Israeli conflict, a resource for causes that became his obsessive preoccupation in the decades following. But in 1946, his soul was still more or less at peace, and his major concern remained honoring heroes of the war just ended. One evening toward the end of my ten-day leave he laid a document on my bed without comment, a draft he had written of an address to be given by a colonel on his staff at a memorial service for the late President Franklin Delano Roosevelt. It ended as follows:

> As truly as the soldier whose Commander in Chief he was, he gave his life in the service of his country. Let us not be downcast that a Divine Providence has seen fit to take him from us on the very threshold of victory; rather let us rejoice that we have been privileged to have the example of his life to point the way as we here dedicate ourselves anew to the fulfillment of the unfinished work for which he gave the last full measure of devotion.

I was pretty sure at the time that his placing the document on my couch-bed was meant to be his way of telling me that I should, in the image of Abe Lincoln, dedicate myself with greater devotion to the unfinished work ahead, presumably by serving the still threatened nation at sea in peacetime, and with less devotion from now on to the selfish pleasures that seemed to be my preoccupation. But of course he didn't say as much when I handed the document back to him for his archive the next day, and all I could bring myself to say was that I too thought Franklin Delano Roosevelt was a truly great man. I now suspect that his motive was, at least as much as anything else, to show me that writing a speech was important to him and might be something that I, as a college student with a year of schooling behind me, could learn to honor in him and maybe in myself as I continued my education. The pity was that neither he nor I could tell the other directly what there really was in us to say.

The second persistent if silent gesture on my father's part to show that he cared about his family, and sometimes others outside his family, was his "treatment" for colds and upper respiratory infections. He had inherited the "treatment" from a practitioner he'd befriended in Montreal, Canada, during his years there, a retired doctor who had passed on the formula, and the faith that went with it, to my father and a few other disciples to carry forward after his death. The "treatment" consisted of balancing vulnerable pressure points along the neck and spine so as to bring the body into an equilibrium that challenged the common cold and its related symptoms. The patient—male, female, young, old—would lie on his or her stomach, arms to the side, and my father, sitting on the bed or couch beside the patient, would test with his finger for a "sore spot" along the patient's neck and spine, then focus on a spot along the spine directly opposite the sore one and press that one with a forefinger or thumb for as long as five minutes before moving on to a spot opposite the next "sore spot" the patient identified, all the way down to the coccyx. The "treatment" would normally last for forty-five minutes to an hour, during which time my father might read a magazine held in his free hand, but the patient had no choice but to think deep or less-than-deep thoughts in silence, face confronting the void on one side of the pillow.

I found the procedure immensely boring and not much help for a cold or anything else, though I never had the courage to tell my father so during these sessions. Others—especially middle-aged ladies—found the procedure a clearly discernible relief for headache, earache, congestion in head or chest, pain in the extremities, who knows what else, and their expressions of gratitude, their faith in my father's faith, was obviously a source of immense comfort to him. My unexpressed boredom and doubt, and that of my younger brother, led both of us to develop strategies for avoiding the signs of a cold until the symptoms became too obvious to hide, and as luck would have it, I came down with a visible cold toward the end of my ten-day leave after boot camp that winter. This cost me a "treatment" whenever my father could catch me for the purpose, until I finally stuffed my nostrils full of Vicks to stem the flow and told my father I was due back in Norfolk a day before that was really the case. What eased my conscience was a sense I got that he himself could do with some relief from further treatments for a patient so obviously capricious in his faith and given to sloppy personal habits. But at our parting, he undercut that sense by measurably softening.

"You know, you can give yourself a treatment at your leisure as far down as your hand can reach," he said as I hauled my duffel bag to the door. "It's better than nothing at all".

"Right," I said. "I'll work on that."

"But one way or another, you take care of yourself."

"Right," I said.

"I mean in general."

Then he smiled almost shyly and put out his hand for the usual quick handshake of our grown-up greeting and parting.

I spent the last day of my leave staying over with a fraternity brother who was busy that evening but gave me a key to his front door. In keeping with the instructions in *The Bluejackets' Manual,* I always wore dress blues while in the open air, but when I drifted over to Western High School I found that even so I couldn't comfortably saunter around the corridors with the assured air of a returning veteran now that the war had ended six months previously and my original classmates had graduated three months before that. I ran into old Mr. Moore, the baseball coach I'd served as team manager, and though he didn't seem entirely sure who I was at first, he ended up saying that he wished me well with my future, whatever that might turn out to be. I finally learned that Mary

Ann was studying design in a school somewhere in neighboring Maryland. One of her younger sorority sisters said she was either engaged or about to be engaged, but she wasn't sure to whom.

I walked around the old Georgetown streets in the Dumbarton Oaks area until school was out, then went back to hang out at the sandwich place across the street from Western on the chance that I might run into Cindy Doyle. Sure enough, she showed up eventually with a girlfriend I didn't recognize. She was very friendly, really happy to see me she said, honestly, and she'd been wondering a lot about what had happened to me all these months she hadn't heard from me, but when I asked her if she might want to join me for a beer at Sam Tehan's a bit later on, she said she'd love to but unfortunately she had a date already. I could tell from the look on her girlfriend's face that this was news to her, and there was something in Cindy's look that made me suspect my uniform some-how intimidated her or maybe just the hunger in my eye. So I ended up spending the evening at Sam's on my own.

Sam, cheerful as ever, came over to stand above me when I'd settled into a booth.

"I hope you don't expect me to show a draft card," I joked. "I turned eighteen some days ago."

"What you mean? You turned eighteen three years ago. When did you first start coming in here?"

"Well, let's say two years ago."

"O.K. So now you're twenty, right? All I know is you always had a draft card."

"I can't argue with that. At least until they took it away from me."

"Well, just think. You may not need one ever again. So now that you're in the service, you get a beer on the house, O. K.? You get one when you go in and two when you come back."

"I appreciate that. I guess it's mostly people coming back you run into these days, right?"

"Some go away, some come back. It's those in between who break your heart."

"I know what you mean. At least we can count on all the old Back Booth Boys making it back now that the war's over."

"I'll drink to that. Even if I never drink on duty. What the hell." And he sat down opposite me for a while.

I decided to take a long route getting back to my fraternity brother's house, so I went along M Street for a ways, then up though lower Georgetown and along R Street to Wisconsin and on up to Fulton Street, past our house and over to the Alban Towers Drug Store and the sandlot near there, then through the back streets of my old neighborhood to the unfamiliar place I was spending the night. It wasn't so much where I went but where I decided not to go that told me I had already moved on elsewhere—the stadium behind Western High, Mary Ann's house farther up, the vacant lot where I'd started out my fraternity Hell Night—and not only moved on but in a way that made it unlikely I could return to that city and recapture the conviction that it was the center of my life, my American life. I realized that maybe there was something positive about that, about moving on, but I can't say that it made me feel very good that evening or for some time to come.

* * *

My new home, the Essex class aircraft carrier Tarawa, CV 40, had been commissioned in December, 1945, and was docked in Norfolk awaiting its shakedown cruise when I arrived at the pier with my duffel bag to join its crew of some 2,500 officers and men. Standing on the pier, you could look up at that monster of a ship and believe, in a moment of wild imaginative flight, that it was some kind of giant cruise ship lying there with its gangway ready to gather up hundreds of tourists for an expensive voyage to the Caribbean or some other vacation archipelago. The one thing that quickly dispelled this fantasy was the character of the hull, a vast spread of blue-gray steel that stretched upward from the pier for what looked like five or six stories, with hardly a porthole to break into the stark image of that metal wall and maybe give you a sense that something human might be living behind it.

There was much evidence of things going on once your gaze reached the hanger deck, all kinds of projecting platforms with guns or machinery on them, here and there an open panel of space where you could see planes neatly parked, and on the flight deck above that, a pyramid of gun turrets and lookout openings forming the conning tower that rose up from that deck another four or five stories. But climbing up the gangway step after step against that blank hull, that sheer cliff of steel, gave you an ominous feeling even before you had any reason to know why it should. This knowledge came soon enough, an intimate knowledge not only of the confining inside of the windowless metal wall that would serve as your living quarters for the next six months but also what could hardly have been anticipated during your first encounter: familiarity with yard upon rising yard of its pampered outer skin.

My naval career aboard the flattop Tarawa actually began with the prospect of much time in the open air. I was assigned to a gunnery division handling one of the five-inch inch guns, and my primary duty while in port and before and after training exercises at sea consisted of scrubbing the outside of the gun turret and those portions of the inside that lent themselves to cleaning at a basic level. It was easy duty on the whole, and whenever you worked on the outside you had clean air, a partial view of the port facilities, and once in a long while, a panorama of the open sea. The physical strain was slight. Even when you had to work with the fatigue that came from too much bar-hopping on liberty or too much boredom passing your scrub rag back and forth over a section of bulkhead that was already cleaner than your own face, you could learn to keep the rag moving at a plausible pace while actually dozing on your feet, and eventually, you could develop the sixth sense that signaled an increasingly seaworthy Seaman Second Class: the capacity for hearing the approach of an officer in good time to respond while your somnolent mind was in another country.

During the third week on board, after much scrubbing of my small corner of the world and several general quarter drills during which my contribution to the action was passing heavy five-inch shells to the seaman next in line with all the concentration and muscle I could summon so as not to drop the thing and thereby maybe send the flattop named Tarawa to kingdom come, I began to wonder if I might not find a better way to serve both myself and my country. There was hardly room on board that flattop for a Seaman Second Class to shape his fate by petition or plea, but there was nothing to prevent him from being keenly available for any opportunity to change his station. I knew there wasn't much chance at my rank of moving up from shellman to loader or anything more exciting in gunnery, but given the size and complexity of that ship, I was convinced that there might be some place other than a gun turret where I could spend my working hours more comfortably and profitably. And an opportunity came my way sooner than I could have hoped, though it was not accompanied by a warning endemic to the U.S. Navy of those days: be wary of volunteering for anything, especially if you are a reserve seaman barred from further schooling and advancement in rank by virtue of the war's end.

What I took to be a chance to move up arrived at a morning muster, while we were heading back to Norfolk from another short run for the purpose of giving the fly boys some time in the air. The boatswain in charge of a maintenance crew in our division announced that he had been asked to provide two seamen volunteers to serve as side boys when we came into the port, and he would be looking to sign up anybody who was not striking for a rate and therefore in training for some other duty. I vaguely remembered mention of side boys in *The Bluejackets' Manuel,* and I liked what I remembered, so I rushed to find my copy and check it out: "In peacetime side boys are non-rated men stationed within call of the Officer of the Deck from 0800 to sunset, except at meal times and during general drills. Their duty is immediately to fall in at the gangway, in the number designated, when it is to be tended, as it usually is for any officer coming aboard or leaving in uniform. Seamen, second class, are as a rule detailed as side boys. The uniform is clean undress blues, with neckerchiefs."

That was clearly the kind of duty I had in mind. I took off to track down the boatswain before too many other volunteers got there ahead of me. I found him on the hanger deck in a forward paint locker kneeling beside a bucket—a short man, slim, all muscle, a James Cagney type, though with short-cropped blond hair.

"O. K., mate," I said, out of breath. "I'm your man for side boy duty."

"You may be my man and you may not be my man," the boatswain said, glancing up at me. "But one thing you're not is my mate."

"You probably don't remember me, but I'm in your gunnery…"

"I know where you are. But I also know we haven't served at sea on the same ship in the same war, so you don't call me mate. You got that?"

"Aye aye, sir."

"And don't sir me either. You know what a boatswain is?"

"Aye aye."

"Already an old salt, right? Anyway. What is it you want from me?"

I told him I didn't want anything, I was just volunteering to be one of the side boys he was looking for. That seemed to please him. He took down my name and told me to report back to him as soon as we'd docked at the pier.

"Undress blues and neckerchief?" I said.

The boatswain stared at me. "Is this some kind of joke? You come as you are, for Christ sake."

It was some kind of joke, but the joke was on me. And on *The Bluejackets' Manual*. When I reported back to him in my dungarees, I assumed it was for further instruction before he sent me back to dress in the designated blues and kerchief, but the only instruction he gave me and another seaman waiting there—a guy named Beaumont, if possible skinnier even than I was and with a serious coordination problem—had to do with what he called a boatswain's chair. This consisted of a plank eight to ten inches wide and maybe ten feet long resting at either end on a two-by-four crossbar supporting a loop of thick rope that in turn anchored a huge length of the same kind of rope coiled up at both ends of the plank. I didn't have to study it long to figure out what it was for and to despise the sight of it.

"This here is your boatswain chair," the boatswain said. "I'll help you set it up over the side and then you're on your own. Though I'll be watching from above to make sure you two coordinate your descent, as the good book says. I don't wanna find either of you dangling out there at the end of the safety rope, cause hauling you all the way back up gets me really tired and really nervous. Getting yourselves back on board is your business. And that goes for any paint buckets you leave hanging over the side. Am I understood?"

So his two new side boys—was he ignorant of the term's true mean-

ing, I asked myself, or deliberately perverse, or simply evil by nature?—
hauled their boatswain's chair to the railing and then their paint buckets
and under the boatswain's sharp instructions and a bit of help got the
chair over the side and secured half a body length below the hanger deck.
Beaumont and I stood there gazing down at it. Despite my acrophobia,
a condition and even a term I didn't dare spell out to the boatswain, I
decided I had no choice but to go over the side. I learned later that a
friend of mine in Middle Dod, who joined the Navy about the same
time I did and who eventually ended up one of the most celebrated
members of my class, found on leaving boot camp that he had a fundamental problem following orders—not specific orders, any orders—and
when he explained to his division officer that his problem was never personal but just a general negative reaction that inescapably entered his
brain whenever he was ordered to do something, a kind of orderopho-
bia I guess, he was sent to the chaplain for consultation and soon after
that was granted a psychological discharge so that he could return to
Princeton for his sophomore year. Whether this was strategy or fact or
both, it did not occur to me at the time as a way of coping with the
boatswain, nor to Beaumont, so over the side we went, and that is where
we stayed while our fellow swabjockeys, sharply saluting at the head of
the gangway, went on liberty by way of the pier yards below us to whatever pleasure they could find in Norfolk, Virginia.

It was not so much acrophobia and the great tilting trip down and up
that ship's massive hull in a boatswain's chair as it was being limited to
only partial liberty or no liberty at all while in port that led me to con-
ceive of a new course of action to counter what seemed unjust punishment for my naïve ambition as a volunteer. What I came up with was
attempting to impress my division officer with the thought that I was
stronger in mind than in body and might therefore qualify for some
more appropriate and less strenuous duty than that of a so-called side
boy. Lieutenant Bragg was a relatively soft-spoken southerner who
seemed to carry no malice—unlike the Tarawa's captain, who was generally regarded as a Queeg-like tyrant of limited experience at sea yet
favoring the kind of excessive peacetime discipline that, so the scuttlebutt had it, alarmed even some of his war-tested line officers. Among

those on board, Lieutenant Bragg remained one of the few I caught exploring a book in the ship's library apparently for pleasure, and whether he was Regular Navy or not, I assumed he didn't harbor the usual prejudice against recruits with some college background and a reading knowledge of English. I decided anyway to exploit that possibility.

I'd brought two books on board for casual reading, one called *Foundations of National Power* hot off the press as I left Princeton and passed on to me as a parting gift by my instructor in the American politics course, and the other a history of American diplomacy, the title of which I forget, as I have most everything else in the book. The former, which I now took to the library with me whenever I had free time for a visit, was a heavy, double-columned book of 750 pages of essays by some 120 hands, not what you'd call easy reading for a swabjockey between bouts of hull and bulkhead painting but a useful tool for my purpose of the moment, which was to recommend it to Lieutenant Bragg when I next ran into him in the library. That took close to a week of reading, skimming, and underlining, as I made my way through essays on everything from the Afro-Asian realm of rival imperialisms to the foundations of peace and the new world order, before the good Lieutenant came into the library to catch the bait.

"What you reading there, boy?" Lieutenant Bragg, asked with what I took to be an amiable smile.

"Nothing much, sir. Just some essays."

"What kind of essays would that be?"

"Well, they sort of go all over the place. Though a few of them seem to be questioning the basic premises of our national policy. Naval and otherwise."

"Such as?"

"Well, let's see. Our assumption of invulnerability, for example. And our assumption of a relatively liberal democratic order backing us up."

"Is that right? Let me see that book, if you don't mind."

I handed it up to him from where I was sitting. I decided I'd better get to my feet since I was speaking to an officer. He leafed through it to the table of contents and was studying that when I told him to feel free to take the book with him.

"I'd be honored," I said. "There are a couple of things I've got marked there that you might find really interesting. Some of the fundamental questions."

He handed the book back to me. He was studying me now, a bit too closely. I tried to look casual, leafing through the thing again to find an underlined passage I might read to him.

"Right you are," he said. "I'll let you think a bit longer about those fundamental questions, O. K.? You keep up the good work. What's your name?"

"Keeley," I said. "And I'd like to keep up the good work. I honestly would. But it's not easy when you have to hang over the side painting the ship during the times you might be free to do some serious reading."

"Yea, well don't think you're alone, my friend. We all have trouble finding time for serious reading. And it's only going to get worse when we head south on our shakedown cruise."

"Well, at least once we're cruising south I won't have to worry about my acrophobia. And about my mate Beaumont with his coordination problem slipping off the boatswain's chair to smash himself flat on the pier."

"Just so. You won't have to worry about it and we won't have to worry about it either. What we do about your acrophobia and your mate's problem in the long run is a touch more complicated, but I'll keep it in mind."

And, strangely, he did. The following week he called me out of morning muster to tell me that I was being transferred to the Plotting Room under the Fire Control Division, which would keep me well below decks and in the heart of the ship, so that heights would no longer be any cause for discomfort and the work with fire control equipment maybe more challenging mentally. He told me all this in a slow drawl with an absolutely straight face, so that I couldn't be sure if he thought he was doing me an honest favor or simply ridding his division of an oddball who read possibly subversive literature—or maybe both. Later that morning I learned that Beaumont had been transferred topside to another section of the gunnery division, which at least relieved him of the perilous boatswain's chair. And later that morning I also learned that fire control had nothing to do with putting out fires but a lot to do with controlling the firing of guns, even if my personal responsibility in the Plotting Room came down to scrubbing the sides of Mark 1 computers and providing coffee for the commissioned and non-commissioned personnel who knew how to plot what all that complex machinery down there was supposed to plot but apparently couldn't function properly without yet another cup of joe from my hand.

I don't remember how many weeks we were out at sea on our shakedown cruise because, without the sun and stars, one day drifted seamlessly into another in the Plotting Room, and there was no way of knowing where we were actually cruising during that period because you got a glimpse of sea water and our passing through it only in those rare moments when some chore you'd been assigned brought you briefly in range of an opening on the hanger deck—though no tarrying allowed on that deck to cleanse your lungs with the wash of healthy breezes and odors of the sea. It wasn't until we finally dropped anchor in Guantanamo Bay, Cuba—Gitmo Bay to sailors—that I had a chance to go topside long enough to taste a bit of salty air.

Yet the Plotting Room wasn't the only life on board during our shakedown cruise. Once you were back in your bunk, that tight but delicious stretch of private space, there was time for reading on your own and time for casual talk with others. Since I was no longer much interested in the foundations of national power, my reading turned to fiction— Hemingway, Fitzgerald, Faulkner, Steinbeck—whatever I could find in the cheap G. I. editions of those days, or the Viking portable editions that you could carry around easily and that chose your reading for you. There was another reader in my row of bunks, a spunky character named O'Dell, stocky, curly-headed, pugnacious if you crossed him but otherwise full of trust. I took to him because he wasn't embarrassed to talk about his reading, which was mostly detective stories, and even less embarrassed to ask about mine. But what he liked most, almost childlike, was sitting at the far end of my bunk to hear me tell stories about where I'd been and what I'd been up to, because he claimed he'd never been anywhere beyond his crummy neighborhood in Worcester,

Massachusetts, until he was sent south to climb aboard this camouflaged prison ship. When I finally felt I was running out of things to tell him and said so, O'Dell insisted that I go on, so I began to make up stories that took me places I'd never been with characters I'd never known. I finally admitted that only half of what I'd been telling him was real, maybe less than half.

"I don't care," he said. "What difference does it make?"

"Well, it isn't honest. I mean it's been mostly fiction for a while."

"What's wrong with fiction? As long as it seems real."

"But you're forcing me to make things up."

"Well you don't seem to mind that much."

He was right. I'd begun to find what I was making up more fun than reliving what I already knew, but at the same time, I couldn't get over the idea that putting myself in those stories was somehow dishonest. So I told O'Dell I would go on telling him stories every now and then, but he wasn't to think they were about me, and that is when I first discovered how difficult it was to make fiction out of whole cloth and make it seem real.

Liberty in Gitmo Bay turned out to mean mostly long evenings in a vast shed with open sides that served as a kind of beer hall. The challenge was how much beer you could get down and still stay sober enough to climb the gangway and salute the Officer of the Deck without falling forward on your face or backward into the swabby behind you, both cause for trouble. The one organized trip by bus into Santiago de Cuba to the west made for more substantial gratification if a less manageable challenge: finding a plausible companion for your hunger. That finally came my way during the late hours in one of the back rooms of a back-street bar catering to American sailors, when what had begun awkwardly with Jeanie Grant and had progressed carefully with Cindy Doyle was completed repeatedly with the skilled help of a shapely black woman some ten years my senior who was professional enough to make the sensual pleasure she provided not only me but herself seem convincingly real. And if the required visit to the local pro station under shore patrol guidance—all salves, infusions, and toilet paper wrappings—added a coda of indignity to this excursion, it was not as depressing in memory's

aftermath as the road to Santiago and back, heavy with images of poverty and sickliness and desolation under the first Batista dictatorship the
like of which no American of my generation on that bus had seen, a
landscape that made returning to our home base in Norfolk appear a
God-given return to health and benevolence.

My career in the U. S. Navy took a turn for the worse when the
Tarawa began to cruise in the waters outside Norfolk waiting for its passage through the Panama Canal to join the Pacific Fleet. In my first days
back from Gitmo Bay I learned that both my brother Ensign Hugh
Keeley and my friend Ensign Bruce Lansdale of Camp Cory days had
managed to get the Navy to assign them to Athens, Greece, as part of
the American team sent there to observe the upcoming Greek elections,
and my brother Bob, now living with my parents in Athens, had been
hired by the team as an interpreter. Greece rediscovered, reunion with
family and friends, escape from the Plotting Room and the traffic in
pots of joe—what more was needed to make this post-war American
enterprise in what was called the cradle of democracy seem a much
grander prospect, surely a more essential prospect, than a tour in the
Pacific on what O'Dell liked to call Captain Bligh's chickenshit flattop?
My imagination traveled gloriously beyond reason, but when I finally
approached the lieutenant in charge of the Fire Control Division and
suggested to him that, with his intervention and support based on what
I could legitimately claim to be an intimate knowledge of Greece and the
Mediterranean, I might be able to offer my country useful service as an
interpreter or clerk on an American team headed for Greece to observe
the elections there, he stared at me as though, now totally out of my
mind, I had suddenly tossed a five-inch shell into his lap. His voice low,
almost toneless, he advised me to see the chaplain as soon as possible. I
finally decided that the chaplain, known to be sympathetic but vague
about worldly concerns, was hardly likely to understand this pressing
interest of mine in my country's new obligations overseas.

I don't know whether it was the failed interview with the Lieutenant
or just the luck of the draw that brought about the new duty I was
assigned to the following day, what the Chief in the Plotting Room told
me, with a touch of irony but no other obvious signs of malevolence,

was my promotion to Captain of the Officers' Head. The duty consisted of my using a good portion of my mornings cleaning the shower and toilet belonging to one of the junior officers in the Division who worked somewhere topside and whose name was to be no concern of mine, according to the Chief, but to whom I ought to feel grateful since this was the least demanding, most independent duty a swabjockey of my rank could expect to take on in peacetime. And there was some truth in what he had to say: you worked entirely on your own in a cool place, with no great physical strain involved compared to handling heavy ammunition or a boatswain's chair, and nobody to demand a cup of joe or an errand the minute you were settled into your cleaning routine. The only trouble: the work was disgusting.

I never did find out the officer's name, but he was a slob. When he took a shower, he left towels all over the place, except where he must have walked around with muddy, tar-spattered feet. The sink was covered with cream and ointment stains sprouting hair stubble. And the toilet—the toilet was so filthy, so casually attended, that it led to my downfall. After I'd swished around my swab in there, I couldn't bring myself to wring it out with my hands the way you were supposed to whenever you swished a swab, but instead I dragged it over to the shower stall, turned on the shower to drench it through and through, then stomped on it to get it fairly clean again for another go at the bowl. During the second swabbing, while I was in the shower stall stomping on the swab, Lieutenant JG Whateverhisname came to the toilet door without any warning.

"All right, sailor, just come out here and stand at attention. What the hell to do you think you're doing?"

"Nothing, sir. Just cleaning out this swab."

"Is that right? And what navy taught you to clean a swab by walking on it?"

"No navy, sir. My own imagination."

"Is that right? Well let me help your imagination find another way, the way we do it in the United States Navy. You pick up that swab and wring it out with your hands. You hear me? On the double."

I was tempted to say that it would sure help my imagination a whole lot if he would show me exactly how it was done, but I just picked up the swab and tried to pretend that the miserable sopping thing hadn't been through the filthiest assignment it was likely to come across in the United States Navy. That in any case proved to be an exaggeration, as I had to admit to myself the following day, when another swab and I, along with another sailor I barely knew, were assigned to new duty: taking care of the seamen's head on the deck outside our sleeping quarters, where there were eight toilets in a row, two of which did not function most of the time. The sailor was named Carnevalle, out of Little Italy, NYC, chubby graduate of an advanced course in meta-lingual obscenity that I sometimes had trouble fathoming. What his crime had been that now led to his joining me in these new responsibilities he chose not to reveal.

Our assignment was keeping the seamen's head spotless by mid-morning and again by mid-afternoon, ready for a sudden inspection of the kind our obsessed Captain liked to call at any hour of day or night. There was no chance of arguing with the inspection team that one or another toilet didn't work. You had to have all of them spotless, the seats and fixtures shining, the full length of the floor swabbed whatever its condition, which was normally such as would surely have turned the stomach even of an officer as sloppy as the pompous Lieutenant JG Whateverhisname. And time was not always on our side despite our best intentions, as Carnevalle and I discovered after failing an inspection twice because a toilet backed up on us before we had a chance to neutralize it, a repeated act of fate that resulted in our transfer to KP duty, beginning with hauling 100 pound potato sacks from the hanger deck down ladder after ladder to the mess kitchen.

The KP training program had progressed to peeling piles of those potatoes as we were heading toward the Panama Canal and the prospect of an endless voyage out into the Pacific. What kept morale on a level keel for the moment was assuming that anything lower in the order of assignments for a Seaman Second Class in a post-war flattop was inconceivable. Then, as the Tarawa slid through the canal with hardly a foot to spare on either side, scuttlebutt reached our sleeping quarters that new recruits were needed for assignment to the boiler room because a large number of naval reserve swabbies with the right credits for time on active duty were to be discharged as soon as we reached San Diego, where we would take on only regular navy types for the voyage into the unknown beyond. Carnevalle swore he would go AWOL in San Diego before serving time in the boiler room. I told him to take heart: if they were taking only regular navy types on board these days, our liberation could not be far down the road, maybe as early as Hawaii. But he was inconsolable, disconsolate, a sailor, like Homer's Elpenor, seemingly defeated by fortune and with no name to come.

That is, until we reached San Diego and the following announcement came over the speaker: "Now hear this. All Seamen First Class and Seamen Second Class in the Naval Reserve who do not plan to sign on for further duty and the many opportunities for advancement provided by Naval training programs are to report to the flight deck at 0700 tomorrow with their gear ready for inspection and transfer to the Naval Discharge Center at Long Beach, California." The cheer that rose in the mess hall was the kind that would warm anyone's heart, even Carnevalle's. I saw him beaming at inspection the following morning—we'd both managed to get away with carrying off our fur-lined jackets as parting mementos of our flattop service—and I saw him one time after that at the foot of the gangway as we were waiting to be bused off to the discharge center and my week in sick bay there with what was diagnosed as the generic virus they called "cat fever" but proved to be a mild case of mumps. On the pier, with the Tarawa for backdrop, Carnevalle and I embraced a last time as released cell-mates might before walking clear of the topless walls behind them into the radiant new world of free citizens ahead.

ELEVEN

When I traveled from California to the East in the late summer of 1946, I did so with euphoria, crossing to my new freedom in a dusty train compartment packed with other released sailors for the many long days and nights that it took to bring us through the Rockies and across the great flat ample fields of grain to the hills of Pennsylvania and the shining sea beyond. I was carrying with me my honorable discharge, a veteran's pin, and the promise of an American Theater Medal and Victory Medal, the latter two citations cause for gratification so transient that I never bothered to find out what they consisted of beyond the print on my discharge certificate. But now that it was all over, I felt fairly pleased with myself, even proud at moments, for having voluntarily signed up when I did, and I could look at the time spent as having fully earned me my citizenship after all those early years in foreign territory, my aspiration to become as American as any other American at last realized in a certain formal way.

At the same time, my short tour in the U.S. Navy had made me, if not exactly a pacifist, ardently anti-militarist except in time of war, an increasingly uncompromising individualist, and what I saw as a committed defender of the common man against capricious authority. And though I was persuaded to stay in the inactive naval reserve by a fast-talking yeoman at the Long Beach discharge center on the grounds that I would otherwise lose the benefit of my rank if called up again, it took me less than half the trip across the great plains to figure out that a Seaman Second Class had no rank worth preserving and not much longer to decide that if I was ever called up again or subject to the draft, I would try the Air Force Reserve—as I did briefly late in the Korean War, a weather man cum travel lecturer finally rising to the rank of T/SGT.

My tour in the Navy had also generated serious doubts about whether, short of wartime necessity, I could bring myself to work inside some government system that would try to dictate how I should think and act, and that included even the mild kind of conformity the Foreign Service was likely to promote. On the other hand, I'd begun to develop a keen interest in politics, which seemed to me at that time the only way you might be able to practice what you believed and shape things for the better without having to serve somebody else's conception of justice and injustice. The problem was that I knew almost nothing about politics beyond the various theories I'd been taught in my freshman year, and I couldn't help wondering how much this new interest of mine was governed by idealism and how much by familiar, if slightly disguised, ambition. With my family in Greece, no place of my own in Washington, and no friends my age I could trust to offer sober advice, I finally decided to retreat for some hard thinking about my future to the only available home I had: the farm house on Alma Hill.

I arrived there in a taxi unannounced in my new gray flannel pants and checkered sports jacket, with my leftover Navy gear in a dufflebag over my shoulder. Things had not seemed the same as the taxi climbed up the hill: only a few cows grazing in the pasture outside the lower barn, some of the fields between the lower and middle farm showing signs of having been fallow longer than was normal, a broken-down wagon parked next to the old water trough opposite Grandma Vossler's cottage. I anticipated the worst, but when Grandma Vossler finally came to the door, looking as tired as I'd ever seen her and confused for a moment by this stranger arriving out of nowhere, she brightened into her usual openhearted smile as she took in who was standing in her doorway.

"So, the sailor has come home from the sea. Only you don't look like a sailor. You look like you're on your way to church."

"Well, the clothes are new. But they won't stay that way long. Not around here."

"Don't you worry. I'm not going to put you to work. There isn't any work left worth the time of a college boy like you, however you're dressed."

When we were seated in her giant overstuffed easy chairs, covered with huge yellow and pink flowers bordered by frills, she told me how things now stood in the region: the farms were disappearing, the leases going dry, the land becoming too cheap to be worth selling, the young men back from the service either trained in new technologies that took them to the cities or studying somewhere on the G.I. Bill or simply bored by trying to scratch a decent living out of the rocky soil of Allegheny County, New York. The house next door was empty. The Rawlins family had moved on, Grandma Vossler said, because Alvin had come back from the army as some kind of newfangled electrician and had found good work right away in Buffalo, and Raymond had back problems that kept him home much of the time, and anyway, the whole family of three generations had moved to Buffalo to stay together. Grandma Vossler had decided to turn the lower farm over to another local farmer for sharing, and he had cut the herd back in order to cope with the new and the old at the same time. She was now content to live off what this brought in, what was left of the lease income, and what she could take care of herself in her nearby orchards and vegetable garden. Of course there was still a lot of gas out back of the house: all you had to do, she said, was pound a stick into the ground and out it would come, enough to run everything that could run on gas. But nobody was interested in developing that kind of thing these days, and Uncle Duffy was struggling to make ends meet out of what was left of the oil leases on the hill and his own property elsewhere.

Grandma Vossler sighed. "Your uncle didn't have the luck your mother did. Or the gumption. He was too good. Stayed around here to work away his years for his family on property that was dying, and where has that brought him now? Your mother was smarter. The minute she got out of college she went off to Turkey and plucked herself a husband with a career and never came back."

"Well, my father didn't have much of a career in those days. He was still just a government clerk finishing college over there at night."

"He may have come out of nowhere and taken his time getting somewhere but look where he ended up. Some kind of ambassador, isn't it? What I'm saying, dear boy, is that you have to take risks if you want to get anywhere. Though maybe no longer the kind your grandfather took digging one hole in the ground to make just enough money to dig another and then another."

"That's the problem. How do you know what risks to take? For example, I'm thinking of giving up on the Foreign Service and going into politics. Which is the better risk?"

"Oh, I wouldn't go into politics if I were you. That's just a way of making money by lying to people and pushing them where they don't need to be. You've got to think of what that would do to your soul."

I didn't bring the subject up again during the week I spent helping Grandma Vossler with her garden and roaming around Alma Hill thinking about past, present, and future. But just that gardening and roaming settled my spirit, and the last day, walking along the ridge at the edge of the forest on the upper farm, looking out over the green and yellow hills toward Bolivar and Olean, I came to see how much courage it must have taken for my mother, just out of her teens, to leave that easy country, with a Vossler relative long since settled into this and that piece of farmland for miles around, and travel toward the other side of the world to that unknown territory in the Near East just emerging out of war and genocide into an untested form of modern civilization. What decision was I facing that could remotely match hers? The risks ahead suddenly seemed small, easily manageable, come what may.

On leaving Alma Hill I told Grandma Vossler so and thanked her for helping me. She gave me a kiss and a hug, but her face couldn't conceal its wrinkled skepticism. I also think she felt that wherever I was heading, it meant that there wouldn't be much chance of my returning for more than a short visit to her part of the world, especially since she must have already started planning for the day she would have to leave that cottage and head into Wellsville to live in the care of others. I doubt that even her kind of prescience could have told her that this would mean living on her own until she was close to *100*, body shriveling and bending to the point where it resembled her husband's in his late years, but her mind sharp as always until its final seasons. I didn't see very far into her future that day, but I realized that my own wasn't likely to find me again taking Alma Hill for my home in the same way it was at that moment, so I put my duffelbag down, gave her a long hug, then turned away quickly to make sure that she—shrewd, compassionate lady—saw no sign of that premonition in my face.

The landscape of Princeton University had also changed while I was away. That September it had become all business, it seemed, all new energy, the entering class large again, the campus crowded with veterans whether students or faculty, some of the older undergraduates three years behind and in a hurry, some graduate students sharing tight space with wives and children, some of the returning faculty now gray-haired and scrambling for their just place in the expanding curriculum. Veteran merely of flattop duty in the quiet American Theater but older by what seemed much more than a year, I took nobody's advice about how to select my courses among the new riches that the catalogue offered. Whether domestic politics or foreign service was to be my future, I decided the focus should continue to be a thorough knowledge of my own country, so I elected courses in American history, American political thought, the American labor movement, and—with a gesture toward practical application—a course in public speaking.

I moved into a three-man suite of rooms in Cuyler Hall once meant for two, with Saleeby and Wilcox for my roommates, and eventually a fourth, John McMurray, all reasonably amiable in those tight quarters—double-decker bunk beds in both bedrooms—all serious enough about their studies to allow me my own rededicated, sometimes frenetic, seriousness. There was no time outside the classroom and library for more than pick-up sports in the late afternoon, mid-week sandwiches at Viet's or the Balt, a beer at the Nass on Saturdays, choir at obligatory chapel on Sundays, a weekend date maybe once a month at best or a trip into The City when that prospect failed. My single committed extracurricular activity that sophomore year was the result of a disastrous decision I made in my attempt to begin a practical education in politics: helping to create a campus Republican Club.

Since almost everybody at Princeton was a Republican in those days with the exception of a few faculty members and some returning veterans, there had apparently never been need for a club to encourage the already converted. And there were hardly enough Democrats around to justify a club of that complexion, though there was an active group of some forty students and faculty called The Liberal Union, considered by some to be mildly left of center and by others to be a Communist Party front. My falling in with those who felt a Republican Club was necessary emerged from profound ignorance and naive ambition. Despite my reading in theory and history, my background in contemporary American party politics was a desert vista. My parents, maybe because professional diplomats, never talked politics in front of their children, and my Washington buddies, without the vote, lived in a political party no man's land. In short, I had no idea what a contemporary Republican, Democrat, Socialist, or Communist stood for, except that it seemed, anyway on the Princeton post-war campus, Republicans were considered respectable and correct, Democrats mostly self-serving and dubious, Socialists sometimes well-meaning but badly misguided (even if Norman Thomas was a Princetonian), and Communists dangerously subversive at best and traitorous at worst. A certain confusion was generated in my mind by the various professors of the time who were stimulating lecturers or sharp instructors—Eric Goldman, Willard Thorp, Lawrence Thompson, Hubert Wilson, among a number of others—and who presented a view of American civilization that cast broad doubt on the easy political definitions and cliches you heard on campus. They also seemed to believe in a still active liberal tradition in American politics that I had learned something about in my freshman year but hadn't connected to the life I actually lived in Princeton, New Jersey.

And I still hadn't fully made the connection by the fall of 1947. My impulse to become politically active and also get some practice in public speaking had led me to take part in the mock "Senate" run by the Whig-Cliosophic Society, where the student debate was mostly taken up by lively amateur rhetoric and vague positioning, except in the case of

several strident defenders of free enterprise and international isolation-
ism and a single voice from the Liberal Union, that of a dark, long-
haired young man who used terms only French intellectuals of the time
might have understood with ease. I was too shy and insecure to speak
regularly in the Senate, but at one point I got up to proclaim with some
fervor against the appalling apathy on the Princeton campus that had
become apparent during the recent Congressional elections—apathy
from "all angles of the political spectrum" is the way I put it—and this
drew the attention of two juniors in the "Senate" named Brooks and
McCormick. They stopped me on the stairway as I was cutting out for
dinner at Commons. Brooks was short, dapper, soft-spoken, but he never
quite looked straight at you when he talked. McCormick—tall, lean, a
touch bucktoothed—was more direct, less subtle, but sometimes hard to
read behind his thick glasses.

"We need people like you," Brooks said, holding my arm. "People
ready to get out the vote. I assume you're a Republican."

"Well I don't really know what I am," I said. "I just think people
around here ought to take more interest in the coming presidential election, even if it's still months down the road."

"That's the point," McCormick said. "And we've got to make sure a
Republican wins. I mean, as my father says, after sixteen years of
Franklin Deal-or-no Roosevelt, enough is enough."

"Sixteen years? How do you figure that? The war was still going strong
when Roosevelt died some..."

"Well, you know what I mean. The point is, any Republican is better
than what else is out there."

"I'd say that depends on who ends up running on both sides. The
Republicans have got four or five people running. Taft, Dewey, Stassen,
and I don't know who else. And the Democrats..."

"The Democrats have got Truman," Brooks said. "What more need
be said? I won't even mention Wallace. We all know where he's coming
from."

"Well, to be honest, I can't speak with any authority, because I..."

"You spoke with a lot of authority," McCormick said. "Apathy is
rampant. We need people talking about the candidates, getting to know

what they stand for, exchanging ideas. That's the democratic process, right?"

This made sense to me, and I made the mistake of saying so. The result was a meeting to explore the possibility of a club that would invite political speakers to the campus and encourage veterans and others old enough to vote to do so by absentee ballot. Five people showed up besides me, four Republicans and a member of the Liberal Union who was immediately labeled a spy and who anyway chose to leave half way through the meeting. Brooks and McCormick offered to draft a constitution for the new organization with the help of a member of the Politics Department but otherwise kept themselves in the background while pushing me into the foreground. Two weeks later we had become The Princeton University Republican Club under a formal charter, and two weeks after that, at a meeting in the Cabinet Room of Murray-Dodge Hall, a group of some ten or so undergraduates elected me president of the new organization and the four other members of the original group to the four remaining offices created by Brooks and McCormick.

An editorial in the student newspaper, *The Daily Princetonian*, declared that the formation of the Republican Club was another positive indication of the widespread interest at Princeton in politics and political problems already demonstrated by the formation of the Liberal Union and thus "well in keeping with the Princeton tradition of taking more than an academic interest in the national scene." It went on to say that most of the aims of the Republican Club appeared praiseworthy as outlined in the open letter from the newly-elected president, but the editors were inclined to be slightly doubtful about the ability of the new club to find the fundamental framework of Republican thought, as the President had indicated was a principal "credo" of the Club, this a commendable motive, but one that would seem extremely difficult to effect, for example, in attempting to find the "common ground upon which men such as Senator Taft and Harold Stassen stand."

The newly-elected president took this editorial as a challenge, even if he wasn't at all sure at the time exactly what ground Senator Taft and Harold Stassen stood upon or the possible difference in their stance. His

fellow officers were vague on the subject, so he did some newspaper
research in the library and asked his instructors in the American politics
and history courses. He learned that Taft was considered on the right of
the Party and Stassen on the left, with Dewey somewhere in the wishy-
washy center, but what each believed in specifically was not clear. He
finally decided to call the Republican National Committee in
Washington to see if Senator Taft and Harold Stassen would be willing
to come to Princeton personally at some point soon to outline their
political philosophies to students and faculty in view of the coming
presidential election.

"I beg your pardon?" the lady on the line in Washington said. "Who
is this and what is it you want?"

"President Keeley from Princeton. I was hoping I might get through
to Senator Robert Taft or the Honorable Harold Stassen to arrange a
visit to our Republican Club up here."

"You are President who?"

It took a while, but I finally convinced the lady that I was neither
insane nor a troublesome prankster, and she ended up putting me
through to somebody in the office down there who explained that it
would be extremely unlikely that either of the two gentleman I had in
mind for a visit to Princeton would be free to accept at the present time,
though I was of course free to send them a written invitation by way of
the National Committee, but I might also consider inviting a young congressman from California in his first term, therefore with maybe more
free time at his disposal, who had received the support of Harold
Stassen and might be able to give my Republican Club the benefit of his
wisdom and knowledge regarding that particular candidate and much
else besides. I wrote the name down as Richard W. Nixon, and that
evening I sent him a formal invitation on our new Republican Club sta-
tionery, which our ten-odd members had paid for out of their first dues.
A week later he accepted. The congressman from California was so
obscure at the time that nobody pointed out the error in his middle initial, even after it appeared indelibly on the poster we put up all over campus announcing his talk, "Congress and 1948."

The talk, advertised as open to the public, drew about twenty people to Whig Hall on a Tuesday evening. Representative Nixon—handsome, articulate, seemingly forthright—did not mention Harold Stassen in his remarks and spoke in broad generalities about the need for a balanced budget, a strong military, and a coherent foreign policy. He did not seem distressed by the small audience, and after his remarks behind the podium, he circulated easily among the gathered students, answering all questions, even smiled occasionally at his or somebody else's effort at wit. Several of us in the audience were impressed, Brooks and McCormick not at all.

"I don't get it," Brooks said. "This man fought a hard fight against that Communist Jerry Voorhis out in California, yet he didn't once mention the need to fight the Communists in Washington. Provincial is what I call him."

"What do you expect?" McCormick said. "If he's supporting Stassen."

"I didn't hear him say he was supporting Stassen," I said.

"Of course not," McCormick said. "He's not going to admit that until he sees if Stassen has a chance. Which in my humble opinion he doesn't."

Congressman Nixon left the group a photograph of himself inscribed "Best Wishes to the Republican Club of Princeton" and took off for New York City without joining the officers and a few stragglers for a late beer at the Nass, as we had hoped. Some forty years later, during class reunions at Princeton, a rumor spread among certain former members of the club that Richard Milhous Nixon had accepted the invitation to be the club's first speaker without fee or other recompense because he was already scheduled to travel from Washington to New York in order to meet secretly for the first time with Whittaker Chambers, earliest architect of the future President's national reputation. The rumor was never confirmed and the timing was suspect—but so was much else in the still unfinished spy story involving Congressman Nixon, Whittaker Chambers, and Alger Hiss.

Several weeks after the brief Nixon visit, the club heard Professor David McCabe of the Princeton Economics Department, famous on campus for his quips against John L. Lewis and his mine workers, argue that strikes in our public utilities could not be resolved by collective bargaining, "which hasn't settled labor disputes but only started them." As a sop to Brooks and McCormick, the committee voted to invite, as our final speaker of the year, Senator Chapman Revercomb of West Virginia, who was said to have been the only member of the U. S. Senate to vote against the creation of the United Nations. The poster announced his talk as "Pending Congressional Legislation: Labor, Communists, Tax Reduction, Foreign Policy." What I remember of the talk, along with his warnings about strikes, Communists in several branches of the government, and the need for broad tax reduction—a theme not yet as thoroughly familiar as it was to become during the half century following— was the Senator's strong opposition to the recently announced Truman Doctrine for aid to Greece and Turkey. Since I felt, whatever the party's argument against involvement abroad, that Greece desperately needed all the help it could get after the devastation of the recent world war and the current civil war, Chapman Revercomb struck me as a ridiculous old reactionary.

I left this last Republican Club meeting that spring in a state of suspended confusion. It seemed to me that everything I'd heard so far in the public sessions I'd sponsored was out of key with what was otherwise reaching my only partially formed political consciousness, and my confusion was compounded by a running dialogue that I'd begun with an older student in the room across the hall from mine, Jack Bunzel, self-confident, quiet in manner, rational in debate if sometimes bitingly ironic in tone, evidently much more sophisticated about national politics than anybody I'd yet come across outside the classroom and often appearing to make perfect sense—but unfortunately President of the Liberal Union. Our mild exchange of thoughts now and then began in the communal toilet in the basement of our entry and finally moved to his living room—never to mine, where this "fellow traveler" across the way was not entirely welcome to my roommates Saleeby and Wilcox. As our dialogue continued, it became weighted heavily toward Bunzel's side not only because of his grasp of the day's issues but because he had a political vocabulary that I sometimes found difficulty interpreting. The more I talked to him, the more ignorant I felt and the more unsure of what I really believed in, though I sensed increasingly that I believed in very little I had so far heard from the Republican Party, and that under-cut my faith in the program of public discussions I'd promoted. By the end of the school year, I decided to put my hope in a possible middle ground to be defined by Harold Stassen, considered by most to be a moderate who might not even be a pure Republican, and in my parting letter to the current forty-five members of the Republican Club, I indicated that, along with plans to promote absentee-ballot voting, I was taking steps to invite Stassen to visit the campus in October. But that hardly served to settle my growing ambivalence.

Along with the distance I'd begun to feel from my political cronies on the right, I found that my enthusiasm had slowly shifted that spring from American history to Romantic poetry as the result of the two courses in those subjects that had consumed most of my academic energy. I still planned to sign up in the history department for my upperclass major, but it was poetry that again seemed to touch my core, at least for the moment. The revolt of the Romantic poets against neoclassicism, rationalism, poetic diction, and conventional morality was a revolt immediately endearing to this young veteran of the American theater. But the poetry itself was what most won me over. Keats came first. Shelley I found cerebral and faint-hearted beside Keats and his grand passions, his bold love forever panting and forever young if doomed to death even as he lies pillowed on his fair love's ripening breast. Then Coleridge's sunny dome with caves of ice to house his dangerous hero with the flashing eyes and floating hair who'd fed on honeydew and drunk something called the milk of paradise. And Wordsworth's Lucy, who made such a difference to him, fair as a star when only one is shining in the sky. But in the end, Byron came over strongest because he could mix his lyricism with wit when he wanted to and because he invented a Greek girlfriend named Haidee for his Don Juan:

> She sits upon his knee, and drinks his sighs,
> He hers, until they end in broken gasps;
> And thus they form a group that's quite antique,
> Half naked, loving, natural, and Greek.

By mid-term, I found myself reciting lines from this or that poem which I hadn't consciously memorized, sometimes writing a line or two of my own during the lectures in the course called "American History Since the Civil War," terrible jingly first efforts that rhymed to a fault and said the obvious but that finally took the place of the awkward abstract doodless that sometimes cluttered my notebook margins. I also found myself getting bored with the piled up facts of one after another 19th century government administration attempting to deal with the immense problems that emerged from civil war and reconstruction and industrial expansion and the labor movement during the accelerating growth of our burgeoning American republic, as our textbook put it. Yet I worked hard after class at getting those facts straight and lined up in my memory for the midterm exam.

I came out of the exam feeling that I'd conquered the territory covered by each of the questions with an array of facts I was sure would stun even my somber instructor, who had always seemed arrogantly remote from me and most others in the class. That I ended up barely passing the exam flabbergasted me—and compelled me, for the first and last time in my life, to make an appointment with the instructor to find out what possibly could have gone wrong with the thing when I was certain I had all the facts right. The instructor leafed through the exam expressionless.

"I see what went wrong," he finally said. "You have most of the facts, as you put it, but the exam is often inelegant."

"I don't get it," I said. "If you have the facts, what else matters?"

"History is not facts. History is writing about facts."

"And I didn't write about those facts?"

"You wrote about them, but not well enough. I'll give you an example. Right here at the start you say, and I quote in part: '...it wasn't only that the South was bad off after the Civil War, but the North's plans for reconstruction etcetera etcetera.' Bad off? Where did that kind of English come from? And where did you develop this looping script?"

"Washington, D.C., sir. That's the way we would say it down there. As for the script, I grew up …. Never mind."

"Well the rest of the country would say badly off. Or maybe something more subtle and elegant. At least those hoping to graduate with honors from an important university."

I was the one now stunned. The instructor must have seen not the flush of embarrassment but the pallor of total defeat, because his expression softened, and as he handed the exam back to me, he assured me that with more care to matters of grammar and style, I could certainly pull up my grade by way of the final exam, because I clearly did have a capacity to marshal facts. When I looked over the exam again in private, there were no marks on it to indicate my failures in grammar or style, but as I read through it again, I couldn't bear to see how casually I had sometimes put things, and the looping script—to find yourself suddenly disgusted by your own handwriting is to cross into a corner of self loathing that even concerted refinement in penmanship and a mastery of touch typing can take months to relieve. I threw the exam across the room, and with it, my obsession with facts. The instructor clearly had a point, which only sharpened the pain and led me to swear that I'd show the bastard. I'd write my heart out the next time and the time after that. I'd never really *believed* in facts anyway. What were the facts in poetry?

What I didn't realize at the time was that the pleasures which satisfy the mind's senses have their own seductive persuasion, and a shift in that direction had already begun to settle in enduringly even if I couldn't articulate it to myself. I never really gave up on history, but the poets and novelists I was learning to understand gradually took over, and the time eventually came when there seemed little need to turn elsewhere. Also, before the end of that term, I found myself trying to write whole poems with some fervor if less than sufficient grace. And I began a short story.

There was another source of pleasure that spring: word that I would be sent a plane ticket to join my parents in Athens for the summer at government expense, what would prove to be the last free ride before I turned twenty-one. This news made up for my barren social life in the late months of the academic year, even though I was supposed to have arrived at Princeton's version of the good life for future upperclassmen by easing my way into Campus Club under the influence and patronage of my two older roommates. It never occurred to me to question what was involved in joining a Princeton eating club and the bicker system that got you there, another sign of how much room there still was for me to grow, but in any case being chosen didn't bring with it all the promise of romance it was supposed to. For the "house party" weekend in May, I invited a graduate of Western High named Beverly, now working as a nurse at Bethesda Hospital, a bouncy, light-tongued girl I'd met while she was dating a fraternity brother of mine who claimed she was the most sensual woman his age he'd encountered. Over the phone she said she'd be thrilled to visit Princeton.

As it turned out, her weekend had to end early Sunday morning to allow time for her to report back for hospital duty that evening, which gave us only Saturday to get to know each other and maybe share some privacy in that sometimes desperately greedy way Princetonians were driven to by their bucolic male isolation. My roommates, who had all of Sunday to cultivate their weekend hopes, were generous enough to give over our communal living room to Beverly and me for Saturday afternoon, but during our tour of the campus and the quiet places around it, Beverly was so taken by the architecture of the university and the green walks along Lake Carnegie that we ran afoul of Princeton's No-Sex-After-Six rule that required women, even sisters and mothers, to be out of the dormitories by that very witching time well before nightfall. Beverly and I had then moved on to Campus Club to dance the old Washington catting dances through an evening with enough nostalgia and easy talk of the good old days at Western to keep us lively and quite happy with each other before she vanished into the dormitory for women guests on the top floor. It was a sweet coda to conclude my separation from Georgetown, if not quite in the mode my roommates had anticipated for me. That fact earned me the ironic nickname of Stud to wear like a brand on my forehead through their graduation a year ahead of mine and, when in their company, into the years thereafter that we survived together.

The truth was that even during that crammed weekend I was preoccupied by thoughts of my imminent return to Greece: what friends from pre-war days would still be there to greet me, how I was going to manage now that I'd almost totally forgotten the language, what would be left of the green fields I'd known during my years there—and most of all, how I would find Lisa. I hadn't written her. I told myself that I couldn't really write her now that I had no specific address for her since she'd moved with her family from the Farm School into town, but the real reason was that I wanted to see her first, get to know her again, give her a chance to see where I was after all these years apart so that we could find the way to speak freely again as we once had, a thing I couldn't quite bring myself to do in a letter addressed to what seemed dusky territory ahead. I was certain she would still be there in the city—surely she would have found a way to let me know if she'd moved somewhere else—and I was determined to find her even if it meant scouring endless unfamiliar streets. But I had no way of knowing just how much spent time and separate history may have influenced the innocent understanding of each other that once was there.

✳   ✳   ✳

In the summer of 1947 the flight to Athens from New York's Idlewild—my first anywhere—involved many hours of idleness both in the air and on sometimes remote runways along that postwar route. But I remember few moments of boredom during those long hours crossing the Atlantic, whether the scene outside the window was cloud forms and tundra vistas in the no man's land of high flying or Quonset hut terminals set out for the time being on weed-strewn ground. And once across the Atlantic, past the hedged-in greenery of England and new-sown farm land on the continent stretching to the sun-lit Alps, there was the thrill of rediscovering a Mediterranean landscape, with its dryer fields and more casual plots of yellow and mauve before you came to the familiar coastal aquamarine of the Adriatic sea deepening to dark blue for its encounter with the rock-rimmed and sandy-coved Ionian islands offshore from the purple mountains of Albania and Greece.

Yet none of it was as brightly colored as my anticipation made it. And when we reached the outskirts of the white city called Athens, it hardly bothered me that its whiteness was here and there dominated by the gray stain of recent concrete or that the old landmarks—Lycabettus Hill, the Acropolis, the Royal Gardens, the marble Olympic stadium—seemed

isolated in the dearth of other open spaces now given over to new building for refugee quarters or for investment opportunities in monotone
cement. It was Greece, and the city was still surrounded on three sides
by an emerald sea, and as the ancient poet put it, who could ever drain
that sea dry?

I did see signs that it was to be a somewhat different Greece from the
one I had left eight years before. For a start, I was met at the airport by
the driver of an American Embassy car who took me to the guest wing
of the villa my father had just bought for the United States government.
It is now not far from the center of town, but in those days it was close
enough to a stretch of open country so that the owner, afraid to house
his family that far out while there was still a Communist threat in the
region, took advantage of the newly-arrived American diplomatic mission to sell it for what both he and father considered a bargain. What
eventually became the guest wing had been set aside for the younger
members of the family, all mine for the time being since Budge was back
in the States in his new post-Navy job in Mobil Oil and Bob was back
in the States as a counselor at Camp Cory. My quarters consisted of a
bedroom with twin beds, a living room with couches and easy chairs and
an elegant empty desk, an immaculate kitchenette, and a bathroom that
was so large it gave the flattop veteran in me a momentary shudder. I
gazed outside at the neatly trimmed shrubs protecting a lawn that
seemed to have no blade of grass out of place and the guard at the gate
dressed to the teeth as though for a party, and when the maid in her neat
black and white uniform knocked on the door to ask if I would like
some tea and biscuits, I sat there on the couch and stared at her so long
she must have thought me deranged. Where in God's name was it that
the gods had now brought me?

I didn't see much of my father during my days in the villa. His meals
were often official, and when he was there for dinner, he sometimes
arrived late and seemed much preoccupied. My mother apologized for
him before I had any thought of complaining: there was a civil war on,
she said, and the Americans under the Truman Doctrine had now taken
over from the British the responsibility of helping the Greek government
during this crisis, and with my father's new position as Deputy Chief of

Mission, his work was almost on a wartime footing.

My mother had put on weight since I'd last seen her, and her hair was now gray, but even with all her official social duties, she seemed more relaxed, more sure of herself, more independent than she had been on Fulton Street—though this may have seemed so partly because, thanks to Grandma Vossler, I could now look at her with more understanding. And for the first time in years, she had all the help she could use. Though she had once been athletic, a badly mended broken ankle in Montreal had kept her from walking easily and even driving a car, which had caused her to be dependent on my father for transportation and had slowly worked to make her overweight. She now had a driver who could take her most anywhere anytime, a maid for her own needs, a cook for the kitchen, and all the other perks that came with being the wife of a diplomat second in rank at an embassy. This meant a degree of liberation, even if she used much of what was available to her rather sparsely, I suppose a remnant of her Alma Hill upbringing. Years later, after my father retired and he again became her erratic and sometimes reluctant chauffeur, I tried to persuade her to call a taxi whenever she had an urge to go somewhere on her own: visit a friend, get her hair done, go buy herself a new hat. "Call a taxi?" she'd say to me. "Why in the world would I want to do a thing like that?"

During those days in Athens my father also appeared more fully in command of himself, confidently professional, his dress and bearing the kind that showed him ready to meet foreign ministers and to stand with authority beside the suave Ambassador Lincoln MacVeagh, classical scholar and early friend of F.D.R. And according to the local embassy scuttlebutt, my father was building a reputation as the kind of senior diplomat who spoke his mind at the right time, reported things as he saw them to the State Department—sometimes with eloquent bluntness— and knew how to transmit his experience to his younger colleagues with rigor yet sufficient tact. But there was still distance between him and his sons, as he himself disarmingly acknowledged at one point that summer in an almost off-hand reference to the difficulty his father had always found talking to him and vice versa. From my perspective, I now took such distance for granted—even if its third-person grammatical phase was over—so that it no longer bothered me the way it once had, and that was not entirely a good thing.

It wasn't very long before I got bored with the isolated luxury of the Villa Lydis (as my father called it), but not before I'd found ways to escape beyond the guarded wall in the company of two free-spirited hedonists on the staff of the Embassy named Sally and Marge, veterans of the American Mission For Observing the Greek Elections, game on any excuse to commandeer an embassy car or jeep and take off for one or another deserted beach on the coast opposite Evia or climb up Mount Hymettus for a long view of the neighboring islands or the olive and lemon groves of the Peloponnese, imagined or otherwise. Sometimes beyond the outskirts of Athens you'd run across a stretch of rusted barbed wire and a sign telling you that there was danger of mines along that section of the shore, and sometimes you'd end up on a stretch of sandy beach that had once been under suspicion of becoming an Allied landing area because it was guarded on the bluff above by a German pill-box that now served as a makeshift toilet, but that close to the city there was hardly any other evidence of the war so recently over or of the one still in progress. You had to travel farther south into the Peloponnese or north beyond Thebes to find the wounded villages left to itinerant animals and a few of the elderly who had returned after yet another Wehrmacht retaliation or the cross-fire of a civil war skirmish, and traveling in either direction was still restricted in places to those with official privilege and purpose.

My companions in search of the liberated life, Sally and Marge, had long since discovered retsina and ouzo, new to me but quickly addictive, and they had also discovered, now in their late thirties or early forties, that a reasonable number of Greek men between the ages of eighteen and thirty loved sex with foreign women of mature age who were relatively blonde and open to adventure and supported by hard currency. They had both learned in due course what so many other foreign women came to know during the decades following: in Greece it usually didn't matter if you were too thin, too tall, too round, or simply not young enough by some standard back home so long as you didn't demand loyalty and so long as you had full confidence in your sensuality, which by their own admission came naturally to both Sally and Marge.

We became ardent if platonic buddies from my first days in the city, I think because they sensed in me a safe subversive much like themselves, tied closely enough to the American Embassy not to be just another anarchic bohemian on the loose in Athens but at the same time a Mediterranean convert with an eye and a heart ready to take in whatever of the local pleasures they could help me accommodate in the interludes between one or another of their erotic excursions. At the beaches we would swim out as a threesome as far as you had to in order to get a wide-angle view of the shoreline, loll there to take it all in for a spell, then swim back hard to build an appetite for the sea's bountiful, and in the right company, aphrodisiac fruit: octopus, squid, clams, crabs, oysters, fresh broiled fish in lemon and olive oil, whatever the sea-side taverna under the few remnant pine trees could provide to absorb the sharp anise bite of ouzo or the lingering resin after-taste of barreled wine. And following the melon or peaches or cherries or all three laid out in style on a communal platter, there was the long siesta on the beach in what shade we could find to restore body and soul for the evening's drive into the neighboring hills and an exchange of lively histories and stories and gossip, some of it real, some of it surely made up, until talk was stilled by distant images of the changing horizon under the dying sun. Then late dinner on a terrace that allowed us to survey the city lights—Henry Miller's sparkling chandelier—as far as the Sacred Way to Eleusis in one direction and the high road to Pendeli Mountain in the other, before the cognac and half-sweet coffee brought in another kind of stillness as we studied and then debated the legible constellations.

What finally made me restless despite these days of adventure and discovery in Athens was a phone call from Bruce Lansdale, my early Salonika pal and Camp Cory mentor, who was now at the American Farm School as a volunteer making an inventory of what resources were left after the German occupation of the School. He wanted to know if I would join him in this work for as long as the spirit moved me during the rest of my summer vacation. I packed a suitcase that afternoon and caught a ride on the next American Mission plane heading for the military airport as close to the School as it took you to smoke a cigarette, in the argot of local villagers.

Bruce met me in the jeep that was his when he needed it, reward for his charitable service to the school and what proved to be our access to recreation along the southern shore of Salonika Bay when the local curfew prohibited a trip into town or regions to the east and west that were still under threat by guerrilla forces on the move toward the northern mountains. Once you reached the province of Macedonia it became clear that the civil war was still hot. Bruce reported that earlier in the week one of the school staff returning to his neighboring village passed by the most popular café on the deserted main square and spotted a severed head on one of the outdoor tables set up among others for the evening's ouzo hour. The head belonged to one of the richest landowners in the region. The next day an army squad came into the square to replace that head with one belonging to a bearded guerrilla. The square remained deserted.

My first days at the school brought me a mix of nostalgia and melancholy, of the familiar and the forgotten, though what dominated was a sense of loss. The closest of my Armenian friends, Kirkor and his brothers, were gone, emigrants to Argentina and the new-world possibilities there, with no evident interest in ever returning to Greece. A few of my other childhood companions were still at the school, those from Greek families still serving on the staff, most of whom had grown so as to be almost unrecognizable and whose questions often remained hanging in the air. My Greek had almost totally vanished, and that early in the summer I could do no more than embrace them in the Greek way, smile as warmly as I could, and try to figure out what each of them was saying to me before turning, embarrassed, to look around for somebody with enough basic English to act the interpreter. It was as though I had crossed the border into a country I recognized as once mine but whose language had changed while I was abroad elsewhere. And my failure to be able to speak easily with those old friends, to catch up on where they'd been and tell them where I'd been, made our encounters awkward and partial, full of gestures and lapses, this long awaited reunion at moments barely tolerable. My Greek gradually came back, but it took the rest of the summer, and it hardly reached beyond the eleven-year-old level of my pre-war departure for America.

On my tour of the School, I found that the building which had been blasted by the departing German occupiers was now restored, and Charlie House, back in charge and eager once again to exercise his Princeton engineering skills, was already laying the foundations of new works for which he was certain God would provide. Theo Litsas, second in command but now with the additional stature of having kept the heart of the School more or less healthy during the years of occupation, was again working hard through the force of his upbeat personality and grasp of village humor to restore the morale of the underpaid and still anxious staff. The farm land was planted anew, the dairy fully back in business, and the recruiting of students for the coming academic year was proving better than expected, even if most could offer only a fragmented record of previous schooling.

But an unresolved civil war so soon after the end of a harsh enemy occupation left many scars and unhealed wounds. The village on Mt. Hortiati that had been the first rest station during our pre-war excursions to the mountain top was now a charred ruin commemorating the last minute German reprisal in 1944. And there were other villages scattered across the Macedonian plains and mountain ridges that had been destroyed or abandoned, whether under the retribution policy of the Wehrmacht and their collaborators or the guerrilla campaign of terror or more recent Greek army clean-up operations. The once open country on the road to Kastania, briefly accessible after the German withdrawal, was again sealed off to all but Greek military units soon to be aided in their rejuvenated anti-guerrilla campaign by American advisers and Helldiver aircraft.

The deepest wound among my former playmates proved to be the one that had penetrated Lisa's psyche, as I discovered soon after I tracked her down at her home on the main road into Salonika. She'd kept in touch with several of our childhood companions still living at the School, so I had no trouble finding her address, but it took several long days of tiring work helping Bruce with his survey of the School's remnant tools and machinery and spare parts before I felt I could ask him for a break so that he could drive me into town to look up the girl I told him had been my surrogate sister before the war.

It was not the easiest of reunions. I'd called Lisa to prepare her for my arrival, heard and recorded the sweet quality of her surprise, babbled of things so trivial that my shyness must have been blatantly evident, promised to answer all that she'd asked me in a flurry of questions as soon as we had a chance to be alone. That took time. The whole family was waiting to greet us when we arrived at the door: mother, father, older sister, all in line, with Lisa stepping quickly ahead to offer me the first almost formal kiss on both cheeks, then the others in turn. And before Bruce could find a way to excuse himself so that he could wait outside for us, he too was swept in by Lisa's mother to share in the round of preserves on a spoon and the saccharine liqueur as we sat in a circle to talk of this and that, past and present, though, ominously, not a word about how things might be progressing at the American Farm School. Anyway, my eyes were mostly on Lisa as hers were on me, mine taking in the ways she'd grown—not much taller but no longer any trace of the child in her—she maybe trying to judge how much was still there of what had once been familiar to her, now that I was six feet tall and thin beyond any expectation.

The chance to make our way across the barrier of years came three nights later when I managed to arrange an after-dark excursion to a stretch of beach near the promontory that marked the outer limit of Salonika Bay. Bruce—too generous by nature to be as reluctant as he wanted to be—agreed to solve the transportation problem by asking Lisa's older sister to come along as his date, and the sister finally agreed out of a sense of obligation to her younger sister and maybe to provide the aura of propriety. Her name was Miranda, attractive in her way but stiffer than Lisa, more self-protective. Yet Bruce's easy manner and accommodation of village humor proved seductive, and Miranda ended up not only trusting him but finding him amusing, especially when he solved the curfew problem at the check point on the southern edge of town by persuading the guard carrying an M-1 rifle that we were legitimate members of some local American mission on our way to the airport, first by flashing his naval reserve card—or was it his life-saving certificate?—and then, after a quick stream of friendly village slang, explaining to the confused guard, who pressed him to say where he came from, that only an American with the right kind of linguistic training in Washington, D.C., under clandestine circumstances, especially an American as blond and Anglo-Saxon as he was, could end up speaking demotic Greek of the kind he was speaking at that very moment. Whether fully convinced or not, the guard, half-smiling, after taking in the special American Farm School license plate, waved us on.

Lisa, though pretty in a way that was no longer girlish, appeared to me as I remembered her: open, spunky, a touch flirtatious especially with her eyes, incapable of not saying whatever was on her mind. The only change I noticed at the start of this second meeting, now that our shared language had to be English, was how fluent hers had become over the years and the fact that it had taken on a certain British coloring. We had so much to say to each other on the long ride out of town that it was some time before I began to notice how barren the coast looked beyond the city outskirts, how much of it was undeveloped marsh-land or arid fields, and when we turned off the main road and headed toward the sea, how desolate seemed the nearer stretches of beach that had once been the liveliest of pre-war playgrounds. When I finally commented on that, Lisa took my hand.

"Much has changed," she said. "You can't imagine. But I'd rather not tell you."

"You mean about the war? I'd really like to hear about that. I feel I missed. . ."

"The war and people during the war. Someday I'll tell you. Tonight we shouldn't think about such things."

But I couldn't stop thinking about such things. The four of us stood there looking out to sea toward Olympus to the west and the mountain ridges to the north, and then, to keep an eye on the jeep, we laid out a blanket on a patch of beach within sight of the dirt road that had brought us there, and we sat down in a row to gaze out across the bay at what there was to see of the city lights miles away now, far dimmer than what you encountered in Athens except for the arc of street lights along the quay that ended abruptly beyond the old harbor. And beyond that, there was nothing to see but the dark expanse of what seemed yet another no-man's-land between the city's perimeter and the far mountains that marked the border of guerrilla country. When Bruce began to tell some of his familiar Nasredin Hodja stories for Miranda's pleasure, I took Lisa's hand and led her off along the water's edge where the sand had been hardened a bit by the sea's earlier coming and going. We walked a long way toward the promontory's rock cliff without talking. Then I asked her again to tell me about the war.

"You won't like it," Lisa said. "You won't want to hear what I can tell."

"We always told each other everything. Remember the cut on your finger and the rabid cat? Why don't you trust me now?"

"It isn't that I don't trust you. I don't think you understand what war does to people, at least over here, and I don't want to spoil your coming back. Besides, that war is over and the other will be over soon enough now that the Americans are coming here to help."

"If it's you, what happened to you, I won't let it spoil anything between us."

"That's sweet," Lisa said. "Even if I only half believe you. But it's some of the people who were once our friends I'm worried about. The ones who betrayed us. And others you don't know. The name of our war was betrayal. And it still is."

The story she told—not slowly, but calmly—began with the notice her father received not long before the Occupation that the year of his retirement as a teacher had arrived and he would be expected to move his family out of the staff house he had occupied at the Farm School for some twenty years—no hurry, just as soon as was convenient. That was the rule, Lisa said, the rule of the committee in America that governed the School and those who ran it in Greece: when you retired, you lost your house. She said her father was too proud to object to this rule even if a war was now close by and the School wasn't really functioning and his family had no other place to go, so his two daughters went in search of a place to rent and found a house part way into town that they could afford on what savings they had. Their father continued to bring home what he could by tutoring people in English wherever he could find private pupils, winter, spring, summer, fall, though teaching English was eventually forbidden by the Germans under the Occupation and that put him in constant danger of arrest.

"During the Occupation he would dress in his best dark clothes and he would put on the only decent hat he still had to cover his hairless head and he would walk with his cane into town as far as the harbor or up the hill into the old city, wherever he would have to go to tutor a pupil with enough money or promise of money to make it worth his while, and every time he left the house you could see his face change as though he didn't really expect to come back."

"That's terrible," I said. "But in the end he was never arrested, right?"

"I suppose dressed like that every day as though going to a funeral he fooled the Germans into thinking he was just a mad old man out for a daily walk whatever the weather with nowhere special to go until he walked into his grave. And that nearly happened. So much for his forced retirement."

"Is that what you mean about our friends having betrayed him?"

"Not exactly," Lisa said. "The retirement rule wasn't the real betrayal. When you get old you have to be ready to retire and lose your privileges, whether you're Greek, American, Armenian, maybe even German. The betrayal came when my father got sick during the great famine, sick with stomach ulcers and I don't know what else, and Miranda and I went out to the place where you and I had grown up, actually where I was born, to ask for some milk as the doctor recommended and we were told that the rule was no milk for those who were no longer on the staff. The milk was for those still working. Even if few were really working. "

"I don't believe they could have a rule like that," I said.

"Of course you don't believe it," Lisa said. "You're American. Though I was told the rule was made in America. By the people who run the school. Maybe true, maybe not. Of course America wasn't really in the war yet, so what could they really know about things over here at the time."

"It still doesn't make sense."

"I suppose it did to those still at the school. Only so much milk to go around in those days. And I'm sure you don't believe in such rules. But we are speaking of war and what it does to people. Here and elsewhere."

"But a bottle or two of milk for an old member of the staff? For God's sake."

Lisa smiled stiffly. "I was told it wasn't personal. Simply a matter of principle or policy or something like that. I suppose that meant war or no war, sick or not sick."

Lisa looked away from me to hide what had come into her face.

It was one of those July evenings when the heat lingers long after the sun has gone down but lingers just enough to keep you warm in the light clothes you're wearing and to keep the chill from coming in early. We had found a raised level of earth at the margin of a once cultivated field on the inner edge of the beach and were sitting down there side by side with our legs stretched out in front of us. Much of the rest of the story Lisa then told has faded in my memory. I remember her speaking of the hunger that fall and winter of '41 becoming so profound she could think of nothing else all day and some of the night, and when the famine extended into many weeks, she and her sister went out like street children to see what trifles they could buy. And both ended up ready to steal from the German occupiers if they could only find something worth stealing. They were never moved again to visit the Farm School to see what might be left of those once beautiful gardens and orchards of our early Eden, now occupied by a Wehrmacht communications unit. And then she suddenly found an opening to help the family through the difficult months that followed: she became a night nurse in one of the local hospitals, which gave her the great advantage of access to some valuable medicines and to supplies of other kinds that helped during the harshest days ahead. It also gave her access to a British officer with severely wounded legs whom she was allowed to care for week in week out because of her good English.

"Will it bother you if I tell you more about this English officer?" Lisa said. "For example, that I fell in love with him?"

"No, that doesn't bother me."

"Or that I became his lover. Does that bother you?"

"No," I said. "I mean yes, in a way."

"Well, it didn't last all that long, because he escaped one day. Just walked out of the hospital when he could finally manage to walk and was taken in by our resistance people to be sent by caique to Turkey. And that was that. Only not quite."

She studied me, I suppose to see if she should go on. And then she told me about hearing from her lover after the war was over and about their correspondence and about her visit to England the previous summer with the last of her savings in order take up his invitation to meet him in his English countryside home, where she found that there was a wife and a teenage daughter who were really very kind and friendly and who seemed willing to have her as a visitor for as long as she cared to stay. That turned out to be longer, she said, than her Greek pride should have permitted, however tolerant of strange English ways she had become by then.

"I guess I just couldn't believe that he wouldn't have told me about the wife and daughter there in his lovely English home surrounded by lovely green lawns and a glorious garden, and so I guess I had to stay there until the truth finally burned itself forever into my foolish brain. Now, my dear long lost American brother, have I told you enough about my war?"

"Yes."

She reached over and held my face in both of her hands. "And do you want me to make it up to you? I mean my being the British soldier's lover? Even if you say that doesn't really bother you and even if you don't deserve it for never having written me all the time you were away except for a simple postcard?"

"Yes," I said.

Twelve

As our work on the Farm School inventory began to ease, Bruce Lansdale and I would pile into the Jeep at any reasonable hour to visit one of the local villages just north of Salonika or in the Chalkidiki peninsula, his purpose to interview the local village leaders for their advice on possible recruits to the School, mine to catch up on some of the history I'd missed out on during the years I'd been away. The stories I heard became familiar. The Wehrmacht occupiers had been bad if you gave them an excuse to be bad and often when you didn't. But, depending on the speaker's politics, the Communist guerrillas were seen as equally bad because they killed their own people without reason under a policy of terror that cost them the support of village after village where the relatives of those they killed turned against them, along with others who simply came to dread the sight of them. The Greek army was seen by some as not much better because it didn't have the time or the heart to choose cleanly among the guilty and the innocent when it entered a village to rid it of insurgent guerrillas or their sympathizers, and the army was accused of sometimes killing or incarcerating those it thought simply out of sympathy with the current royalist government. Fear, and the muffled tones that came with it, colored most talk in the villages. Those who preferred not to talk at all about politics went after the capriciousness of nature, especially its devastation through drought that particular summer, just as farmers were getting their crops back to a certain healthy rhythm after the catastrophes of war.

Bruce had the gift of earning the trust of anybody in a village not too wounded to talk, and I simply listened, at first with difficulty, but gradually with enough grasp of the local idiom and grammar to ruin my Greek for decades in the minds of cultivated Athenians. When our School inventory was finally ready, we decided to take a day off for a trip to the foot of the Kastania pass and the village of Verria where my father had created a sensation those many years ago by passing through the square with a house behind his car. Since we couldn't offer an official reason to travel that distance, we headed out without formal permission from anybody, hoping that our vague American Farm School credentials and our usual blarney about undefined connections to foreign missions would get us through.

We made it past the first roadblock at a makeshift bridge across the Vardar river, but some kilometers farther along we were turned back by an armed patrol that had suddenly sealed off the region beyond the possibility of debate as they waited for the passing of a large band of guerrillas on their way to the Grammos and Vitsi ranges to the west, what would eventually prove the final battleground of the civil war. We had no choice but to head back to Salonika. Since we still had the rest of the day off, we decided to have a leisurely lunch at a taverna famous for its wildfowl and local fish on the main road out of town to the south, and that gave the two of us a chance to talk over wine in an uninhibited Mediterranean version of the fraternity bull sessions in high school that had once attempted to reform me and other incorrigible adolescent hedonists.

As often happened with Bruce, three years my senior and already a man given to enriching his inner resources, the conversation turned serious enough at one point for me to tell him that I wanted to write about Greece someday soon, about the war now past and the war still in progress, try to understand what had gone on during those tragic years I'd missed, including what I'd learned in the villages and what Lisa had told me but also the larger picture—all that I hadn't seen myself and had yet to learn but might be able to recapture and eventually put in perspec-

tive by writing about it, whether as history or fiction or both. I also told
him that I wasn't sure any longer about trying out for the Foreign Service
or any other kind of government service, though I didn't know what else
I might do to earn a living. I wasn't even sure about how much time I
should go on giving to the study of American history and politics when
it was poetry and fiction and plays that had now begun to claim the center of my attention.

Bruce was a pipe smoker in those days, and puffing slowly on his pipe
and gazing into the distance gave him an aura of quiet authority. He didn't
answer me directly but by personal parable, another characteristic stance.
When faced with that kind of unsettling dilemma, he told me, he took
out a piece of paper and drew a line down the middle of it, then put
arguments in favor on one side and arguments against on the other side,
and when he'd done that, he tore up the paper, threw the pieces away, and
followed whatever argument remained in his heart. As an example he
told me that he had gotten his degree at Rochester in engineering, but
happy as he felt working with his hands on this or that minor engineering project, he was planning to give all that up and do a graduate degree
in rural sociology so that he would be better prepared to return to the
American Farm School, where he planned to spend the rest of his life,
his professional life, if they would have him as they had promised they
would, whether as a teacher, administrator, recruiter, fund-raiser, or all
of these. He said he'd come out of the Navy feeling as unsettled as I now
felt but that after his visits to the School during the American election
mission in Athens and his stint this summer, he had come to see that
only the work this School provided to help untrained villagers in the
country he'd now rediscovered and learned to love as his own would
quiet his unrest and satisfy his need to serve.

I was astonished. What possibly could have made him so certain
about how and where he wanted to spend the rest of his life?—and there
was no doubt in my mind that he was certain. I finally had to ask him.
Bruce puffed on his pipe.

"You just know," he said finally. "And when you do know, you won't
need to ask yourself or anybody else a question like that."

On our return to the Farm School that afternoon I took a long walk, first around the School grounds, then along the back road leading up to the village called Kapujida, where legend had it that Paul the Apostle had been stoned during his travels in northern Greece, as many other unwanted visitors had been since. I stopped short of the village, above a wheat field that seemed barely to have survived the war and was clearly in need of water, fertilizer, affection. The sun was on its way down across the bay a bit north of Olympus, but it was still strong enough to paint the bay with dappled light wherever the breeze didn't cut that short. Now, the height of siesta time, the city stretched out below me was quiet, almost silent. It seemed that calm had spread all around.

I sat there turning over what Bruce had said in the taverna. Suddenly things began to appear simple, uncomplicated, clear: when I was back in Princeton, I would switch my major from History to English, and that would signal the end of any ambition to enter the Foreign Service. And politics, theoretical or practical? I asked myself how anyone serious about writing could restrict whatever one might have of the writer's free-roaming spirit and humane impulses and ironic view of life by wasting time on abstract theories and party politics—at least Republican Party politics as I'd then come to see them. The question answered itself. Only how could I be sure I was serious about writing and ready for the risks that would involve? This too, at that moment of calm, become a question I no longer felt I needed to ask myself, whoever else might ask it, and if this meant I was now making a life-long commitment, the thought, far from frightening me, brought on a rare elation.

I didn't tell Lisa about these thoughts and their effect on me. They seemed too private to share even with her, and the fact that they did bothered me—but not for long. I told myself that I couldn't expect her to understand about things like a Foreign Service career and Republican Party politics and majors in History or English, let alone my novice literary ambitions. And her bitterness about what had happened to her and her family at the School during the Occupation made it difficult to talk about Bruce's decision as well. There was still too much distance between my partial rediscovery of the place and her withdrawal from it, and I wasn't at all sure how that distance could be crossed. During our last date the night before I flew back to Athens, we took a long walk down to the

Depot and along the bay-side Alatini road heading out toward the king's northern palace. You could still get down to the rim of the bay between the villas along that route, and that is where we went for a bit of privacy, sitting side by side on a section of retaining wall overlooking what had once been rocky beach.

"So you have to go to Athens when you really don't have to yet, is that it?" Lisa said, only half teasing.

"I'm afraid I've already stayed longer up here than I should have. I'm giving my parents only a few days before I have to go back to America."

"Well go ahead then. Even if they have no reason to complain. They had you for eight years while I had nothing. Just one postcard."

"I didn't know what to write in the first years when the situation was so confused. And then I forgot how to write. I mean in Greek. So I just, well I..."

"You don't have to make excuses. I understand. War excuses everything, isn't that so? Only I won't understand one bit if you don't write me when you go away again now."

"I'll write. I promise."

"And I promise to try to believe you."

"You'd better," I said.

Lisa sighed, then turned her head to gaze out at the distant esplanade, her eyes narrow.

"You know, it isn't only that I'll miss you again now that we've been together like we've been. I'm jealous."

"Jealous? Of whom?"

"Not of anybody. Unless you tell me there is somebody. Is there?"

"No. There isn't anybody. Not anymore."

"Well, I won't ask what you mean by that exactly. No more old love stories, right? What I mean is that I'm jealous of your traveling to another country. I'd give anything to leave this city and go somewhere far away. Even England again."

"Maybe you will. Maybe we will together. You just have to be patient while I'm still in school."

"You see, dear boy, patience isn't easy for me. I don't have what you have. No money for school or travel. No help from my parents. No road

I can see for finding another kind of life."

This turn in the conversation made me uncomfortable. The mention of our different circumstances reminded me of Kirkor and the space that had come between us when I tried to get him to look inside the newly arrived trailer those many years ago and he said that thing was for me and my family and looking inside it wouldn't do him any good.

I stood up to stretch with my back to the retaining wall.

"I wish you wouldn't stay so far away," Lisa finally said.

"Well it isn't so far away anymore by plane. And I'll be coming back soon enough."

"I mean now."

I sat down beside her and put my arm around her. "Is that better?" I said

"Yes. And this is even better."

"And this?"

"Yes. That too."

* * *

Sometime soon after I returned to Princeton for the fall semester as an English major, I wrote an article on Greece for a newspaper or journal that, in my euphoria as a first-time published writer, I failed to identify in my scrapbook. The article was well-meaning if hardly subtle in style or perspective, all about the days when raids and murders by Communist guerrillas would bring equally severe raids and murders by government gendarmes, days when the villager would feel that England had let him down and when he would have only skeptical optimism that the American dollar could do the impossible and restore his country "under a royalist regime now disguised under a thin coating of liberalism."

The article was not well received by some of my companions in the Republican Club, nor was my later declaration that I would not stand for re-election in mid-year. But to my immense discomfort, I still felt an obligation to chair the public events I had already scheduled, some that now embarrassed me: Representative Fred A. Hartley of the highly dubious Taft-Hartley labor law, accused of being a fascist by the shop-steward of Local 50 AFL and "heartily endorsed" on a mock "Save Somaliland Committee" placard outside the hall in which he spoke to a packed audience, then Representative Hugh D. Scott of Pennsylvania who wrongly prophesied that the Republicans would win the 1948 presidential election and so end "sixteen years of incompetence" (as *The Daily Princetonian* put it), and finally Harold E. Stassen, more liberal than most in his party, reasonably informed, but so tepid and unimaginative that his career as a perennially unsuccessful presidential candidate was almost predictable at the very start. After I'd handed over my gavel, I announced that I would be leaving the Republican Club to join the Liberal Union. The announcement, picked up by *The Daily Princetonian*, was received, in my hearing anyway, with thunderous silence.

My only political activity during the rest of that year and the next, aside from supporting the left wing of the Democratic Party, focused on efforts to reform the Princeton eating club system, which normally accommodated ninety percent of the sophomore class each year, while rejecting the remainder as undesirables for reasons generally not specified, at least not openly. The effort to achieve one hundred percent admission of those choosing to enter the "bicker" system by persuading one club or another to be generous toward these presumed misfits failed in my senior year, but it energized the next sophomore class, which took the bold position that the spring "bicker" had to end with all candidates admitted or none would join. In the long run that didn't solve the anti-intellectual and exclusivity problems endemic to the selection process and to the pattern of life in the clubs. Nor, as some had hoped, did the admission of women undergraduates to Princeton and the open admissions policy that most clubs adopted some years later, at about the time Princeton fraternities and sororities, including those initiated by blacks, began to come into existence to keep selectivity and exclusivity alive in some form, if so secretly and discreetly that most members of the faculty remained unaware of their presence. Early in the new millennium, my own club started another trend by reverted to selective admission.

During my senior year I joined my brother Bob (then a sophomore at Princeton) and other literary types in a different kind of political activity: trying to persuade the English Department, by way of a series of unofficial lectures, to offer a course in contemporary literature, which at that time meant D. H. Lawrence, T. S. Eliot, Joyce, Faulkner, Fitzgerald, Hemingway, Thomas Wolfe, and Gertrude Stein, the syllabus that a highly popular young instructor in the Department named John Hite finally volunteered to present on his own authority to a mix of students and elderly town residents in the Engineering Building auditorium. His reading the first evening from *Lady Chatterley's Lover* created a breathless silence among both young and old and insured a substantial return audience that somehow survived his presentation of excerpts from *The Waste Land* the following week. The English Department apparently took note of the series' success, and most of that syllabus was eventually brought into the curriculum by Carlos Baker, the Hemingway biographer. But John Hite, choosing not to complete his Ph. D. because he thought it irrelevant to what he felt ought to be primarily a teaching rather than a research institution—and said so with quiet disdain at a packed faculty meeting—was not re-appointed by the English Department and left the University, eventually accepting a position as training lecturer at the Johnson and Johnson Company outside New Brunswick. He subsequently became the misunderstood and misunderstanding hero of a three-act play I wrote immediately after graduation, modeled on a violent yoking together of *Billy Budd* and *Death of a Salesman.*

I did not go back to Greece in the summer of 1948. That spring my mother and father were on their way to Syria, where my father had been appointed Minister (the State Department then considered Syria only important enough to merit a legation rather than an embassy), and with my G.I. Bill running out after two ample years, I was again about to take up the scholarship route with no spare cash. I had been writing Lisa regularly, filling her in as best I could on my round of college activities that I'm sure meant little to her but gave me a way of easing into more personal territory and more passionate prose. Yet all passion vanished and a kind of stuttering inelegance appeared on the page when I tried to explain to her why, in my Anglo-Saxon insistence on maintaining what independence I could from my parents, I was not prepared to ask them for their help in getting me to Greece for the summer and to the girl still

at the center of my consciousness. She said that she of course understood, but it took her the best part of the summer to say so.

I spent some of that time working my way across the United States
by way of odd jobs—everything from blister rust control to slaughter-
house hosing to harvesting hops—that kept me and my three accompa-
nying classmates solvent enough to pay for our modest portion of food
day in day out and the gas guzzled by the Lincoln Continental that
Roger Saleeby had borrowed from his father to take us from New York
City to California and back. I kept a journal when I could, *Midnight
Memoirs,* full of lush descriptions and profound responses, sometimes
translated into rhymed verse, and for this purpose I fell in love for the
moment in Peoria, Illinois, and more fervently if just as briefly in Mesa
Verde, Colorado, grist for the journal but in the end not as rich a source
for the verse as the Petrified Forest and Yosemite and Mount Rainier.

When I returned to Princeton, now fully taken up by the writing of
a senior thesis on the novels of F. Scott Fitzgerald, I showed my summer's poetry to R. P. Blackmur on the off chance that he would accept
me at that late date into his Creative Writing course. Blackmur, who in
future years became my closest senior friend in the English Department,
suggested that I put my full heart into my work on my thesis: though he
was prepared to say that the poetry I'd shown him was perhaps no worse
than what Keats wrote at eighteen (I was then twenty), I would probably learn more about the demands and prospects of a mature style from
studying F. Scott Fitzgerald's fiction in depth than I would from writing
more poems about America's national parks. I took Blackmur's advice,
then and always thereafter. Except for the occasional Christmas poem
and a line or two in moments of passion, I gave up writing poetry and
turned to fiction and plays.

In the spring of my senior year I had a new dilemma to deal with.
Bruce Lansdale, about to earn his M.A. at Cornell in rural sociology,
had notified me early in the year that he was applying for a Fulbright
teaching fellowship to return to the American Farm School that fall in
the technical division and in training as the director's assistant. He wanted
to know if I would be interested in applying for a like fellowship as an
English teacher. He said that whatever else I might have in mind doing

after graduation, he hoped I would give this possibility at least equal consideration because there had been a dramatic event at the school which made it imperative that any foreign teachers who came over at this time be familiar with the country and its problems: on a cold night in January, the whole of the senior class of students and a few of the junior class had been kidnapped by three armed guerrillas and marched off at gunpoint toward the mountains. Many had escaped the first night, and all had made it back in the weeks following. But there would be traumas left over to deal with during the coming academic year, language classes to be taught imaginatively to distracted and largely unprepared students, recreation to be organized, athletics to be supervised, etc. I should think about this opportunity for special service very seriously, he said. Besides, since the civil war was surely nearing its end, there would be ample room for excursions into the high mountains and trips to the nearby seas. I thought about it for a whole day and most of a night, then wrote the Fulbright people for an application. At the same time, encouraged by my advisers in the English Department, I applied to graduate school at Columbia and Harvard in case fate sent me in that direction.

I learned in May that both Bruce and I had received Fulbright fellowships to teach at the high-school level in Greece for a generous stipend to be paid by treaty agreement in what I guessed would be enough inflated drachmas to fill a small suitcase. At the same time I was awarded a Woodrow Wilson Fellowship for a year of graduate study in English at a university of my—and their—choice, with the understanding that during this year I would begin to think seriously about the possibility of a teaching career at the college level. I thought, I consulted, I didn't know what to do. Most of my English Department advisers argued that my going to Greece would kill graduate school prospects at Columbia or Harvard or most anywhere else because it would not only mean losing vital graduate fellowship support but would signal an eccentric and capricious streak in my character. Only Ben Merritt, classicist at the Institute for Advanced Study and devoted philhellene of the old school, suggested during a private conference that a year in Greece might actually enlarge my soul enough to make graduate work at Columbia or Harvard a whit more tolerable than it otherwise would be. I lined up the

pros and cons on a piece of paper, tore it up, sat down and wrote a letter accepting the Fulbright offer to teach the English language and basketball and amateur acting to village boys in northern Greece.

Word also came to me that spring that Lisa and Miranda had moved
to London to work for the Society of Friends. That settled where I
would spend the summer on my way to Salonika. I had worked hard
enough during the Christmas season as head of a student sales agency to
have put some cash aside for the summer, and with the prospect of all
those Fulbright drachmas coming in during the fall and winter, I felt as
carefree about money and just about everything else as I could remember ever having been. My father had sent me a $1000 check as a gradua-
tion present from his new post in Syria, and out of what to me is still
unintelligible pride and insensitivity, I returned the check to him with a
note thanking him kindly but stating that I was now on my own and no
longer needed to burden my parents financially. Despite my plural reference, this must have hurt him personally, and it must have further
cemented the border between us, though at that time and at that distance
I had little sense of this. In any case, he chose not to respond.

Some years later I learned why the summer of 1949 may have been a
watershed season in my father's life, dominated by events that reveal how
much else he had on his mind at the time beyond communicating with
his sons. The story of those events was told by Miles Copeland, who
served under my father in Syria and who wrote a book about his career,
covert and otherwise, in the Middle East. It was a complicated story that
told of the effort by Minister Keeley, "a career officer of the highest
integrity," to promote "democratic processes" under General Husni
Za'im, who had been recently installed as head of the Syrian government
after an army coup in which the U.S. was to some degree complicit.
According to Copeland, Minister Keeley, "overestimating our influence
on Za'im (as we all did)," thought the new leader would create law and
order of a kind that would eventually allow him to introduce "free elections, free press, and all the rest." The minister also didn't share the
Syrians' low opinion of themselves, in fact, according to Copeland, he
"loved them" and persisted in a belief that they were "naturally democratic." Copeland adds that "most of our other ambassadors and minis-

ters in the Arab world were to tell me that had they been in Keeley's place they would have seen the situation as he saw it."

The problem was that others in the U.S. government saw the situation otherwise, especially after Za'im proved recalcitrant toward American influence in certain ways, interested in receiving aid but not much interested in a return to parliamentary government, ready to put corrupt politicians in jail and institute much needed social and economic reforms but arrogant toward his American contact, one Major Meade, who tried to advise him the very day after the coup as to who his ambassadors ought to be and which officers ought to be promoted to official positions. Perhaps most revealingly, Za'im indicated that he hoped to do "something constructive" about the Arab-Israel problem, and this, according to Copeland, was what "neutralized any inclination the [State] Department might have had to give us explicit instructions to lay off."

On August 14, 1949, less than three months after the Za'im's coup, a group of his immediate subordinates surrounded his house, killed him and simultaneously his highly competent Prime Minister, Muhsin al-Barazi, and buried Za'im in the French cemetery (what was apparently a diversionary favor to his American sponsors). Za'im was replaced by a figurehead who lasted four months under the actual dictator, Colonel Adib Shishakli, who lasted only two more years, replaced in another coup that further promoted a series of coups and countercoups in the years following, so that, as Copeland put it in the late Sixties, "even those of us who know [the country] well are unable to keep track of which predator is currently in charge."

Reading the story of this sorry 1949 affair so many years later jogged my memory of an evening I had spent in the Damascus Legation during a short visit there before my father was transferred back to the States. He told a tale that evening that caused his voice to break. Za'im, he said, had been his one hope for establishing an early and enduring peace in the Arab-Israel conflict of those days; in fact, he had managed to arrange a meeting between the Syrian President and Prime Minister Ben-Gurion through the good offices of the Syrian Prime Minister, Barazi, who had become my father's friend during his earlier Syrian tour and had remained faithful. When both Za'im and Barazi were murdered that day in August, within a few weeks of the scheduled meeting, my father said he realized that whatever influence he might have brought to a settlement of the issue had died with Za'im and his friend and would remain dead so long as clandestine forces, his own country's included, had the power to destroy the working of conventional diplomacy.

In the years after my father left Damascus, he continued to be deeply concerned about the situation in the Middle East and remained emotionally immersed in the issues there almost to the end of his days, but in my presence he was never again at ease in discussing the Foreign Service or his long devotion to it. He had clearly become disillusioned, one cause of his slow retreat into a private world from which he emerged only sporadically during his late years. And when my brother Bob decided that his future might lie in the Foreign Service and began to prepare in earnest to take the required exam, my father, after reviewing the pros and cons with Bob, suggested that his advice could no longer be considered either up-to-date or objective, yet ended up trying quietly to discourage him. As it turned out, my father didn't succeed.

✻ ✻ ✻

When I reached London in June of 1949, I found Lisa and Miranda living on wages of a few pounds a week in a Friends hostel in Swiss Cottage where the lodging was free and the food—what there was of it under still strict rationing—almost free. I was taken in on the same basis despite my efforts to pay my way, and this, along with the general if often silent tolerance of an unemployed guest, eventually began to burden my conscience. But what burdened more than my conscience was trying to find secret places to meet Lisa alone in those crowded quarters, none satisfactory for more than a few minutes, even the far corners of the garden, dense with flower beds hardly made for hungry lovers. And the few times we wandered over to Primrose Hill on her return from a hard day of work south of Camden Town, we would hardly get settled into a spot that seemed far enough off the worn pathways for private pleasure when the rustle of one or another Peeping Tom nearby would cause us to rise suddenly and get ourselves tidied up. I finally persuaded

Lisa to ask for a two-week holiday without pay so that we could break free of the hostel and take a tour of literary England and Wales, and the ever-accommodating Friends agreed. We set off for the Lake District with a knapsack each, a blanket, a single sleeping bag, and a strict budget that would allow for a bed and breakfast overnight twice a week to have an easy bath and a full-size double bed.

What I remember most of the public landscape at the start of that tour more than fifty years ago is not so much the literary charms of the Lake District, with my selected editions of Coleridge and Wordsworth in hand, as the quiet generosity of those in the countryside who put us up night after night, whether inside their homes or on an outside porch or in a barn across the way, and often fed us a meal as well, whatever they were providing themselves, within or outside the stringent rationing. I came to have an abiding affection not only for the countryside but for just about everyone we came across living there, hardly a cold or overly curious English man or woman beyond the outskirts of London. Most were interested in where we came from and might be going, but nobody ever asked questions that might have made us feel uncomfortable. And most seemed to have a sixth sense about when it had become time to leave us to ourselves, with no more than very general instructions about where or how we were to make our bed, as though they remembered, whatever their age, that young lovers could best do that on their own.

One night, now deep into Wales and the poetry of Dylan Thomas, the two of us lying on a mattress of hay at one end of a cow barn with a single cow in it, our sleeping bag spread open to take in fresh air, Lisa sat up suddenly and crossed her arms over her knees.

"You know, how many nights has it been, not counting the bed and breakfast nights? Has it been seven or eight? And not once have we been asked: How long have you been married? Or engaged? Or even together?"

"Well I guess that's England. They take things for granted. Or maybe they just feel it isn't their business."

"But think if it were Greece. Would anybody ever offer to put us up if they didn't think we were married or at least engaged? And how long do you think it would take before they asked?"

"I don't know. I haven't been in that kind of situation."

"You poor thing. Well I can tell you even if I haven't exactly been either. Traveling with a man when you're not married makes you a whore. At least in the provinces."

"And what does that make the man?"

"A normal healthy human being," Lisa said.

"Is it really as bad as that?"

"If you don't believe me, try it sometime. No, don't try it. At least not without me."

"I wouldn't think of it."

Lisa glanced at me. "Yes you would," she said. "You don't have to pretend just because we're in another country."

"I'm not pretending."

Lisa reached over to touch my face. Then she dropped her hand. "I have to tell you something," she said without looking at me. "I don't think I can go back. Ever. Except now and then to visit my parents."

"To Greece?"

"To that city. Or anywhere else in the country. I just don't feel free there anymore. Maybe it isn't the country's fault. Maybe it's my fault."

"But things are going to change. They're bound to."

Lisa shook her head. "Not for me. I think it's too late."

I was flabbergasted. I didn't know what to say, and Lisa saw that. She reached over and touched my face again, really a caress. "Forget what I said. I don't want to spoil things for you. Not when things have been as sweet for us as they've been these days."

She reached over with her other hand to ease my head in next to hers.

Our private landscape had been more than sweet: the most intimate kind of adventure in discovery, she more experienced than me and without inhibition, I as eager a pupil as she could have expected to entertain. But I couldn't get what she had said out of my mind, and though it didn't really change our access to pleasure through the end of our tour of Wales and during the remaining days of walks and galleries and especially theater in London—always the cheapest tickets, but almost any production anywhere in the city would do—I nevertheless felt that she and I had come to a turning point that night leading I knew not where. At the same time, my days in London and the countryside convinced me that if

I finally decided to go to graduate school, England is where I would head first of all.

My first weeks as a teacher at the Farm School that fall were demanding, in part because I tried to impose an alien system on thirteen- to nineteen-year-old students who had barely had time to adjust to a post-war classroom and who seemed in any case to have been trained in some previous academic life to think of their teachers as adversaries out to prove that students were either mentally retarded or morally delinquent. I immediately set up an honor system during tests, on the Princeton model—no teacher present, a signature at the end signifying that the answers were the student's own—and after I found that the first test I offered the freshman class of some thirty students resulted in answers that were hardly perfect but had exactly the same errors, I modified the system in all four grades to allow my occasional unannounced intrusion during any test.

While popping in several times on an hour-long test given to the senior class, the class that included four heroic students who had been kidnapped during the guerrilla raid of the previous year, I was able to record at least four methods of advanced cheating, two requiring expertise in minuscule calligraphy, one requiring extraordinary eyesight, and one that seemed to presuppose a kind of ventriloquist musical talent. The first and most popular method consisted of a scroll of thin paper full of minuscule words that seemed in code and rolled to the thickness of a cigarette for storing behind a belt or in a shoe, the second a vocabulary list in ink covering the length of the inner side of a forearm initially hidden behind a gauze bandage binding a non-existent wound, the third a Greek-English dictionary the size of a matchbox that could be concealed on the person most anywhere, and the fourth a quiet kind of humming that allowed several of the brightest students to send singing messages to their neighbors in an English so broken in rhythm and intonation that I had trouble at first convincing myself that it actually was the language being tested.

When I gave those caught cheating a failing grade on the test, the response was strident but short-lived, as though that, like the referee's red card in soccer, was simply part of the game. But when I decided that my strategy would have to be that of making all tests essay tests which called for individually creative answers, with dictionaries permitted, whether the essays consisted of only a few lines for beginners or a full page or two for seniors, I was sent a delegation of the older boys to complain about unfair examination procedure. I stuck to my guns but added an oral exam for those who could convince me that they had not performed adequately in this new mode of testing because it had brought on a serious case of writer's block. I suppose that softness on my part was influenced by my interview with the pedantic Princeton instructor in American history who had acknowledged my grasp of facts but had challenged my grammar and handwriting. Only two candidates for the oral exam appeared at my door and both did poorly.

Gradually, by hard work coaching soccer through the fall and the exciting newly imported sport called "basket," and by distributing soccer boots and sneakers to the badly shod and shirts stenciled AFS, all charged to my suitcase of inflated drachmas, I won over the athletes, and then the group who put on a spirited Thanksgiving one-act play full of tall-hatted Pilgrims and feathered Indians, and finally a group of school leaders elected to a new organization I created called the Student Council. The latter bewildered and alarmed most of the Greek teachers at the school until Theo Litsas saw its value as a way of managing self-discipline outside the classroom, especially since the toughest soccer players and tallest basketball players were inevitably elected to the Council. By the end of the academic year, I had earned the public nickname "My Teacher" (pronounced "Teetser"), and as a parting present, a delegation of the senior class invited me to join them for an outing to the beautiful waterfalls of Edessa town to the west and a farewell dinner there, followed by a visit to the town's first-class brothel. I joined them for an ample meal above the waterfalls but amicably begged off the brothel visit, suggesting that it would violate Anglo-Saxon convention on such occasions. That passed, but barely.

It had taken me only to the Christmas vacation to decide that teaching those sometimes wild if mostly open-hearted potential farmers emerging from a ghastly civil war finally had its strong virtues and rewards, a thing that Bruce Lansdale had discovered some time since and had already managed to persuade a lovely Rochester University coed nicknamed Tad that it was worth her life's commitment as well. I began to ask myself if it might not be equally rewarding to try teaching English at the college level, perhaps a plausible calling even for a writer who wanted to be independent, in fact what might prove the best of possible callings, with its own particular gratification for a neophyte humanist who had begun to believe with some passion in the redeeming value of literature. I decided to take that Christmas vacation in England, first of all to see Lisa but also to track down the possibility of graduate work in one or another university there.

Some former Oxonians in the States had told me that Oxford's Balliol College was especially sympathetic toward Americans, so that is where I began my university tour. But the tutor who interviewed me, no doubt in part as strategy to test my cunning or nerve, was so disparaging of my committed interest in American literature, beginning with Hawthorne ("Specializes in children's stories, what?") and Melville ("Writes about fishing, isn't it?") and finally F. Scott Fitzgerald ("Afraid I haven't heard of him. Could you perhaps mean Edward FitzGerald?) that I thought seriously about taking the next train to Cambridge or maybe Edinburgh. Yet after a visit to Blackwell's bookstore and some research there, I discovered that the classicist Sir Maurice Bowra, whose recent book of essays included one I scanned on the Greek poet C. P. Cavafy, then only a name to me, was now Warden of Wadham College around the corner. Audaciously, I phoned the distinguished gentleman for an interview. When he heard that I had just come from Greece, he invited me to tea. Early in the interview he asked me bluntly: "Now tell me, why are you really here? Certainly not to discuss Cavafy." I told him that I would like to be admitted to his college, and by the end of the interview it had become apparent that, as a raging philhellene, he was generous enough to overlook certain glaring deficiencies ("What? No Latin? No Anglo-Saxon? Little European literature?") in any candidate for admission who had a love of Greek poetry, ancient or modern—and that is what I had managed to pretend. Some weeks later I learned in the same mail that I'd somehow been accepted at both Balliol and Wadham. I chose Wadham.

London was cold and wet during that Christmas vacation. Lisa and

Marina were still at the Friends hostel near Swiss Cottage but had plans to move to their own place as soon as they could find new employment that brought in a plausible wage above the dole. I tried to offer Lisa enough funds from my still ample drachma income to bide her over until that day, but she refused. I could see that I had again raised the malevolent specter of our differing situations—and that kept appearing in one form or another between those tender moments that recalled the good days of our summer excursion. We went to plays regularly, ate at the best Indian restaurants we could find, and disappeared into my own bed and breakfast room in Swiss Cottage for long after-theater retreats into our private space. I also persuaded Lisa to spend our last weekend at a country inn that I had spotted on the road to Oxford.

It was not a brilliant choice. Aside from the problem of feeding an inadequate heater from an insufficient collection of relevant coins, the bed was lumpy, the décor depressing, and the aura of Oxford—no fault of the innkeeper—an ominous presence. It must have been three in the morning when I woke up to find Lisa sitting up with pillows behind her gazing at a painting of nuzzling deer on the far wall.

"So now you will come back to this country next year and go to the great university and I suppose that will be the last I see of you."

"Well, I haven't been admitted yet. And if I am, it's only an hour or so from London."

"It's years from my London."

"Why does that have to be? I don't understand."

"Because I can never be at ease with your friends at that university. I have no education that will make it possible for them to take me seriously. And I never will."

"What friends? I don't have any friends there. And anyway, you're years ahead of anybody my age I may meet there."

"Not in the ways that count. I know what I speak of. Education, money, what they call class in this country. I've already seen it often in London."

"That doesn't mean a thing to me."

"Well I wish it didn't mean a thing to me, but it does. And it will to you, you'll see soon enough. Anyway, I'm thinking of going to

Switzerland. Or Scandinavia. Some place where I can use my talent for foreign languages. Now you go back to sleep and we'll talk of all this another time."

But I couldn't go back to sleep. And Lisa couldn't either. At some point before daylight she came over to me, and we lay there tight against each other as though threatened by a huge wave about to engulf us. Then I heard her say softly: "Mikey, my little brother, why did I have to love you this way?"

And a bit later we finally slept.

After my return to Salonika that winter, we kept up our correspondence more or less regularly for a while. I wrote about the excitement I was beginning to feel teaching those once seemingly unteachable Farm School boys, and about my being accepted at Oxford, and about maybe writing a dissertation on the plays of W. B. Yeats. And then the correspondence faltered. Lisa must have felt that I was now working my way back into old territory that she had already left and new territory that she didn't care to enter. When she wrote that she had taken on extra work in a hospital in order to save her money for a trip to Switzerland that summer to see what might be available there, the distance between us appeared to have become too great to bridge. I decided to spend the summer trying out the grand tour of Europe in reverse, beginning with the Balkans and ending in England in time to report to Oxford for Michaelmas Term in October. Bruce and Tad Lansdale drove me to the border with Yugoslavia and stood behind the barrier on the Greek side to wave goodbye and watch me disappear with my suitcase into that desolate buffer zone between the two countries that Tito had then opened to Americans as his newest allies.

The story of my grand tour—Belgrade, Graz, Salzburg, Vienna, Florence, Rome, Paris, London, partly in the company of a sophisticated and adventurous young heiress from California—became the subject of my first novel, written the year after I finished a dissertation not on W. B. Yeats's plays but on two Greek poets relatively unknown at that time, C. P. Cavafy and George Seferis. The novel was fortunately never published, but it helped me to earn an advance on a second novel that was. The dissertation topic emerged from a bitterly cold and underfed first term at Oxford. I had arrived there that fall ill-equipped with clothes for the season, deplorably unaware that food and coal rationing was still in force in England, naïve about the casual role of lectures in the Oxford curriculum—I had signed up for at least two a day—friendless, alien, but unquenchably ambitious.

After several weeks of wearing my gabardine raincoat under my academic gown into the clammy Wadham dining hall and carrying my ration clump of butter with me to all meals for however long it might last—saving it for afternoon tea wasn't yet remotely within the range of my transatlantic perception—I had by then earned a certain notoriety in my college as The Gabardine Kid. Within the first month, I found that the choice of plausible lectures had diminished to two or three a week, the coal in my college room remained good for only two or three hours of lounging pleasure, and Yeats's plays—as distinct from his still exquisite poetry—had proven barely readable by my restless, dramatically untrained mind. My year at the American Farm School had taught me what warmth of various kinds could do for a lonely, disoriented young man's morale, so I now went looking for the Greek community in Oxford, first of all by way of a course listed in the catalogue as "The Modern Greek Short Story".

It took me some days to find either the professor or the lecturer in Byzantine and Modern Greek, both apparently preoccupied with intellectual and social enterprise other than that focused on students, since at that time there was only a single student in their subject at Oxford, a young lady named Mary Stathatos-Kyris, whom I found lingering in the more or less centrally-heated Byzantine and Modern Greek library of the New Bodleian. Without further delay this young lady led me to the Modern Greek Lecturer Robin Fletcher, her fellow student of the previous year, and he to the distinguished Professor Constantine Trypanis, then re-working his annual lecture on a poet I had never heard of, Kostis Palamas, a name famous in the Greek community but still barely recognizable outside it. As could be the practice at Oxford, the course in "The Modern Greek Short Story" was either a phantom course or had been cancelled.

I will try to make this rather complicated academic history succinct.

Professor Trypanis's initial response to the news from Robin Fletcher that "an American chap" had appeared with an interest in studying Modern Greek literature had apparently been: "We'll soon discourage him" (so Miss Stathatos-Kyris later reported to me). But it seems that my grasp of village Greek and my persistence during a conversation with the Professor after his lecture were sufficiently powerful to earn me an invitation to a sumptuous spread of good things to eat under the warm roof of the Trypanis household at 9 Norham Gardens, with Mrs. Aliki Trypanis an ample hostess, and soon after that, under the guiding hand of Constantine Trypanis, to a discovery of the work of a number of Greek poets who proved to be life-long literary companions. Also soon after that I became engaged to my single fellow student, now simply "Mary," and by the end of my second term, committed to hard work on a new dissertation topic that had to do with the poetry of Cavafy and Seferis in its relation to poetry in English (Professor Trypanis assured me at the start that I was bound to discover a certain relation of that kind in due course).

I don't want to suggest that any of this was hurried or easy. Though I had spent almost five years in Greece by that time, I knew nothing at all about Greek literature. Moving from Yeats, Eliot, Pound, Hardy and the earlier English tradition to unknown twentieth century poetry in a totally new linguistic tradition was a demanding change of direction, except in the case of George Seferis. I found his poetry immediately accessible to some degree, especially the 1935 volume *Mythistorima,* which revealed a comfortable affinity to some of T. S. Eliot's poetry that I had studied at Princeton. With the help of Constantine Trypanis and the future Greek man of letters and Harvard professor, George Savidis, at that time a student at Cambridge, I began to read extensively in other contemporary Greek poets: Cavafy first, then Sikelianos, Elytis, and Karyotakis. But Seferis was the poet closest to my heart, and he really served as the excuse for abandoning Yeats and turning to what I hoped would be a focus on Seferis and his relation to T. S. Eliot.

The problem arose when I solicited permission for the new thesis topic from whatever mysterious committee considered such solicitations. I received word that it was not permissible at Oxford to write a doctoral dissertation on a living author, let alone two living authors, and when I asked why, I was told: "Do you really think that would be fair to either Mr. Seferis or Mr. Eliot? After all, those gentlemen would very likely still be alive to read what you might choose to write in your dissertation." So I decided to resubmit the topic with several dead authors to accompany the living, and in the end, as I ran out of time and energy, this came down to C. P. Cavafy, who was close to twenty years dead at the time. That compromise proved sufficient for the relevant committee, I suppose largely to honor Constantine Trypanis and Maurice Bowra, my philhellenic Warden at Wadham, and the first effort at a doctoral dissertation of any kind under the faculty of Byzantine and Modern Greek.

Soon after the topic was approved, I decided that I had to give up my thespian ambitions under the Experimental Theatre Club, and, newly married in the spring, to begin writing in earnest on my dissertation before my savings ran totally dry. As luck would have it, I was into a first draft of the Seferis section when I learned that George Seferis had been appointed to the Greek Embassy in London as Counselor. I saw an opportunity, before I moved on to Cavafy's oeuvre, to check out what I had written so far about George Seferis's poetry with George Seferis himself and maybe dig up what clues I might from actual dialogue with the living poet. That impulse may reasonably explain why writing a dissertation on a living poet was normally forbidden at Oxford. In any case, I immediately wrote Mr. George Seferiades (the poet's real name) at "Foreign Office of Greece, Athens, Greece": "Dear Mr. Seferiades: I am currently doing research and preparing a thesis under the supervision of [etc., etc.]. As an American, I am interested in the influence of English on Modern Greek poetry, though the poetry itself is of course my primary concern. Having spent five years in Greece... I [want to do] what I can to acquaint the English-speaking countries with the active, modern culture of Greece. I have been recently studying your poetry with great interest, especially since I sense that you have introduced the same stylistic renaissance in Greece that T. S. Eliot accomplished in England, and I am a devout admirer of Eliot. However, I find that it is more difficult for me to trace the symbolic pattern of your poetry than that of Eliot. This is perhaps because your symbolism tends to be more personal, and because I am not always familiar with the necessary background. I realize that a poet wishes to allow a certain amount of elasticity of interpretation, but I also realize that this elasticity, of undeniable poetic value to the native, causes confusion and unintentional obscurity in the case of foreign readers …"

Instead of simply admitting at this point that I was swimming in rather murky waters, I went right on to pose six general questions about matters of influence, symbolism, historical background, biographical background, what have you, and concluded: "You may feel that I am asking too much, and that may be the case, but I would appreciate any enlightenment, no matter how limited, even if it consists of a more or less candid reproach for my ignorance."

This letter never received an answer, though it reached the poet's archive at some point, despite its rather vague address. In any case, I didn't wait for an answer before I followed it the next day with what was clearly the product of a sleepless night. "Dear Mr. Seferiades: In reconsidering the letter I mailed you yesterday, I feel that I may have given you the wrong impression as a result of the way I worded several questions. I do not wish you to feel that I have not read your poetry thoroughly or have been lazy in expending thought over the interpretation. To the contrary, I feel that I do understand a great deal and have certain positive theories regarding your symbolism and the ideas I believe you are interested in expressing. My questions are more for the purpose of corroborating an already established analysis on my part. However, as a foreign reader, I find your poetry sufficiently difficult and obscure so that I do not feel as secure in my interpretation as I might with poetry of [sic] my own language. In other words, I do not wish to deceive anyone who may read my thesis, and get them started on a tangent at odds with the intended direction of your poetry.…" I then went on blatantly to speak about my difficulty in interpreting certain specific symbols "such as the statues, stones, the woman who appears continually, and any number of others." This letter also received no answer, nor did a third sent ten days later, though both again can be found in the poet's archive. Whenever one or the other actually reached Mr. Seferiades, it must surely have taken great generosity on his part not to tear them up into small pieces.

My next letter to Mr. Seferis (as I now began to address him) is dated a year later, when I was very close to submitting my dissertation, this letter addressed to the Greek Embassy in London, where my spies told me the poet was actually in residence at that moment in an apartment near Sloane Square. What I had to say now makes me smile, then blush with some chagrin: "I don't know whether you remember me, but I am the young man who approached you over a year ago in connection with a thesis I am writing on Modern Greek poetry, i.e., Cavafy and Seferis. I am about at the end of the thread, and with a slight push will emerge into the light. I wonder if it would be possible to see you sometime in the near future, preferably towards the end of this week, in order to clear up a few points. I am sorry that the notice is so short, but things always become rushed at the end. I must say that the way has been long and hard, but I have enjoyed it."

When I think back on it, I find it difficult to believe that my persistence in this mode actually resulted in an invitation to my wife and me to join Mr. and Mrs. Seferiades for tea on Sloane Avenue, surely evidence of George Seferis's quite unusual indulgence and magnanimity. I have sketched that meeting over tea in the strictly limited edition of my twenty-year correspondence with Seferis (that has continued to remain strictly limited in sales since its publication). After Mrs. Seferis—a strikingly beautiful woman with delicate features and braided golden hair—had served my wife and me a tea that included more delights than we could possibly have anticipated, the poet and I withdrew to the other end of the room to talk a bit about his poetry. Almost six hours later we were still talking, or rather I was still talking, the poet by that time heavy-lidded, bleary-eyed, slow of response, gazing around, it seemed to me, for a way to escape. He finally suggested that I must by now know his poetry better than he did, and perhaps to know more was to know too much.

Our dialogue, if it can be called that, had gone on for so long because I had tried to reassure myself about my interpretation of certain images and themes in the various poems I discussed in my thesis, and the poet had been very reticent about telling me directly what this or that line might mean, so we had played cat and mouse during what I assumed would be my first and last chance to record his valuable insights into his own work. In fact I recorded nothing except the few things that became etched in my memory because of the emphatic way he responded every now and then. For example, at one point he suggested that I try not to look at everything I came across in his work as a symbol or a symbolic statement. "Those statues you mention, my dear. Those statues are not always symbols. They sometimes exist as statues. When you travel in Greece you will actually find statues, real statues, everywhere. And the stones. You will also find stones everywhere under your feet, my dear, or there in front of you for your hand to caress if you choose. And the woman. The woman too is real enough, [here with a little cunning smile] as perhaps you have discovered already."

Responding to his exhaustion, I finally said: "Just one more question, please. The punctuation in your poetry is rather free, and there are moments when a line, a passage, that is ambiguous would cease to be so with the addition of a coma or a semi-colon." And I read out a troubling line from *Mythistorima* that seemed to me a case in point. "Here, for instance. A comma here could make all the difference." Seferis simply stared at me. From the other end of the room, where Maro Seferis was still sitting patiently with my wife Mary, Maro's voice suddenly rose up as in a profound lament: "Give the young man a comma, George, help him, for heaven's sake."

* * *

The lesson I learned from my first encounter with Seferis was a valuable one that remained with me whenever I met this poet again or any other writer of like stature and shrewdness. However accommodating a poet may feel toward a student or critic or interviewer, if he is as wise as this poet was, he will be reluctant to allow the richness of his work to be restricted by the kind of detailed commentary on specific poems that seems to carry the imprint of the poet's approval. That Seferis was particularly sensitive on this point is illustrated not only by his reticence during our first meeting but by his second-thought effort to suppress sections of a "public" letter to his friend George Katsimbalis for publication in the Athenian literary journal, *Angloelliniki Epitheorisi.* The letter took the form of an introduction to the poet's complex three-part poem called "Thrush" and was meant to guide the reader through some of its more obscure territory, but when it appeared later in his collected essays, Seferis eliminated most of what had seemed a direct explanation of certain passages in the poem.

In any case the poem has survived Seferis's commentary, as *The Waste Land* has survived Eliot's extensive notes. But after my first six-hour tea with the Greek poet, I never again attempted to grill him about this or that passage in his poetry, and I think this made it possible for us to become friends during the twenty years that followed and to allow our talk to ramble over literature, politics, personalities, and the absurdities of daily life in the free-wheeling way that made his company always highly entertaining and instructive, especially during his more relaxed days in his Athens home above the old Olympic stadium.

Not that he couldn't sometimes be aroused to passionate disagreement with anybody who might offer what he considered a dubious or strictly prejudiced point of view. Another lesson I recall occurred during a second meeting in London some years after the first while Seferis was back there serving as the Greek Ambassador and while my wife and I were passing through. That meeting was a small dinner that included another visitor in town, Michael Kakoyannis, the celebrated Greek film director. At one point the conversation touched on the poet Angelos Sikelianos, and Ambassador Seferis remarked to Kakoyannis that people in Greece had not yet fully recognized how important the poetry of Sikelianos had been to the linguistic progress of the modern Greek tradition. Without giving much thought to what I was saying at that moment, I suggested that what a poet contributed to the development of his or her linguistic tradition was of course important, but there were poets who were great quite beyond that particular criterion—and perhaps even greater than Sikelianos. Seferis fixed me with his sharp eye. "For example?" he asked. "For example, William Butler Yeats," I replied. Seferis exploded. "How can you compare Sikelianos and Yeats? Sikelianos is a Greek and Yeats is an Irishman. They belong to separate traditions. I'm a Greek, so Sikelianos is greater to me than Yeats. You're an Irishman [sic], so Yeats is greater to you than Sikelianos. My dear friend, both are great and neither is greater than the other." The lesson I learned that evening from this remarkable poet and diplomat was never to make such casual international comparisons—at least not in public within his hearing, or that of others with a like suspicion of quick evaluations across national borders.

The one occasion when the poet in George Seferis let down his guard a bit was during an interview I conducted with him for the *Paris Review* series late in our relationship (1968, three years before his death). I was still careful not to raise questions of specific interpretation, but Seferis, once he got over a certain nervousness about speaking with a tape recorder present, allowed himself to offer some general observations about his poetic career: the influence of his Smyrna childhood "among certain old sailors" (as it appears in his verse), his long struggle for precision and stylistic economy, and given the instability of Modern Greek, the necessity he and other demotic writers had of creating their own language "all the time we are writing." And he was voluble about his association with other writers and intellectuals who had been good companions in his progress to maturity as a poet, those from abroad, in particular Eliot, Henry Miller, and Lawrence Durrell, and those at home, the group headed by George Katsimbalis, who came to be Miller's Colossus of Maroussi.

But at one point Seferis put on his protective mask again as he indicated that he sometimes kept what he called "poetical notes" which he returned to while "elaborating" the form of a given poem in his mind, and these notes he usually destroyed or forgot that he had—and he cited his recent failure to find certain notes he had written about his relatively early poem *The Cistern*. When I suggested, off my guard for the moment, that in view of how obscure I found that poem in places, those notes might have helped me understand it better, Seferis replied: "Don't complain about it. They might have made the poem much more obscure, you know." And again, while we were reviewing the question of imagery formed during his early years, the poet distinguished between conscious and subconscious imagery, and he concluded the discussion with a statement that struck me as an essential warning to those who try to dig too deeply into a poet's personal sources: "I think it is always a bit dangerous to make unconscious images conscious, to bring them into the light, because, you know, they dry out immediately."

There was another moment near the end of the interview when Seferis became legitimately protective not regarding his poetry but regarding his possible role as a Nobel Prize spokesman. Our conversation took place during the second year of the Colonels' 1967-74 dictatorship in Greece, the political situation at home one reason Seferis had decided to break into his retirement and accept the invitation from the Institute for Advanced Study in Princeton to gather his thoughts for a season abroad in a quiet if stimulating new environment. When I asked him if he, as his country's only Nobel laureate, felt any responsibility "toward the cultural life around you, or any position you may sense you have to maintain in relation to your country," Seferis immediately caught the drift of my question and shot back, with some irritation: "I should from the beginning tell you quite bluntly—if I can say it in English— that the Nobel Prize is an accident, no more than an accident. It's not an appointment... Otherwise, if you are over-dazzled by that sort of thing, you get lost and founder... After all, I don't recognize the right of anybody to take you by the back of your neck and throw you into a sort of ocean of empty responsibilities. Why, that's scandalous after all." And he added a bit later: "I'm sorry to say that I never felt I was the spokesman for anything or anybody. There are no credentials which appoint anybody to be spokesman for something."

Yet the issue gnawed at him. During the question period following his reading at the YMHA Poetry Center several weeks earlier, Seferis had been asked by a Greek student in the audience what his attitude was regarding the political situation in Greece, and the poet had refused to answer on the grounds that he didn't think it proper to criticize his government while he was safely abroad in a foreign country during days when others were suffering back home for their opposition to the dictatorial regime. The mixed response of the audience showed that some there did not consider this an adequate posture under the circumstances, and that failure to understand his position much disturbed the poet during the dinner that evening and in the days following.

That his answer was not an evasion became apparent soon after his return to Athens, when he decided that enough was enough and issued his famous uncompromising denunciation of the dictatorship: "It is a state of enforced torpor in which all those intellectual values that we have succeeded in keeping alive, with agony and labor, are about to sink into swampy stagnant waters.….. Everyone has been taught and knows by now that in the case of dictatorial regimes the beginning may seem easy, but tragedy awaits, inevitably, in the end…. I see ahead of me the precipice toward which the oppression that has shrouded the country is leading us. This anomaly must stop. It is a national imperative."

The reluctant spokesman had become the prophetic voice of his country. His public challenge to the regime, the first of its kind during those years, became the focus for passive—and sometimes not so passive—resistance to the Colonels by other writers and intellectuals inside and outside Greece. And his funeral two years later proved to be an unsponsored national event fit not merely for Greece's first Nobel laureate but for a heroic forefather of the eventually reestablished democracy.

* * *

During my days at Oxford I found that I actually enjoyed translating the poetry in modern Greek that became a necessary part of my dissertation. But at that time I had no premonition that translation, and my effort to merge Browning and Whitman and Yeats and Eliot with the newly discovered Greek poets, would eventually make for a life-long commitment to the literature of Greece and even to the exploration of its modern history. My heart as a writer continued to remain first of all with the American novelists who had taught me the most about the prose possibilities of my native language: Twain, Fitzgerald, Faulkner, Hemingway. Still, whenever I could, I grafted the Greek poets—sometimes secretly—onto this or that course that I taught in contemporary English and American literature, and whenever I was between novels, I used the translation and occasionally the criticism of their poetry to refresh mind and spirit before my next long engagement with writing fiction. This was one way I attempted to combine the two cultures that, in their separate fashion, brought me the greatest pleasure over the years.

Another way, far riskier, was by setting most of my novels in Greece, always with a mix of American and Greek characters, both talking in their particular idiom—the risk, anyway at the start, not so much in this necessary linguistic stratagem as in what my first American editor rue-fully identified as an ongoing cross-cultural problem: "I'm afraid Balkan novels just aren't likely to do very well over here this year or next."

I returned to the States from Oxford to my first job as a college English teacher, a nine-month stint at Brown University that ended with a trip back to Greece on a Liberty Ship that had survived the Second World War (free passage arranged by ship-owning friends of my father-in-law, an Admiral in the Greek Navy). This was followed by a year as a Fulbright Lecturer at Salonika University and by annual trips to Greece in the summers or when I was on leave, a pattern unbroken during the subsequent forty years of my teaching English and Creative Writing at Princeton and beyond that into the new millennium. Greece meant a new family, my in-laws not merely hospitable in the warmest Greek tra-dition, but taking me in as though I were not only husband but brother to their only daughter. It was an unusually easy-going family, all banter and jibing and ready affection, with much shared travel by car wherever the Admiral and his Alexandrian wife found their compass pointing toward some landscape that promised undiscovered adventure—that is, as long as the gods granted these adopted parents their portion of time to navigate the earth easily. When they were gone, their apartment in Athens still remained our home away from home.

During my first years on the Princeton faculty I made a few gestures toward converting parts of my dissertation into publishable articles in the fashion of the day, but after writing one or two, I gave myself entirely to a new novel, the first of mine to be set in Greece. I didn't reveal what I was up to nor that the work was under contract until it was too late to take into account the contrary advice of well-meaning colleagues about such a reckless and unscholarly preoccupation, except for R. P. Blackmur and Alan Downer, neither of whom had bothered to pick up an advanced degree (shades of John Hite) and early on devoted themselves to promoting creative writing and living theater in the University.

The novel I wrote during my first leave was dedicated to my parents, with an epigraph from Aeschylus's *The Libation Bearers* that begins (in the Penguin translation of those days by Philip Vellacott): "Father, father of sorrows, O can I, /Severed from you as far as pole from pole, /still by some loving speech or timely deed /Send a fair wind of comfort to your soul...." I could never be sure that my father caught a waft of that fair wind as I'd intended or that he saw himself among my novelistic transformations—as I hoped he wouldn't too clearly. Since he was very generous in his response the one time he spoke to me about the book, I assumed he was either impervious to any similarity between him and the character who plays the role of American father in my story or preferred to pretend imperviousness.

And what my mother may have seen of herself or others in the novel she kept hidden behind the quiet appreciation and relief she expressed—still the conscientious home school teacher—regarding what she found to be the generally fluid English and correct grammar of what had emerged as my post-graduate prose. It appeared that this first effort to create a fictional account of my coming of age, if not exactly a timely deed, at least avoided adding more distance to a separation from my parents that was gradually becoming substantially less than that of pole from pole.

The story I told in the novel belongs in some measure to Timothy Gammon, a young American—modern sibling of Orestes and Electra—who returns to Greece after the Second World War to search out the truth about his missionary father's death. His access to the truth is first opened to him by the recent history he hears from his childhood friend Helen as they lie side by side on a beach gazing out across Salonika Bay. By the final pages of the novel, Timothy and Helen, now lovers, discover that they share the same inheritance and the same father and mother. Mostly under Helen's persuasion, Timothy comes to recognize that the two of them can live on together as brother and sister if he learns to temper his Anglo-Saxon sense of sin by a larger portion of the local tolerance and pride that are also his inheritance.

Such are the prerogatives of fiction. Memory, whatever its willed and unwilled constructions and whatever its compensations, can't always provide that kind of benevolent resolution. I made one more attempt to transform the positive influence of Lisa into a fictional recognition through the ending of my sixth novel, where the young protagonist writes the woman he finally realizes he has to leave forever that, whether or not he will find someone else in his life he might love as he has her, he will remember her as the one who taught him what was possible and impossible about it in the beginning, and he can't help believing that their beginning was the best there is likely to be. But the protagonist is still a young man when he writes that parting note, and true as it may have been for him at that moment, there was still much time left for him to learn more about both the possible and the impossible in love, as those the gods sometimes favor are given a chance to do in real life.

✻ ✻ ✻

I've known children of Americans serving abroad—those you hear called Foreign Service or Army or Business World brats—who lived outside their country in one or another foreign post for some years and always carried what they considered the disadvantages of a double vision, a fractured sense of identity, a longing for national wholeness that they felt could never be theirs. As I've tried to show here, there were times during my early years when I felt the need to piece together an American identity and to build toward a wholeness I never really had. Laying claim to something called national wholeness would have been more than difficult when so many of those I befriended and came to know best belonged to other worlds and other ways of seeing, whether outside or inside America. And in the years following I could be passionate in defense of my native country at times and passionate in defense of my adopted country at other times. I could also be critical of both. If I felt nostalgia for the early days I lived in one or the other country—and at moments I did—it was the kind that can accommodate the ambivalence of gratification and regret. At some point I finally came to see the double vision I grew up with and later cultivated, even the double loyalty, as a potential resource, both for my attempt to understand the corners of the world I was given to know and for my long effort to put that understanding on the page.

The Author

Edmund Keeley was born to American parents on February 5, 1928, at Damascus, Syria. The son of a career diplomat, he attended schools in Montreal, Canada, and Thessaloniki, Greece, and graduated from high school in Washington, D.C. He received a B.A. from Princeton University in Princeton, New Jersey, and a D.Phil. from Oxford University in Oxford, England. He has been Fulbright teacher at the American Farm School in Thessaloniki, Greece, and a Fulbright lecturer at the University of Thessaloniki and the University of Athens, both in Greece. He was visiting lecturer at Oxford University, the University of the Aegean, the University of Michigan, and the University of Iowa. Additionally, he has taught at the New School for Social Research, the School of the Arts at Columbia University, and Brown University, and has been writer-in-residence at Knox College. He is Charles Barnwell Straut Class of 1923 Professor of English, Emeritus and Professor of English and Creative Writing, Emeritus, at Princeton University.

He has been a Hibben Scholar, Woodrow Wilson Fellow, Guggenheim Fellow, McCosh Faculty Fellow, Fulbright Research Fellow, and a Fellow at the American Academy in Rome, the University of Crete, the Virginia Center for the Creative Arts, Oxford University, Princeton University, and the University of Michigan. Additionally, he has been a resident scholar at the Rockefeller Foundation Bellagio Study and Conference Center.

His awards include the New Jersey Authors Award, the Council of Humaities Award from Princeton University, the Guinness Poetry Award, the PEN Translation Award, the Harold Morton Landon Translation Award, the NEA/PEN Fiction Syndicate Award, the Premier Prix Europeen de Traduction de la Poesie, the Academy Award in Literature given by the American Academy of Arts and Letters, the PEN/Ralph Manheim Translation Medal, and the John D. Criticos Annual Prize given by the London Hellenic Society. A finalaist for the National Book Award in Translation, he was also selected for a Pushcart

OPrize and for a NEA/PEN Fiction Syndicate anthology.

He has been a board member for *Translation Review, Princeton Alumni Weekly, Byzantine and Modern Greek Studies, Journal of Modern Greek Studies, Delos,* and *Mediterraneans.* He has served as a judge for the Harold Morton Landon Translation Award and for the Poetry Society of America/Wesleyan University Press Translation Award.

He has been married for over fifty years to Mary Stathatos-Kyris. They divide their time betwen homes in Princeton, New Jersey, and Athens, Greece.